RAISING THE BOTTOM

RAISING THE BOTTOM

BOUNCE MUSIC AND BLACK QUEER PERFORMANCE IN POST-KATRINA NEW ORLEANS

ALIX CHAPMAN

DUKE UNIVERSITY PRESS   DURHAM AND LONDON   2026

© 2026 DUKE UNIVERSITY PRESS
All rights reserved
Project Editor: Lisa Lawley
Designed by Matthew Tauch
Typeset in Merlo Tx and Anybody by Westchester Publishing Services

Library of Congress Cataloging-in-Publication Data
Names: Chapman, Alix, [date] author
Title: Raising the bottom : bounce music and Black queer performance
in post-Katrina New Orleans / Alix Chapman.
Other titles: Bounce music and Black queer performance
in post-Katrina New Orleans
Description: Durham : Duke University Press, 2026. | Includes
bibliographical references and index.
Identifiers: lccn 2025036189 (print)
LCCN 2025036190 (ebook)
ISBN 9781478038610 paperback
ISBN 9781478033707 hardcover
ISBN 9781478062226 ebook
Subjects: LCSH: Ethnomusicology—Louisiana—New Orleans—History—
20th century | Bounce (Music)—Louisiana—New Orleans—History—
20th century | African American gay people—Louisiana—New
Orleans—Music | Queer theory | Gender identity in music
Classification: LCC ML3798 .C43 2026 (print) | LCC ML3798 (ebook) |
DDC 780.89/96076335—dc23/eng/20250929
LC record available at https://lccn.loc.gov/2025036189
LC ebook record available at https://lccn.loc.gov/2025036190

Cover art: Photo by Chris Granger

*In loving memory of Velmer and Joseph Alix—
mister done good*

CONTENTS

ix   *Preface: Bourbon Street Blues*

1	INTRODUCTION	Project Music
25	CHAPTER ONE	*Catch Dat Beat*: Performing Pleasure and Coalition
49	CHAPTER TWO	Get It How You Live: Twerking for Survival
71	CHAPTER THREE	Back of Town: A Bottom Geography
96	CHAPTER FOUR	Touching the Rim: Gentrification, Popular Culture, and the Collective Asshole
122	CHAPTER FIVE	Raising the Bottom: Church Girls and Secular Music
143		*Acknowledgments*
147		*Notes*
163		*References*
175		*Index*

PREFACE
BOURBON STREET BLUES

I was nine years old, out with Mama and Grandpa Alix on Bourbon Street, Halloween 1987. They were enjoying their to-go drinks and walking too slow for me, so I began to walk ahead. Mind you, this was before tourism in the city had really begun to boom, and I was only a block away, not far out of their range.

A tall black man, oiled from head to toe and wearing nothing but a red sequined thong, came dancing out of a club. He two-stepped, twirled, and shook his ass to a song blasting from inside. I don't remember the sound of the music, or what he said as he shouted for passersby to come in and join. He didn't seem to notice me standing in the middle of the street, frozen in awe. I can't tell you if I wanted him or wanted to be him, but a world of possibilities suddenly leapt into existence.

I turned and started heading back toward my family. On the other side of the street, a boy about the same age as me, covered in sweat, tap-danced on a flattened cardboard box for whatever money people would put in a can beside him. I saw splotches of dark skin that resembled my own, but his shirtless torso and arms were covered in what appeared to be burns. I kept walking and joined my family. I tried to walk and match their steps, but I couldn't find the rhythm.

....

There's a long tradition of touristic and romantic narratives that speak to the transformations, not least of them death, that might occur in

New Orleans. That walk down Bourbon was the first of many trips to the city, and in many ways, it was the beginning of a lifelong interest.

Beyond that experience, the little I knew of New Orleans I'd received through my paternal grandfather. Big Alix was born and raised there before joining the Great Migration of the 1940s and heading west and north to far-off Washington state, where I was born. He was my step-grandfather, but that didn't stop my parents from giving me his name.

Back home in Washington, Big Alix didn't speak directly about his youth in New Orleans. All most of us knew of his past was that as a young man in his early twenties, he'd been in a fight with a white man of prominence, and that his family had told him to flee. As the story goes, he got on a train and never moved back. But distance didn't get in the way. My grandma would call her New Orleans in-laws for counsel if Big Alix acted up, and my sister and I would wonder at hand-me-down clothes from far-off cousins we'd never met.

My grandparents' history is important in framing my path to New Orleans. Drawn to the Northwest by plentiful jobs in agriculture and infrastructural expansion, they experienced a great deal of upward social and economic mobility between the Depression and the 1960s. Despite growing up in Washington, I was surrounded by a small black community with serious pride in their accomplishments and local contributions. Once, driving through the Cascade mountains on I-90 in my grandparents' 1973 Monte Carlo, a state trooper stopped us. The officer approached Big Alix behind the wheel. "Sir," he said, "do you know you were swerving in the road back there?" The first thing to come out of Big Alix's mouth was "Man, I built this road."

My grandfather's brand of masculinity was tough, but he never took comedy and a good time for granted, something I think he brought with him from New Orleans. As soon as church was out, we would start watching kung fu movies. At sixty-something, he let me wrestle him and play bartender, making virgin cocktails he'd pretend to get drunk off of. Now that I think about it, he might not have been pretending. I'll never forget him clarifying the difference between a prostitute and a ho while watching reruns of *Miami Vice* at 2 a.m. He passionately explained to me that one was free and the other was not. I was seven.

Nana and he divided cooking from day to day, and I always looked forward to his Creole dishes. Rice was an important part of our diet; how to go about cooking it was a matter of life and death in our kitchen. If I even attempted to lift the lid before that magic moment, rather than setting a timer, he would make me stand there and use all my senses till a voice inside my head said *now*, to which he'd respond with one of the only Creole words he ever graced us with, *konprann*, meaning understand. These small aspects of his, and by association *our*, cultural differences always gave me a sense of being local but also connected to a broader lineage. They were also my first lessons in learning that blackness was not a monolith, and that we could follow various roots and routes to come to see ourselves as a community, a diasporic one.

Indeed, both my grandparents made life lessons out of their small home, which, despite being right in the industrial center of our small town, was also a small farm. We had peaches, apples, watermelon, strawberries, mint, cucumbers, a grapevine Nana made juice and eventually wine from, and a big chicken coop. We ate their eggs and occasionally wrung their necks, rather than buying the store-bought ones my sister and I preferred. They also came in handy when it was time to potty train me: My grandparents would take me to the coop and make me focus on the chickens as they sat. Big Alix would say, "See how they just sitting there and being patient till something happens?" and Nana would say, "That's what you gotta do." I did as instructed and went to the toilet *to roost* until something happened. To my surprise, they were right.

This way of inverting the everyday into performances of self-making showed up in our lives, proving that nothing was to be taken for granted—not even the smallest of god's creatures. These early lessons in cultivating a sense of self while making do with what's at hand served as a prologue to the "bottom knowledge" I'd later observe in my fieldwork.

Beyond our family's household, there were two primary avenues connecting us to blackness outside our region: the church, and secular black music and performance. Big Alix was one of a few "sometimes" Catholics in our community, and he never converted to Nana's Pentecostal faith. He wasn't a musician, either, but his ambivalence around Protestant morality and his love of a good time led him to give my dad his first guitar when he was six—what he often called my dad's starvation box. Despite never spending time in New Orleans, Dad was firmly rooted in the blues tradition; playing by ear, he sought to live up to idols like Muddy Waters, Big Mama Thornton, and Fats Domino. Big Alix had an eclectic ear and liked everything from Cab Calloway to Elvis Presley. With all these influences and support, Dad started playing professionally by the time he was twelve—at church, in his own bands, or hired by community groups like the Elks Lodge. Nana certainly was known to party before she got saved, and she also supported her son's musical talent. By the time I came around, my dad had performed throughout the West Coast. He'd once opened for Chaka Khan, he'd played in the studios of the Isley Brothers and Ike Turner, and he'd established relationships with other Washington-affiliated musicians and black celebrities, not least of them Quincy Jones and Alex Haley.

My dad used these contacts to start a limousine service in the early '80s, acting as a driver and fixer for black entertainers visiting the area. When he brought Cab Calloway to visit my grandparents' home in 1986, I breakdanced for him in the living room, and he gave me money for my bank account. As the story goes, my dad cringed as Calloway and Big Alix swapped stories of their youthful partying days in the Oakland jazz scene of the 1940s, with Big Alix recounting, "Man, the coke was flowing!"

There was a gendered divide between my grandparents' and parents' investment in the church and secular music. I literally lived (and often was torn) between them. By the time I was born, my parents' marriage was off and on, and they were often separated. Dad performed for a network of hotel clubs and bars, where he also lived when he wasn't at home. I would spend weekends and summers in the back of smoky hotel lounges, behind the bar eating bowls of cocktail cherries, and at the pool playing with other kids I'd never meet again. I loved it; the funk, glamour, and general sociality of Dad's world was fascinating. Between his limo service and my attempts to perfect my signature while charging room service to his tab, I developed a false sense of class consciousness.

Life with Dad was in stark contrast to Mama's religiosity. Her disdain for Dad's life as a performer and artist grew once they divorced. Mama was the one who paid for my classical piano lessons and encouraged me to go to church, where I began singing in choirs. She also instilled a love of travel in me, taking me on cross-country road trips to visit our big, spread-out family. It took years to appreciate, but she had a diverse curiosity about music and art that often found its outlet through the small adventures she tucked between years of graveyard shifts as a registered nurse. Nevertheless, as a child, I struggled with the possibility that the devil was real, that secular music was a vehicle to hell, and that my dad was the chauffeur.

I learned early on and in quite personal ways that spirit was assumed to move in one realm while erotic desire lived in another. In music, assumed lines were drawn between good and evil, what would lead to a full life or a precarious death, and what would bring about wealth or poverty.

These lines were racialized and classed: becoming a good civic participant meant sublimating artistic passions into good, honest, hard work or the church. I saw the cracks and crevices in this logic, though. First, Dad was just as likely to perform at a family or community wedding, birthday, funeral, or reunion as he was to go to the club. He was a small-town celebrity even my friends at school knew and liked. Second, everybody at church had at one point danced to and enjoyed his music. Quite possibly many of them were at the club Saturday night and then in the church Sunday morning. The divide was more talk than practice.

Big Alix usually refused to go to church with the rest of the family because he found most church folk hypocritical. He and Nana had healthy debates and conversations about these issues. When Big Alix did join us on Sundays, he spent most of his time smoking on the front steps, keeping an eye on the ministers and deacons he didn't trust around his wife and family.

Just before that first trip to New Orleans, Mama decided to leave Washington and move back to her family in Oklahoma, and I went with her. It was devastating to be separated from my grandparents, my dad, my older sister, and the family dog. When Mama arranged for us to meet Big Alix in New Orleans later that year, it was a much-needed reunion, but for me, it was also filled with grief. I had changed. From the age of nine, I'd been in a perpetual state of longing for what I'd known. First the dog died, then Dad got a gig playing in Hong Kong and I would only get to see him every few years; then Nana died, and something broke inside.

Through all these changes, I was also coming to terms with my queerness. Nana and Big Alix had often joked with me about being weird, and I like to think there was an implicit solidarity. I never heard homophobia come from them, but even more, I never felt pressure to grow up and be anyone or anything other than a child of god. It was partly because of music that I never felt the need to go to church to connect to a higher power. Divinity knitted together the fabric of everything, from what I could tell. It connected us as a family despite distance, connected me to the chickens out in the coop, to the garden and food Nana canned, to the magic in Big Alix's pot of rice. Despite the binary logic of secular and sacred, good and bad, or what it meant to be human versus animal, it was all love. Nothing was more important than simply finding a reason to live and securing the spiritual and emotional provisions to do so. This was what shaped and supported me throughout life's changes.

After that first trip to New Orleans, I maintained a connection to the place through music and books; in some ways, this allowed me to stay connected to my grandparents. I was always reading comic books and loved anything with fantasy, sci-fi, or magic in the mix—a sensibility Mama shared with me more than anyone. When I got into reading Anne Rice's books after the film release of *Interview with the Vampire*, Mom would enjoy listening to me describe all the details, but she didn't quite grasp the appeal. For me, it was all about gothy, immortal queer longing, set against the libidinal street life I'd glimpsed in New Orleans. The mixture of unorthodox love and melancholic desire for transformation and power was appealing. This period also coincided with the emergence of New Orleans–based Nine Inch Nails, one of my favorite rock bands in the early '90s. Future rendezvous with Big Alix in the city included trips to landmarks described in Rice's books, which slowly added to my awareness of and fascination with the landscape and its history. I craved more knowledge of the city and read and watched everything I could.

Big Alix had a long battle with dementia that reached its peak in 2005, the year the levees broke. In the end, he could remember addresses, but not the name we shared. I would sit with him as he recounted his childhood in New Orleans. In some ways, he became young again, Benjamin Button–like. There was no way to explain to him the devastation of Katrina and the breaking levees, or that his two sisters who'd stayed in New Orleans had died. It was only a few more months before we finally lost him. Three siblings, all gone within a year. I was on my way to Big Alix's funeral the day I got the call that I'd been accepted to graduate school.

When I started visiting New Orleans again, I didn't know I was going to take up this research right away. It wasn't until my first Mardi Gras in 2008, deep in my cups, sitting at the iconic Mother-in-Law Lounge on Claiborne Avenue. Out of nowhere, I heard Big Alix: An older man beside me spoke, and a quality to his voice made me feel my grandfather's presence nearby. Suddenly, I felt called upon.

I've never had an experience like that since, but my time in the city has proved culture is truly a repository of feelings—a resource we can access in the wake of loss, displacement, and death. Given this past, it's hard to say when my research really began. It takes time for the head to catch up with the heart.

INTRODUCTION

PROJECT MUSIC

It was summer 2010, and we were leaving a gig on Bourbon Street. I was performing with Vockah Redu and the Cru, a group of local artists who'd gained popular appeal through the commercial phenomenon of sissy bounce—a fast-paced black queer offshoot of the larger New Orleans bounce music scene. Bounce music, like Vockah and most of the group, came from the city's public housing projects and their surrounding neighborhoods. For a few months, I'd been working with the group as a DJ, cuing prerecorded tracks they would rap, sing, and dance to.

As we stopped to sit on a stoop and figure out the next move, it felt like a good time to switch hats and move from performer to anthropologist. I pulled out my recorder to do an interview, hoping to capture what was on everyone's mind.

Vockah, the principal leader of the group, went first. "The Magnolia itself was the beginning of everything," he said. "It really was the best project ever—not just 'cause I'm from there, and you know Uptown is the best. You know, like, *Uptown!* Just picture it: 'Uptown!' How's that sound?"

Vockah continued to reminisce about his past in the "'Nolia" neighborhood. "Daily life was like me and a bunch of black women walking the streets," he said. "Clara Street, to the Callio, the Melph—now that was the dirtiest project—but it's just like, Uptown, Uptown hoes! I was supposed to be the first sissy of Cash Money, but I didn't like that word ever since then. That's what they use to say."

"Sissy," often used locally as a catchall for black subjects who live outside masculine expectations, is generally directed at gay men and trans women. Cash Money Records, the music label that launched hip-hop stars like Drake, Nicki Minaj, and Lil Wayne, began in New Orleans; in its earliest days, it showcased bounce acts.

Many of Vockah's lyrics spoke to friendships and just hanging out, walking the streets. Even as we strolled along as a group, laughing and reflecting on our show, the call-and-response lyrics to one of his early songs came to mind:

> Fresh ideas, fresh face to the world
> Easy, breezy, beautiful avenue girls!
> C'mon, c'mon, avenue (girls!), diamonds and (pearls!)
> Avenue (girls!), diamonds and (pearls!)
> Make ya tiddies (twirl!) avenue (girls!) on top the (world!)

"Avenue Girlz 2Gs," recorded when Vockah was a teen in the '90s, playfully remixes the "Easy, Breezy, Beautiful, CoverGirl" jingle, redefining feminine beauty and sexuality in the everyday life of ghettoized black youth. The song's background vocals were delivered by some of the young women he'd walked those streets with; many of them had since been displaced, along with a great deal of the public housing community he'd grown up with. The song is just one example of what I call *raising the bottom*: performances that redirect common hierarchies of value in an effort to sustain what's been cast to the bottom of social relations.

Vockah and the other group members' memories functioned much like his songs—recalling relationships, places, and circumstances that would otherwise be forgotten. This was in great part what fascinated people about sissy bounce. The music and performances paid tribute to, and expressed the joy of, people living at the intersection of multiple forms of marginalization due to race, gender, class, and sexuality, in places defined by generations of alienation, displacement, and exploitation.

As we sat talking, it was getting late. People were beginning to exit the clubs on their way home. The cassette tape in the recorder slowly rolled as the cars cruised by. One member of the group after another spoke while the others danced. Somebody started to bend over and twerk to the music coming from the nearby club, flirting with the occupants of the cars passing by. Everything was great until one older black driver made eye contact with something he didn't like: us.

The man behind the wheel began cursing: "Sissies! Faggots! You punks!" He described to nobody and everybody what he'd do to us. At first it seemed like the car would slowly pass, but then it came to a full stop and the driver began yelling about shooting us. Arguing with his two women passengers, he backed up until we were face to face. Then he leaned down as if to reach for the gun he claimed to have.

No one in our group moved, let alone attempted to run. We were together, silent, inching closer toward that annoyingly familiar refrain, "vulnerable and at risk." If I'd been alone, I would have run, but in our group, it felt as though we were caught together in a net—that if any one of us moved or spoke, our decision could mean everyone's fate. For a moment it was just silence and a lot of eyes. Then the driver began arguing with his passengers again. Instead of bullets, he punctuated his exit with a run of curses and skidding tires.

"I wish he would have!" said Fatman.

"If that had happened back in the projects, I'd have slipped away and come back and got his ass from behind," Vockah said.

Mundane threats like what we'd just experienced were as familiar to the Cru as the positive attention and applause we'd received an hour before at our show. Haters gonna hate. I found Vockah's consistent reference to the projects telling. Good or bad, it was home. Most of the public housing projects the group came from, like the Magnolia, were gone and had been for some time. Despite this, the memories and conditions everyone had experienced within them were often reproduced, in moments of violence but also great joy.

When I got home that night to jot down my field notes, I picked up the recorder and pressed play. It had caught the interviews, but also the scary encounter. It was a haunting sound.

....

Sissy bounce is an amalgamation of black queer vernacular, R & B, blues, and US and Caribbean performance traditions. It also highlights New Orleans's mixture of sexuality and black political struggle. The genre became a central ingredient in pop cultural treatments of liberation in the 2010s, when shaking and twerking amid assimilation and respectability politics garnered widespread appeal.

This book, *Raising the Bottom*, is a performance ethnography. Over two years, I examined everyday life from the stage and the moments in between each show and situated bounce and its surrounding culture historically and globally. My research required paying attention to community members and cultural practices marginalized not only by race and sexuality, but also class disparities within black communities. I conducted the ethnographic portion of this research, focusing on my time with Vockah Redu and the Cru, between 2009 and 2012.

Sissy bounce helped define more inclusive notions of black belonging in the wake of Hurricane Katrina in 2005; that disaster had caused the mass displacement of black New Orleans and led to a radical shift in neoliberal governance.[1] Why and how, I wondered, did a black queer performance genre from the projects come to represent home and kinship for the broader black community in a time of crisis? Although commercial interest in sissy bounce peaked around 2015, its reach can't be taken for granted. Sissy bounce increased black queer and trans people's visibility in mainstream social media, dance culture, and hip-hop throughout the 2010s. Its traces can still be seen when someone twerks, face down and ass up, on the dance floor; when a song samples bounce's unique rhythms and voices; and when contemporary black queer representations combine equal parts urbanness and Southernness.

The popularity of bounce artists both within and outside New Orleans reveals that their lives are far more broadly significant than apparent at first glance. As black queer Southern performers, they've played a key role in defining alternative notions of black power and liberation. Their lives, and the culture that fostered them, also challenge dominant assumptions that black kinship, home, and community are inherently homophobic, transphobic, and antiqueer.

This book offers a path toward reconsidering and redirecting personal and communal assumptions about good/evil, pleasure/pain, and dirtiness/cleanliness. Readers can also make various connections between the text and debates about difference, power, and social justice. I'm of the mind that none of these topics can be engaged without first doing the undervalued labor of digging deep to observe our own unconscious biases. Anthropology presupposes an interrogation—a view usually imagined as neutral and downward-looking—of the world around us; that position, like many others within this book, might need to be inverted to consider what the people and stories within these pages have to say. I discourage, too, taking up this book in the name of multicultural bridge-building if the end result involves annexing black queer experiences into a passageway for those already afforded power.

For readers who are struggling to embrace what they've been told is unworthy and excessive in themselves, consider the acts of self-love, intentionality, and manifestation in these pages as a condition of possibility for your own capacity to define, grow, and act. Like music, dance, or language, this book won't produce better access and resources for systemically marginalized peoples in and of itself. But perhaps, through playing with entrenched ideas about the how, where, what, and why of power and powerlessness, we might tip the scales that undergird today's intellectual force, and thereby change material conditions. Redirection as a practice of revaluation is inherent to this work: If you've ever caught your foot tapping to the beat despite what your mind tells you is cool, pleasurable, and of good taste, I encourage you to pay attention to your felt connection to the text. You could be a few steps away from raising the bottom yourself—and if so, what would that mean about you and your own worth?

AN EPISTEMOLOGY OF THE BOTTOM

Toni Morrison's novel *Sula*, and its fictional black neighborhood, "the Bottom," feel especially relevant in situating black queer performances of bounce. *Sula*'s account of the people and geography of the Bottom is a blueprint: It brings what black feminist scholar Barbara Christian referred to as the felt knowledge of black life into contrast with the "real," self-evident yet constructed, mapping of spaces.[2]

Raising the Bottom traces the structure of what I call an *epistemology of the bottom*: a way of understanding, navigating, and countering the interconnected narratives and (de)valuation systems that merge black and queer bodies, spaces, and sex with the bottom of social hierarchies. I insist on rethinking who is an authority as we rank knowledge from doctors, clergy, academics, artists, musicians, and dancers. If hospitals, churches, and universities are formal social institutions that attend to the former, how can we conceive of the stage, nightclub, and street as informal equivalents of the latter?

This epistemology of the bottom is a toolkit for deconstructing commonly held notions around bottom locations, whether those locations are geographic or embodied: for instance, black queer vernacular, public housing projects, the body's own physical bottom, and deviant stereotypes of the sissy. *Raising the Bottom* will highlight the ways performers have taken these and other stereotypes and their everyday effects, remixed them, and redirected the result into counterintuitive notions of power, pleasure, and solidarity.

Other thinkers I lean on include anal theorists like Kathryn Bond Stockton, whose 2006 book *Beautiful Bottom, Beautiful Shame* brings *Sula* into conversation with psychoanalysis through Freud. Stockton makes a compelling case for the Bottom as a metaphor for a range of representational fields, as well as a signifier for a racialized economic basement. I'm also grateful for the guidance of Jennifer C. Nash, whose 2014 essay "Black Anality" explores "how black pornographies represent the anus—the Bottom—as a passageway through which black pleasures, perils, and pathologies are made visible" (446–47).[3] Morrison and, by proxy, her critics draw on the history of black peoples living in real black bottoms, poor, often segregated urban areas low-lying land throughout the United States (Davis 2018; Summerville 1981; Williams 2011). *Raising the Bottom* furthers these literary and political economic histories in ethnographic vignettes that exemplify bottom epistemes, aesthetics, and praxis.

The bottom, Nash explains, is tethered to black sexualities—and here we must trace this connection specifically to the figure of the sissy.[4] In "Sissies at the Picnic," Roderick A. Ferguson frames critical thought on the matter through childhood memories of a black queer choir director named Edward. Outlining shifts in black communal attitudes toward sissies, Ferguson reveals how sissy figures have been indispensable yet also disavowed and often scapegoated as pariahs amid larger systemic oppressions.[5] The sissy in bounce, much like Ferguson's, is also imagined through cultural labor: part of the everyday, rooted in the working class, and tied to performances that the black community solicits, learns from, and takes pleasure in. The sissy is an alternative figure of black power and liberation's attachment to masculine ascendence who is not "necessarily, or only feminine" but "exceeds or overruns" the masculine (Scott 2010, 19).[6]

In the parlance of New Orleans, *sissy* is generally used to describe queer men and trans women who break with tradition.[7] This figure exceeds heteronormative and nationalist bonds; it challenges classical notions of pleasure, power, and desire for the "black family." Personhood is historically modeled on successful masculinity, and black liberation is stubbornly linked to the rise of black men as patriarchs. The figure of the sissy in bounce is, by this reasoning, an affront to notions of freedom and the self. Despite this, bounce's sissy figures offer counterintuitive potential, (re)producing blackness in spaces, moments, and relationships that might otherwise succumb to the conditions of displacement and dispossession.

An epistemology of the bottom is aimed at exploring the imagined and real meanings of varied bottom positions, revealing logic that conflates ghettoized space, black queer bodies, and, by proximity, the extended community. I'm by no means arguing that the subjects of this book are actually pathological—they simply exist in a shared representational field around waste, sexual excess, and moral and economic deficit. This interlocking system brings people from the ghetto, sissies, and New Orleans (despite its historical status as the most northern Caribbean city) together in a racialized and economic bottom. Morrison's work has provided a pathway through which the bottom becomes a metonym.

THE BLACK QUEER PAST

Sissy performances, or "punk shows," have been a staple within New Orleans's black communities for generations; they took on a special place following Hurricane Katrina (Chapman 2014). Meanwhile, sissy bounce artists join a long history of black queer performers who have acted as translators of cultural meanings around race, class, and locality.

Throughout my time in New Orleans, people interested in the origins of sissy bounce mentioned the career of local soul singer and producer Bobby Marchan, a black cabaret and soul vocalist who was publicly gay and performed in drag at legendary ballrooms like the Dew Drop Inn.[8] From the 1950s through the 1990s, he produced a series of hits and collaborations with famous singers. Marchan was an early promoter of New Orleans hip-hop, providing seed money and connections for young artists who would eventually become significant figures in Southern rap—namely, the Williams brothers of Cash Money Records.

Marchan had performed in drag since his youth, inspired by the cross-dressing acts incorporated into the jazz and blues tours of the chitlin circuit (Ankeny, n.d.). Originally from Ohio, Marchan made a home for himself in New Orleans, living right between a lively club scene and the public housing projects where a significant portion of his audience must have lived.

In his 1987 song "Strokin' Part 2," Marchan represents the city, the projects, and residents' sexual prowess in a fashion not unlike bounce:

> *All around the world, everybody's strokin'* . . . *but all the strokin' comes down to New Orleans.* . . . *I heard the best strokers in New Orleans was in the*

I.1 Rhythm and blues singer Bobby Marchan performing in drag.

> *project. Somebody said the best strokers were in the Fischer Projects; I can't tell, because I heard the deal that the best strokers was in the Iberville! But then, if you must know, some woman told me she strokes best in the Callio. Then I had another cat tell me he stroked all the way from the Bahamas—but he never got down right till he got to the St. Thomas.*

It's important to understand that black queer performance in bounce, New Orleans, and the greater South is not exceptional, but part of a broader history that has contributed to blackness and popular culture at large (Davis 1998; Johnson 2008).[9] Marchan's life establishes a genealogical thread that links black queer performance, black working-class life, sissy bounce, and bottom locations in New Orleans.[10]

Just as much as Marchan's own career connected black people throughout the United States and Caribbean on the basis of shared pleasure, his legacy and mentorship of emergent artists affected the scope and reach of their artistry. Through his label, Manicure Records, Marchan managed musicians and producers who'd go on to influence the global face of popular culture—New Orleans's own Ronald "Slim" Williams, his brother Bryan "Birdman" Williams, Mystikal, and Lil Wayne. Here is a critical juncture between the beginnings of bounce music and the development of Southern hip-hop, as well as continuity between black queer performances ranging from early R & B to blues to sissy bounce.

Marchan passed away in 1999, right when queer and trans artists began to make names for themselves in bounce.[11] Still, it's clear that hip-hop icons like the Williams brothers were in close proximity to black queer culture, as they were mentored by Marchan.[12] This means that the emergence of Vockah Redu and the Cru and other performers wasn't contradictory to urban black culture—these artists were very much part of the family.

PERFORMANCE ETHNOGRAPHY AND THE STAGE

Big Freedia, né Freddie Ross, is a gender-nonconforming, gay-identified rapper using both he/him and she/her pronouns. Freedia has done more to popularize bounce beyond New Orleans than any of her peers—and I owe her a great debt for introducing me to the bounce stage (and later to Vockah Redu and the Cru).

Prior to this research, I was a musician and performance artist, active in the United States and abroad throughout the 2000s. Aware of my background and scholarly interest in black queer performance, Big Freedia's manager contacted me about performing as a backup dancer for her. I joined her on her first tour at the 2008 SXSW Music Festival in Austin, Texas. Although I'd seen Freedia at a few parades in New Orleans and was familiar with her music, I wasn't prepared for how generous, humble, and dynamic a presence she was. Only hours after we met, I took to the stage with her, and her own larger than life spirit emboldened me.

I really knew little about the customary dances and movements associated with bounce, but before long the music, mixed with Freedia's directorial call-and-response, had me shaking, twerking, and popping.[13] Up until that point, I'd only seen one live bounce performance at a community block party. Not knowing if I'd have another chance to connect with an artist like Freedia, I shook for my life. Wearing nothing but my shoes and hot pants, I set my glasses and notebook aside and danced. After our performances, Big Freedia thanked me. When I described my research plan in New Orleans, she encouraged me and began connecting me with clubs and performers. From the start, I knew that my presence

1.2 Big Freedia photographed for the 2010 *Where They At* bounce music exhibition. Photo by Aubrey Edwards.

1.3 Photograph taken by Angeliska Polacheck of Big Freedia and author performing at the 2009 SXSW Music Festival.

onstage and acceptance by Big Freedia was somewhat justified by my being a black queer person, as opposed to someone with any real knowledge of bounce.

Later that same year, I attended a Big Freedia show in the French Quarter. It was here I first met Vockah Redu and the Cru. I approached the VIP section to say hello, and Freedia turned and introduced me to Vockah. The music was so loud I could barely catch his name. Shortly after, we ran into each other in the bathroom while washing hands. I took the opportunity to reintroduce myself and explain my interest in researching bounce music. "Well, you should be talking to me!" Vockah exclaimed. Almost on cue, Vockah's backup dancer Fatman walked up, and we exchanged introductions. Fat was less friendly; he went out of his way to act aloof. I would become accustomed to his apprehension toward me, and I'd also come to appreciate his overall wariness and discernment. I would learn that Vockah and Fatman alternated between good cop and bad cop, always tempering each other in a rocky yet deeply committed friendship.

I was asked to participate in rehearsals and shows very quickly, and my enthusiastic participation was also a means of securing research data. Group members would introduce me to people, saying, "He's our historian," owning the fact that they stood, or should I say, danced, at the center of a significant historical moment. Once I started meeting everyone in the group for rehearsals, I realized I was out of my league. I was five to ten years older than everyone, and keeping up was a challenge. But I was determined to make myself useful, not just as a participating observer but as a contributor. I knew Fat's initial wariness changed as he and the others observed my commitment. Once, laughing, he exclaimed, "Alix got to shake, just like us!"

Over two years, group members took me into their homes, families, and churches, giving me opportunities to see the spectacular and everyday aspects of their lives. Through them, I began to experience the black queer club scene—in particular, Club Fusions, Club Vibe, and The Page, all of which played bounce music almost exclusively. I went to church revivals, birthdays, funerals, and other gatherings. At private homes, block parties, and bars, I was increasingly surrounded by the group's extended community of friends and fans.

My preliminary research began in the fall of 2006 with frequent short trips to New Orleans. I began making connections with performers in

2008. I conducted primary fieldwork and interviews with at least sixty community members from 2009 to 2011. During these years, I met and performed with Vockah Redu and the Cru and shared stages with Big Freedia, Sissy Nobby, Katey Red, and others. I continued to follow the careers of particular artists throughout the 2010s.

After 2011, my attention shifted from fieldwork to the movement of sissy bounce from its local context to national and international circulation in popular culture and social media. I paid close attention to three areas: (1) Big Freedia's career, which led to greater national and international interest in both Freedia and the genre as a whole; (2) the annexation and circulation of sissy bounce (and attendant representations of New Orleans) in popular culture throughout the 2010s—particularly the music and performances of Beyoncé, Drake, and Miley Cyrus; and (3) sissy bounce's influence on the mainstreaming of twerk. Twerking, I argue, isn't a neutral act, but a performance that brings ideas about blackness, sexuality, and anality to the fore.

I approach this study of black music not through ethnomusicology or music studies but through various streams of performance studies, African diasporic genealogies, black queer and black feminist thought, and theories of space-making. Through methods of performance ethnography and coperformance specifically, I met most of the people who contributed to this research; I engaged questions of memory, embodiment, and geography; and I became more sensitive to cultural expressions I encountered within music and everyday life.[14] My ethnographic practice required more than observing and documenting—I learned what to listen for in bounce music and vernacular expressions, which deepened my understanding of performance as a tool and strategy within my coperformers' lives.[15]

This ethnography documents a rupture and its structural effects. This book moves between my respondents' memories of life before Katrina and our collective post-Katrina experiences. Interviews and observations return to memories of loss and hopes for renewal. Part of everyday life was always noting what no longer was—lost relationships, destroyed homes, razed community centers. Renewal and reconstruction projects, meanwhile, often furthered the work of ideological and structural oppression, obscuring people's memories of the past and awareness of current conditions.[16] In these conditions, cultural performance becomes a high-stakes power struggle in negotiating the production of knowledge and history.[17]

MUSIC AND CULTURAL GEOGRAPHY

Music can take you places. Bounce rapper Kilo once said, "Bounce isn't hip-hop. It's not R & B. It's project music" (Miller and Thomas, 2007). This is a critical distinction: The genre is intrinsically different from nationally recognized black musical genres while defined by its origins in public housing—a nationally familiar infrastructural object and symbol associated with an economic bottom.

I was getting my hair cut in a makeshift shed-turned-barbershop when bounce artist Sissy Nobby's song "Break It Down" came through the speakers. With no pretense of the lyrical devices of other forms of hip-hop (or earlier forms of bounce), Nobby drives home one point:

Break it down, break it, break it down, break it, break it down . . .
I'm not finished, you know how we roll
Put your hands to the ground, now do it on the floor
Where's the uptown? You know how we roll
Put your hands to the ground, now do it on the floor
Do it on the floor, do it on the floor, do it . . .

When the barber exclaimed, "Here go that sissy shit!"[18] another patron replied, "Yeah, but you can't deny him. Nobody got a voice like Nobby."

The other patron and I began discussing the differences between bounce and hip-hop from elsewhere. He explained why he'd rather listen to bounce, even if it came from a self-proclaimed sissy. "Gay or not, I feel this," he said, "because we don't got time for some long story. We still on the plantation down here, and you can hear it."

The reference to the plantation, like references to the projects, points to an imagined geography about racial-economic bottoms. Sissy Nobby's voice—guttural, locally accented—grinds the lyrics in a combination of Southern drawl and labored breath that harks back to the work songs of sharecropping days. The voices of jazz and blues greats like Louis Armstrong and Howlin' Wolf would be hard-pressed to achieve Nobby's gravelly vocal quality. Whether they were being received by passive listeners at the barbershop or fans at shows, black queer performances like Nobby's conjured feelings that then influenced communal perceptions about race, sexuality, and what it means to be local.

Music functions as a portal, taking the listener on a geographic and historical journey. Hip-hop artists like Kanye West regularly pay homage to New Orleans's public housing projects; West's song "Blood on the Leaves," like many others, specifically references the Magnolia, or 'Nolia, where Vockah and a number of internationally famous rappers like Juvenile and Jay Electronica come from. The notoriety of New Orleans projects extends way beyond local ties, serving as a kind of hip-hop mecca. Pilgrims may not be able to visit these locations physically, due to the displacement of people, brick, and mortar, but they symbolically recognize and pay homage to them.

Many people don't catch these local references, and initially I was one of them. To be honest, when I first heard bounce music I didn't understand it. To me it sounded nonsensical, random, messy—too loud and fast to take in. The songs never mentioned the most familiar parts of New Orleans: tourist attractions Bourbon Street, the French Quarter, and the Garden District or well-known symbols like gumbo and Mardi Gras. Though the meaning was often lost in translation, I witnessed the passionate dancing and, at times, tears the audiences were moved to—and saw something much deeper at work. Understanding what the culture meant to the community would require more than me working in proximity and neatly situating an outside, top-down analytical framework around what was happening on stages and street corners. I needed to learn about the culture from the inside—living, working, and performing alongside artists and their broader community. Physically becoming part of the action was a must.

Although I moved beyond my first impressions, for many people, conflicts over the meaning, legibility, or aggressiveness of black music or culture don't happen on neutral ground. Consider the murder of Florida teenager Jordan Davis in 2012. Davis, sitting in the passenger seat of his friend's car at a gas station, was fired upon by a disgruntled white man who was upset by the loud hip-hop they were listening to.[19] "Ghetto" or "ratchet" music and dance are assumed to exist at the bottom of the barrel; to people like Davis's assailant, these forms offer real proof of the low morals, sexual deviance, and poverty that define black stereotypes.

To understand this project music would mean rethinking ideas about high and low culture; learning how to listen and engage; and developing an understanding and appreciation of local vernacular, knowledge, and histories from within the community. For example, another popular Sissy Nobby song, "Josephine Beat," incorporates a number of classic samples and features from other bounce artists. It also mixes in Beyoncé's "Partition" and Enya's "Boadicea" (the latter popularized among hip-hop crowds through the Fugees' 1990s track "Ready or Not"). "Josephine" refers to a street in New Orleans's Uptown that ran through and alongside public housing communities like the Melpomene and Callio projects. In the track, Nobby engages in a pattern that runs through much of bounce: the poetic merging of black geographies with figments of desire and love. "You know that Josephine ain't nothin' without that Josephine Johnny," he raps. "She got that Josephine boy." Similar references run throughout a great deal of hip-hop culture—but here, Nobby speaks to a space and community that's been all but displaced due to years of political effort by local elites to rid the city of the projects. Due to these efforts and the acute impact of urban shifts related to Hurricane Katrina, Nobby and other sissy bounce rappers' songs appeal to young audiences who have seen their homes and neighborhoods disappear within their own lifetimes. The lyrics take on an even deeper sense of urgency considering who they come from. The precarity of black queer desire intersects with the general sense of longing and need felt throughout the community; if a sissy can find love and union, might we all?

Sissy Nobby's music was special partly because he'd started out as a dancer, then begun producing his own tracks. Nobby understood from experience that what local audiences wanted more than anything, "dat beat," the unique rhythm that's key to a real bounce song.[20] Mixed between the particularities of bounce is something any hip-hop head can recognize and identify: the locomotion of a syncopated 808 bass and drum, key to so many hits from the 1980s onward. The rhythm is held up high as if on a pedestal, shaking black ass.

There's a profound relationship between the black body and bounce's reclamation of bottom geographies. Dat beat—the golden thread, the rhythm that defines bounce—cannot be separated from the visuality of ass-shaking. The perpetual driving force of dat beat carries speech and dance on a journey, directed by call-and-response chants: "Shake that ass like a saltshaker!" "Face down, ass up!" "Bend it over—touch ya toes!" (and one of my favorite responses, "Hit me with dat turkey neck!"). In clubs catering to bounce audiences, a DJ bold enough to break from dat beat and put a regular hip-hop song in the mix runs the risk of people abandoning the dance floor en masse, offering choice words to the DJ booth, and even leaving the venue entirely. Audiences take rhythm dead serious in New Orleans. The focus on forward motion may have emerged from what occurs in the city's parading culture. When a marching band takes too many breaks or gets out of pocket in terms of keeping the beat, losing the locomotion that propels the parade, bystanders feel entitled to tell the musicians to do their job. "Baby, it's always fashionable to make an exit before the music ends," one old-timer remarked. "When the beat don't drop, people come back to reality, and things can get ugly." The number of shootings and fights that have occurred after parades and at venue closing times is evidence of the imperative to catch the beat and keep it going.

A good DJ can play to this sense of something urgent at work in the rhythm—something to do with life and death—and in this sense bounce resonates with genres like gospel, punk rock, and rave music. Sissy bounce garnered large nonblack and nonlocal audiences, and Vockah Redu and the Cru would often share stages with punk rock acts. Black queer musician, performer, choreographer, and author Brontez Purnell, discussing the intersections of his experiences in the black church and do-it-yourself punk rock scenes, notes:

> I think church is where I first performed—and this was back before the church had a microphone, so I think most of the songs went to whoever could project the loudest. How well you sang was secondary. First, who could project? I carry a sense of projection in everything, even in [my] writing. . . . I grew up in probably the midst of, like, DIY culture. And what DIY culture teaches you, of course, is "The powers that be are never gonna talk to you specifically. If there's something that needs to be addressed, you yourself have to take control of that." (2019)

Bounce's primary audience has always been black New Orleanians. After Hurricane Katrina, a new audience grew, paralleling the expansion of gentrification due to an influx of reconstruction volunteers, tourists, and college students. This circulation and movement brought a national spotlight on sissy bounce that was bright and promising—albeit temporary, as trends go. After Katrina, throughout the city, people across differences of race and class were thrust into a context where daily life required making yourself heard, lest you be drowned out by a multitude of talking heads. Sissy bounce carried a sense of projection across the city and beyond; it served as a model for people struggling to find their voice amid political silence.

COUNTERINTUITIVE FREEDOM

In a brief series of interviews with straight and queer rappers and fans, the 2007 Miller–Thomas documentary *Ya Heard Me?* covers Katey Red and Big Freedia's remarkable entry into the bounce scene.[21] In an interview, Red, a black trans woman, remixes street callouts into a means of self-making, challenging notions of private and public space: "I use to walk down the streets, [and] they use to be saying, 'Katey Red, you dick-sucker.' So why don't I get on the mic and call myself a dick-sucker? Just get it on out, feel free—so now, when they call me a dick sucker, they singing my song" (Miller and Thomas 2007).

In this instance, Red uses the cultural labor of music to express counterintuitive notions of freedom and personhood. She contests discrimination against her body, gender, and sexuality—and by association, against those like her.[22] When I call these notions "counterintuitive," I mean they require us to rethink what we generally consider unproductive, shameful, or illegible—and reenvision these things as valuable challenges to norms that pathologize blackness and queerness.[23] We can't assume music will decrease high rates of violence against black trans women—representation doesn't determine survival—but music can effectively shift the moving equilibrium that naturalizes such violence.

Raising the Bottom focuses on intersectional and antiassimilative practices—like Red's—in a community attempting to reconstitute home and kinship in post–Hurricane Katrina New Orleans. Emphasizing communal self-understandings and vernacular performances, the chapters examine how performers and audiences express the joy of cultural labor and alternative kinship. They also highlight the limits of community and agency in the face of persistent discourses of pathology and violence. These conflicts and impasses are made stark in both mundane aspects of daily life and in the dramatizations of staged performances.

Following Cathy J. Cohen's "Punks, Bulldaggers, and Welfare Queens" (2005), my approach to black queer studies emphasizes solidarity and coalition across categories of identity. In delineating an epistemology of the bottom, I consider how similar experiences of violence and pleasure crosscut queer, heterosexual, and working-class black lives. While highlighting relationships between black queer men, trans women, and cishet black women, I recognize not everyone subscribes to a particular gender

I.4 Katey Red's 2000 album *Y2 Katey Millennium Sissy*. Take Fo' Records.

or sexual category, and some may prefer to remain fluid. Blackness and locality, however, provide an undergirding foundation throughout the community, overriding other forms of difference.

Historically, music and dance have helped stabilize black social movements and formed some of the most salient expressions of freedom and emancipation since the turn of the twentieth century. *Raising the Bottom* explores black queer cultural production in a *superstructural* rather than an *infrastructural* sense—a difference Samuel Delany explains in his astute critique of urban transformations in 1970s New York. "Infrastructure makes society go," Delany writes. "Superstructure makes society go smoothly (or bumpily)" (1999, 162). I'm interested in black queer culture's role in the moving equilibrium of knowledge—what it contributes as dominant and marginalized groups vie to assert interpretations of what's "real."

My focus on New Orleans situates sissy bounce's origins and its reach.[24] As historian Clyde Woods (2017) points out, New Orleans is central to understanding the development of both the US economy and global popular culture. Through what Woods calls the blues epistemology, we come to understand the blues as a form of black working-class thought that comments on and explicates the undertaking of living through capitalism and white supremacy.[25] I build on these insights by extending Woods's blues theory to bounce. To do this, I draw from Angela Y. Davis's use of the blues as an aesthetic domain that challenges oppressive cultural ideals that abounded in both white America and black respectability politics. Performers like Ma Rainey and Bessie Smith represented forms of black womanhood that defined sexuality and gender beyond white, middle-class, heterosexual norms. Davis shows how respectability, within and outside black communities, is defined by the private expression of nationalist ideologies like heteronormativity and the gendered division of labor.

In dominant (that is, whiteness-centered, heteronormative, and bioreductive) frames of family and future, blackness and queerness aren't productive; they represent incoherence in ways that might destroy familial bonds or a person's sense of self. The bottom, in terms of anal desires, is presumed not to build communities or produce new generations of people. I'm interested in countering these bioreductive notions. Black queer pleasure, culture, dialogues, spaces, social frameworks, and relationships—presumed nonproductive because of liminality or alleged moral deficits—have actual reproductive power, providing the fertile ground on which intersectional and antiassimilative futures are birthed.

To claim counterintuitive powers is to lift what's been devalued—to raise up what's been naturalized as the bottom of social, economic, and political relations. My framework for doing this incorporates embodied experiences in dance; it also expands outward to consider the devastating effects of exclusionary and exploitative state infrastructures, such as the decimation of black urban communities by federal freeway projects.

Racialized and economic bottoms map onto the body as much as environments do; these notions must be deconstructed and reimagined. Katey Red, Vockah Redu, and other bounce artists encourage audiences to rethink their relationship to their bodies—and to reconsider geographies like the public housing projects and streets the artists hail from. This kind of bottom knowledge can express resistance to antiblackness, and it can be a means of finding and creating place and community across time and space. To what narrative of black freedom and liberation do those who claim it belong?

"AZZ EVERYWHERE"

Big Freedia's hit "Azz Everywhere" gestures to the global resonance of bounce. While I discuss a bottom epistemology that articulates the racial-sexual landscape of New Orleans, this way of knowing is part of a diasporic felt knowledge, often expressed through regional sensibilities. New Orleans has bounce; DC has go-go, Chicago juke, Oakland hyphy, Florida Miami bass, Houston chop and screw. Detroit has more forms than I can count. In African diasporas outside the United States, Brazil has baile funk, Trinidad and Tobago have soca and calypso, and Angola has kuduro. In every case, music and dance are "not only *of* the body, in the sense of object, but also *from* the body, that is, deploying the body as tool of inquiry and vector of knowledge" (Wacquant 2004, 21–22). This knowledge is formed in relation to particular ecologies, environments, and conditions of racial capitalism.

Progressive scholars must take seriously the body as a site of decolonization. As the sexologist Herukhuti (H. Sharif Williams) writes in his incisive critiques of black studies scholarship, scholars "must be willing to engage body, mind and spirit, eschew respectability politics and get funky if they have any chance of connecting to the multidimensional lives of Black people—a people who have survived but not yet liberated themselves from the multidimensional trauma of colonization and kidnap" (2016, 21–22).

Incorporating Audre Lorde's development of the erotic into his own epistemology, Herukhuti states, "Bodies have just as much ability to save minds, spirits and souls. We can move, dance, and fuck our way to decolonization. Our bodies have the capacity to show our minds new possibilities for liberation if we pay attention" (12).

Herukhuti and scholars like L. H. Stallings (2015) have developed black funk or funk studies into an integrative framework, bringing the erotic, spiritual, and political into a research practice I deploy. An epistemology of the bottom requires acknowledging physical and erotic energies that are most certainly in the body, but also extend and inform the way we experience the world. For example, throughout the twentieth century, major shifts in black music were birthed through working-class experiences of labor. Through the auto industry, assembly-line workers entered a relationship with machines so intimate they used those experiences to inform the factorylike production of Motown and the postindustrial programming of 808 drums and samplers (Che 2009; Nkiru 2019).

In bounce, a similar relationship is informed by the ways blackness has had to negotiate space in a sinking city. Many nonlocals are familiar with the flood-prone nature of New Orleans, due to Katrina and the potential disaster the city encounters every hurricane season. But what many don't know is that when New Orleans was settled by colonists, it was above sea level. Anthropogenic subsidence—the compaction and gradual sinking of the land, due in major part to humans pumping water out of marshland and swamp to expand the city—has led to a nuanced racial topography. Areas like the Lower Ninth Ward, once home to one of the country's largest populations of black homeowners, are also floodplains.[26]

Race, sexuality, and the uninhabitable are conflated in bottom geographies. In New Orleans, as in other urban spaces, white vice—sex work, sex trafficking, the drug trade—is often positioned in proximity to black neighborhoods, reflecting and deepening those neighborhoods' imagined associations with toxicity, excess, and waste. New Orleans's Congo Square, an origin site of African diasporic performance in the New World, was presented in colonial depictions as an abject, ghettoized space. The Faubourg Tremé, the first black neighborhood in the United States, and Storyville, the iconic red-light district that travelers ventured to the city to experience, are adjacent to each other on the periphery of the French Quarter, the city proper. All this is to say that black cultural expressions of home and belonging are produced and maintained through a relationship to the bottom; learning to live in and through these spaces has both a local specificity and a relevance within global African diasporas.

An epistemology of the bottom constitutes sissy bounce artists' attempts at redressing the queer and black working-class plight within these geographies. Rather than tuck away or restrict what's generally estranged, the artists raise and dispense forms of social wealth in antiassimilationist, egalitarian acts of joy and caregiving. This bottom knowledge and strategy are a condition of possibility, an artistic awareness, and an emotive framework; it reorients norms concerning the distribution of power and its justification. It also resonates with other groups who know what it's like to always and already be the underdog.[27]

Diaspora is key to understanding home and community—and also bounce—in New Orleans and the US South. Racial, ethnic, and queer conceptions of diaspora can speak to global cultural flows, memories, and structures of feeling—unlike white Western ideologies that attempt and fail to determine alternative notions of personhood. These concepts and frameworks have the power to address far more than the current or historical context of global migration across national borders. They can bypass reductive beliefs about "developed" and "underdeveloped" worlds—and they can invert heteropatriarchal and racist systems of thought that reduce black queer bodies to pathological objects. Afrocentricity is a common (if marginalized) ideology underpinning global black life. Bounce music expresses Afrocentric and queer notions of diaspora as an erotic and sacred resource—one with the potential to destabilize oppressive and inadequate ideologies and point toward a more livable future.

New Orleans is one of the most African cities in North America. Here, music and dance are far more than leisure and entertainment. They're forms of world-making, old and new. New Orleans has historically been portrayed as a peripheral and exceptional geography (Anthony 1978; Blassingame 1973; Dessens 2007; Hall 1992). Countless narratives about New Orleans offer images of racial otherness usually reserved for "distant and alien" geographies such as Haiti and the African continent. These places have been symbolically pushed to the edge of white Western civility and moral rectitude, while simultaneously used by the West in its accumulation of material and existential resources. This might explain why news outlets, in the years after Katrina, labeled displaced evacuees "refugees," as if they weren't US citizens.[28] Following Hurricane Katrina—or, more accurately, the failure of the Army Corps of Engineers' substandard and neglected levees—the city has become a symbol of urban decay and twenty-first-century disaster.

THE BEGINNING, NOT THE END

Each chapter of this book follows a similar organizational structure. The ethnographic context of my coperformances with Vockah Redu and the Cru and other black queer figures provides context for the analysis. Music lyrics, excerpts, and/or notes engage additional artistic and scholarly voices in order to develop the bottom epistemology described above. Members and former members of the Cru, as well as their friends and family members, share oral histories and self-understandings. Beyond the ethnographic vignettes, I'll situate the local and everyday within larger historical and global networks. That said, the ethnographic accounts and the voices of black queer people are what shine and are privileged, as this is the goal of *Raising the Bottom*. The political economies I touch on are by no means exhaustive; I make no pretense toward in-depth histories or an extensive understanding of contemporary media in global popular culture. *Raising the Bottom* is concerned with the past and theory inasmuch as I can find touchstones that support, balance, and lift my coperformers' understanding of their own material conditions.

Chapter 1, "*Catch Dat Beat*: Performing Pleasure and Coalition," explores the daily lives and staged performances of Vockah and the Cru while attending to the broader context of post-Katrina displacement and reconstruction. I connect black queer performances to a larger network of informal economies (in this case, unlicensed barbering and beautician services). These forms of social wealth attend to life in an economic bottom defined by generations of capitalist extraction, particularly within the tourist economy. These bottom locations and sissy figures will be connected to counterintuitive notions that redirect pathologizing narratives toward pleasure and coalition. My coperformers serve dual roles, as interpreters of cultural meanings and caregivers. Survival tactics they used at the time of Katrina had already been well honed by conditions shaped by pre-Katrina attacks to social welfare. The Cru's life histories reveal that performance has always been an available means of engaging in an economy that constructs black people as deviant when it isn't exploiting their labor. Performance is also illuminated as a stabilizing force that maintains communal ties to symbolic and material spaces.

Chapter 2, "Get It How You Live: Twerking for Survival," illuminates the Cru's struggles over conflicting narratives of belonging and individualism that pose limits to their freedom. This chapter follows the Cru's attempts to capitalize on sissy bounce's commercialization while navigating stigma in public health discourse, popular culture, and mutual aid. This section describes the social and economic challenges the Cru faced while performing across New Orleans and touring in New York city. I show how conflicts within the group highlight the limits of a bottom episteme. Conversely, a longtime friend of the Cru recounts the ways he has raised the bottom through twerking as a praxis of personal growth and transformation.

Chapter 3, "Back of Town: A Bottom Geography," identifies a conceptual bottom geography, "back of town," that has circulated in public discourse for over two hundred years. Connecting bounce to twentieth-century blues and the colonial period, I explore histories in which black people navigate exclusionary, unsustainable infrastructural development. This exploration will extend from the racialization of Congo Square in the early nineteenth century to the more recent and nuanced context of the black neighborhoods bounce music represents. All these bottom locations serve as a poetics of landscape that sustains working-class black communities (and former public housing communities in particular) against ongoing dispossession and displacement.

Chapter 4, "Touching the Rim: Gentrification, Popular Culture, and the Collective Asshole," examines the demographic changes that emerged in the wake of Hurricane Katrina and shifting urban gentrification in the city. I highlight the twinned processes of housing gentrification and the annexation of black queer figures into the self-understandings of predominantly white and nonlocal audiences. I trace the crossover of sissy bounce—looking particularly at Big Freedia's successful career and the popularization of twerk dancing—from a local cultural form to a global phenomenon. Like the minstrel performances that followed the Civil War and the Reconstruction era, I argue, sissy bounce and twerk came to represent "safe" avenues toward experiencing myths of black sexual pathology.

In the fifth chapter, "Raising the Bottom: Church Girls and Secular Music," we go to church to consider the division of body and soul in conservative theology. We enter the sanctuary of the black queer club scene and witness the work of sissy figures as alternative authorities of the sacred, exploring their use of music and dance to foster social bonds, and facilitate communal joy that is both spiritual and erotic. New Orleans's unique forms of life-affirming, death-witnessing performances, including twerking, are derived from African diasporic traditions that can mend body and soul (Pérez 2016); bounce's bottom epistemology highlights the importance of the flesh in the sacred labor of the dispossessed.

I hope this text inspires readers toward new possibilities in scholarship, music, and the arts in general. As you read, I encourage you to cue up the referenced songs, find and read artists' biographies, and look up related maps and images. I hope this book encourages us to rethink the power of culture to narrate home and kinship among those often denied a voice. There is always more than one story.

CHAPTER ONE

CATCH DAT BEAT
PERFORMING PLEASURE AND COALITION

> A shucking, knee-slapping, wet-eyed laughter
> that could even describe and explain how
> they came to be where they were.
>
> **TONI MORRISON** | *Sula*

"I will put your perm in," Vockah would sing to the audience as the Cru, including myself, echoed him. He'd reference products that, while unfamiliar to some, were mundane aspects of black hair care: "There isn't a perm too deep—a perm! Not even a TCB—you need an Optimum." He'd call out, "Say it loud!" and we'd respond, *"I'm black and I'm proud!"* Then, "Say it loud!" as we switched the lyrics up to answer, *"I ride big dicks now!"*

Mimicking the gospel-choir breakdown from Diana Ross's version of "Ain't No Mountain High Enough," the whole stage would sing:

Ain't no perm high enough
Ain't no perm low enough
Ain't no perm wide enough to get through them roots!
Ain't no perm high enough
Nothing can get through them kinky roots!

Vockah would continue:

Three ninety-nine, you got a perm on sale
Don't try to steal it or your ass'll be in jail
When we can't do nothin' with our hair
What we fuckin' do? *(Put it in a ponytail!)*

Vockah would then reach for a small black doll shaped like a girl named "Symphony," that he'd costumed in a twinkling, light blue princess dress. Singing to the doll and the audience at once, he'd chant a series of calls we'd respond to: "Spritz it! (*Yeah!*) Nappy-ass! (*hair!*) Comb yo'! (*hair!*) Spritz and! (*gel!*)." He gestured to Symphony as if the doll were the one the message was meant for. Then he'd pull out a large aerosol bottle of hair spray and begin spraying her. He'd sit her down, then spray his own exaggerated wig—in some performances long extensions, in others a larger-than-life afro—as well as the doll, his whole body, and sometimes the audience. The skit would conclude with a four-part choral breakdown of the lyrics "I beweave it." Performing the role of choir director, Vockah would instruct us and the audience—first sopranos, then altos, tenors, and basses—to beweave it.

When we performed "U Need a Perm," the rhythm of bounce became the foundation for a song full of call-and-response highlighting the performance of caregiving, particularly among black women and queer and trans people. The live act used background vocals and props to dramatize the type of everyday socializing that happens among beauticians and their clients. These exchanges, drawing on the music of James Brown and Diana Ross, including the enactment of a gospel choir scene, mirrored elements of everyday life.

Sissy bounce performances like these embody an epistemology of the bottom. The artists' performances of pleasure, mutual aid, and coalition—within bottom locations, and in relation to sissy figures—are used to redirect pathologizing ideas and narratives. These bottom locations are defined by an economic basement, but in the three contexts

1.1 Vockah Redu photographed for the 2010 *Where They At* bounce music exhibition. Photo by Aubrey Edwards.

shared below, sissy bounce figures transform everyday experiences into spectacular dramatizations of social wealth.

The lyrics of "U Need a Perm" satirize rather than reinforce beauty standards that suggest combing, spritzing, perming, and getting rid of one's "nappiness" is a necessary move toward becoming black and proud. The recording and public performance of the song also suggests a dialogue about blackness and self-worth that cuts across gender and sexuality, as represented through the call-and-response between Vockah, the Cru, and the diverse audiences.[1]

Responses to the song ranged from positive to negative. I found that as the stages and audiences of these performances changed, so did the representations people took from them. After Hurricane Katrina, bounce music saw an emerging audience made up of nonlocals outside the black community—particularly white audiences who saw in bounce a piece of "authentic" New Orleans. During performances of the song, I often watched white audiences, men and women, enact the lyrics, attempting to respond to Vockah's gestures and calls to spritz, comb, and indeed perm their "nappy-ass hair." Attempting to participate in the fun, these audiences came to enjoy mimicking and parodying what they saw onstage.

The varying responses to the representations in "U Need a Perm" were manifold. Some audiences sought out a cultural authenticity in which black pathology became a self-fulfilling prophecy. For some, the performances weren't parodies that played on black representations and questioned beauty standards defined against blackness; instead, the performances offered confirmation of ideas they already held.[2] For certain audiences, black people's efforts and inability to transcend dominant standards of beauty became the object of comedy; people failed to understand that the performance was aimed at dislodging those normative standards of beauty to begin with. Nonblack people were not the only ones missing the point; I watched and spoke to black people who'd never seen the act—or at least hadn't seen it in predominantly white audiences—walk out and denounce what looked to them like an updated minstrel show.

Sissies, I argue, are people who create kinship through caregiving. One of the oldest definitions of being a sissy is being perceived as feminine—and the domesticated labor of caregiving is understood as the normative, biological province of womanhood. Gender, here, is not a matter of biology, but the social construction of feminized care. Sissies are associated with devalued feminine labor—an economic basement (and form of bottoming) that connotes a waste of potential masculinity.[3]

In performances like "Perm," the labor and performance of care were specifically privileged, however devalued they might be elsewhere. My coperformers and I deployed a bottom epistemology in that our performance redirected devaluating assumptions toward counterintuitive notions of power, pleasure, and solidarity. The Cru and their audiences drew this solidarity from their differing but shared experiences of racialization, gendering, and sexualization; they all are seen as "surplus" in relation to traditional masculinity.

Many of my coperformers made their livings as beauticians, serving women, children, and people throughout the black community. Black queer men, and trans women in particular, tended to work by day as unlicensed beauticians, while straight and queer members of the black community comprised both audience and clients. What was really funny, and what audiences didn't know about "U Need a Perm," is that Vockah was also a father, with a young daughter he shared with a former high school girlfriend. The doll was a gift he'd given his daughter for Christmas; one day, he'd asked if he could borrow her for a performance.

The theatrical roles and everyday contexts in which these community members fashioned a sense of personhood were shaped both at home and in the club. Offstage, I would come to see the continuities between formal bounce performances and the everyday cultural expressions connected to them.

FATMAN

As I thanked Fatman for giving me a fresh haircut, I asked, "Where's the broom?" He passed it along, and I started cleaning so he could move on to his next client. I looked around. "Hey, where's your dustpan?"

He side-eyed me, grabbed an envelope, bent over, and swept up my hair. Shaking his butt, he said, "Chile, this how you sweep in the hood." I looked him in the eye, we giggled, and I mock-deferentially clutched imaginary pearls at having been taught a life lesson. I grabbed the trash and curtsied as he deposited the trimmings.

We were at one of Fatman's "sometimes homes" in New Orleans's Bywater, a section of the Upper Ninth Ward that was quickly becoming gentrified post-Katrina. Unstable housing had been a continuous issue for Fatman since he'd returned from his displacement to Texas. Vockah had resettled in Houston and was making regular trips back to perform and visit his daughter and mother. For this reason, I'd been spending more time with Fatman—and I was learning that while Vockah may have been the head of the Cru, Fatman was the backbone.

Like all the other members, Fatman seemed to hold on to "the hood" as a kind of cultural capital, aesthetic, and sense of home he took with him. We both took pleasure in comedically going to this place momentarily, reflecting less on my naivete than on our shared appreciation of a sensibility shaped by material conditions of race and class. Our practices formed a kind of archive or toolkit toward reproducing home and relationships, in daily life and on the stage.

Fatman called himself "doing heads" to make ends meet. He was hard to find any day of the week—unless you were a woman pursuing his skills or a bounce fan going to see him dance, it wasn't going to happen. Fat's inaccessibility and constant movement made clear the conditions and context of displacement after Hurricane Katrina. For many of the young black people still living in New Orleans, institutional racism and structural neglect led to a life of constant precarity. Informal labor, such as unlicensed hairdressing, was one of the few options available in a city predominated by service economies and tourism.

I originally thought I'd be able to schedule meetings with members of the group to conduct interviews but had to settle for a scavenger approach to fieldwork, looking for any random moments of contact. I eventually focused on club life because it was one of the few places I could count on seeing people. Integrating everyday life with research demands also led to Fatman becoming my barber. I sometimes had to bike upriver and across town, through humidity thick as gravy, in hopes of catching up with him. He moved almost every month, living with family members, lovers, and friends—at one point, when he needed a place to stay, he even considered living with me. Over time, I developed a list of contacts to keep up with him and the rest of the Cru. Before long, I had compiled at least ten temporary numbers from prepaid phones, plus names that included Fatman's mother, grandparents, boyfriends, and other clients. I would call them all to try and learn where he was currently living, where he was working, and how he was doing in general. No doubt, a similar process was involved in their own efforts to stay in touch. I began to see that these attempts at keeping up with Fat weren't specific to him, but part of a pattern in the lives of people dealing with multiple and interlocking forms of marginalization and differential access to employment, housing, and healthcare.

With long dreadlocks, meticulously styled eyebrows, and a voice and physical demeanor that reflected a bustling energy, Fatman could do heads as effortlessly as he could dance and sing, which he sometimes did all at once. Given his constant moving about and the need to keep up with his clients, Fat required a highly pragmatic life. Everything he needed to survive and work was kept at hand, and everything else was scattered about the city. In between doing heads in people's homes, he hitched rides back and forth, from Uptown to farther out in New Orleans East, always relying on others for a ride. When I asked why he didn't take the bus, walk, or ride a bike like myself, he said, "Boy, you know I got asthma! You think I'm gonna be power walking from here and there with all this stuff, looking retarded?" By "all this stuff," he meant his personal belongings and all the equipment he needed to do heads: bags of curlers, irons, different combs, and a compact portable hair dryer for clients to sit under, stuffed in a large knockoff Louis Vuitton tote bag. The bags themselves spoke of the multiple techniques, skills, and knowledges he'd acquired over a lifetime of doing heads.

When I asked him how he came to do hair, he said, "My mother did hair from our house—and after she found me trying to copy the curl sets she gave herself and other women on a mop, she said, 'You kinda good at that,' and decided to teach me how." As a teen, he said, he did so many heads that he began to hate it, but now he depended on the income it brought; he'd never had any other job. When I asked him how his father felt about a son who did women's hair, he replied, "Oh, my dad was cool and always knew I was gay. He would let me play with dolls and things like that—just as long as I did 'boy' things, too, like going and playing horseshoes with him and his friends. He didn't care, as long as I wasn't weak or act afraid of anything." Years later when I had the chance to meet Fat's dad, Mr. Eddy, he said just as much:

> You know, Mardi Gras is the one day of the year when it's okay to take your kids to the bar. So I got my kids dressed up, and we went out looking good. I could see that my older boy loved the attention he got from the girls, but Fat wasn't interested. He was shy. Wasn't interested in going out on motorbikes with us or any rough stuff. But I remember I got him one of those My Buddy dolls and he wouldn't let it go. That's when I started to see that he was different.

Over the years, I got to meet Fat's whole family. I felt privileged to be in their company and experience the love and acceptance they had—not only for Fat, but also for his friends and clients.

One particular day, I went to Fat for a haircut in his grandmother's kitchen. She lived in a shotgun home uptown; you had to walk through the whole house, greeting and exchanging pleasantries with everyone in the extended family ("Hey Grandma, Uncle John, Cousin Rhonda," and the list would go on) as you walked through the living room, past the bathroom, through the bedrooms, and back to the kitchen. The decades-old pink floral wallpaper was peeling here and there. From the back door, which was open to the yard, a nice breeze drifted through in lieu of central air, allowing the heat from Fat's curlers and dryers to ventilate. The faint smell of hot combs and burnt hair complemented the stray hair on the floor.

From a certain perspective, a number of incoherent and messy circumstances were at work. I didn't enter Fat's family home through a white picket fence to greet a nuclear model of kinship. Fat's own life story and relationship to his parents speak to the demands of capital and the need to monetize Fat's talents, while also nurturing his queerness. It's normal for black working-class families to be fractured and interrupted by the demands of keeping up; maintaining private "domestic" space is difficult, and personal life is often open to the public and/or a more broadly defined notion of kinship. There was a general acceptance and lack of shame regarding these material and economic conditions, and it seemed to parallel the family's acceptance of Fat's queerness. Despite dominant notions of blackness as inherently heteronormative and antiqueer, among Fatman's family there was no apparent judgment on the basis of sexuality.

Once, I showed up too early and ended up waiting two hours for Fat to do another head. My wait turned into a long afternoon in which Fat, myself, and a group of black women talked about sex, relationships, and style. While we didn't directly address the context we'd gathered in, our conversation reflected the fact that we were all cultivating a sense of personal and social wealth, in a space produced and maintained by oppressions we all experienced in our daily lives.

Ms. Pat was a friend of Fat's and had brought her daughter to get her first weave, a hairstyle in which synthetic hair is sewn into natural hair. Never having seen the process and needing to wait for my own haircut, I watched for over two hours as Fat intricately braided, laced, and wove. The hair appointment was a birthday present and coming-of-age gift. As Fat began braiding the young girl's hair into a circular pattern, we all got to know each other.

Seeing Ms. Pat's daughter, I remembered my own childhood enjoyment of being privy to grown-ups' conversations and general shit-talk. In later years, I'd go out of my way to find barbers who wouldn't make me endure homophobic and/or misogynist banter; I'd come to find those conversations—paired with sharp objects and barbershops full of mostly straight men—undesirable. As a result, I ended up seeking out queer beauticians and barbers who usually worked in home kitchens and bathrooms. There, I could be more comfortable and still talk shit.

Fat's other clients were there for myriad reasons, including personal friendships, family ties, and Fat's popularity as a bounce performer. He often talked about his years of dancing, his skill, and their relationship to his embrace of a black gay identity. "We are behind everything," he'd assert. "When people see Beyoncé and those divas onstage, they looking at our work too." I found these statements and Fat's other personal narratives telling, and often contradictory. When he wasn't speaking about himself as a confident, knowing black gay man, he often talked about the difficulties he faced growing up, particularly with his own self-image. He expressed the challenges he faced fostering a positive identity, not just because he was gay or black but because he saw New Orleans as a "masculine" place that everyone—gay, straight, man, woman, black, nonblack—had to face. His recognition of patriarchy was more than a matter of masculine power emanating from male bodies; he spoke to a form of oppression that affected everyone's personhood and movements. Fat suggested that dealing with this—even among women and "t-girls," slang for transgender women—meant confronting the people you feared most and surrounding yourself with others for protection:

> In high school, I wasn't tall enough or bold enough to dance in the marching bands, where there were some effeminate men, so I went into the drill team and color guard. But even then, they were all studs [masculine women]. . . . We would dance and perform at parades, especially around Mardi Gras, and sometimes people would throw things at us, but for the most part everyone loved it. . . . After a while, I started to realize, I am beautiful . . . and even if I knew people were looking at me funny, I'd give them a little extra [shakes his body and smiles].

Public performance was central to Fat and other black queer youths' development in New Orleans; personal growth could emerge from those collective experiences. I began to wonder if the social network and affinities created by Fat and his hair clients functioned similarly. As Fat's clients and I got to know one another, I noted our shared desire to create a sense of self-worth amid masculinist and heteronormative oppression.

Fat's relationship with the women in his family, and with his women clients, reflects the dialogue between sissy figures in bounce and their audiences. Fat and Vockah often reminisced about the black women they spent time with in their youth, as they took over the streets, moving from project to project. Similar narratives—about solidarities, mutual aid, and resistance to patriarchy and racism—ran through my fieldwork interviews and bounce music itself. Whether the issues involved controlling men, the police, or their homes, black women's struggles often intersected with the lives of black gay men and transgender people.[4]

This may explain why the primary local audience of bounce music was black women. I'm not just talking about teens or twentysomethings: I saw black women of all ages disregard conservative respectability in favor of dancing with abandon for one another's pleasure. Multiple generations of black women would gather on porches, in parking lots, and on dance floors to get a shakedown going, playfully showing and telling who got the best moves. The original members of the Cru were also black girls. "Yeah, I had a lot of girls with me in the beginning," Vockah would say, "but they would meet guys and go have babies. I started using more boys for the shows, and the girls would come to the studio to record, but most of them left to Houston to raise their kids."

Black women, both cisgender and transgender, make up the backbone of bounce, and performers know this is the choir they're preaching to. When I asked Ms. Pat how she knew Fat, she described their tight relationship by crossing her fingers and saying, "Oh, we're like this."

Once Fat finished braiding Ms. Pat's daughter's hair, he produced a wig cap that he shaped and molded. Pulling out a circular needle, he sewed the cap onto the braids. Throughout the process, he was careful not to poke the girl's scalp or pull too tightly on her hair. As he worked, our kitchen conversation turned toward other matters—namely, bounce music. Who was going out tonight? What were we wearing? What could we expect? Another client said she wanted to cut off all her natural hair to reduce the maintenance it required, but was sure everyone would think she was a lesbian. She didn't go to gay clubs to meet women, she explained, but to have a good time; she jokingly added that if she did pick someone up, she'd have to play the woman in the relationship because she was so femme.

She liked going to the gay clubs, the client said, because she didn't feel pressured to get done up. Fat argued with her, saying the gay club was the worst place to get "read" or "rang up"—in other words, suffer the scathing critiques and standards of people who'd publicly and unapologetically tell you if you didn't look right and needed a makeover. Ms. Pat agreed, laughing. Once, she said, she'd worn a bright pink outfit to a club, and before she knew it, the emcee was calling her out over the microphone, referring to her as "Pepto-Bismol." "Yeah," Fat shot back, "and I bet they looked a mess." Our conversation was threaded with expectations and assumptions about hair, beauty, blackness, gender, and sexuality.

Fat sat down to take a break and whipped out his inhaler. After hours on his feet, he had the same look on his face he got after a performance.

His asthma was a chronic issue. He began to plot his next move, asking who could give him a ride to his upcoming appointment. Both his work as a hairdresser and his mother's decision to teach him the skill were intentional efforts to survive an unstable economic and racialized domain that never had enough good jobs, particularly ones that wouldn't leave you feeling exploited. Fat was tired of doing hair; he wanted to be able to make a living from his frequent performances and his other skills as a stylist. When I'd mentioned having to do my taxes one day, he screamed. "Boy, you do your taxes! You go!" A bit shocked, I told him it didn't necessarily mean I was getting a tax return; I might even have to pay. "So what?" he replied. "I've never been able to get a job on the books in my life." This was yet another example of the economic basement he and others found difficult to escape. It was also a clarifying moment. Fatman wasn't much younger than me, and he was incredibly talented and hardworking. The difference was that he, like many of the young working-class black people I met in New Orleans, didn't have the opportunities, cultural capital, or financial literacy I'd received as a token of employment and education.

Fat didn't have a hairdresser's license, and he'd never gone to beauty college. In part, he'd never found those formal steps necessary because he'd acquired his skills and clientele through other avenues. Returning home to New Orleans with relatives after a year of displacement in Texas, Fat discovered that most of his clients were still displaced. Many would never return, which threatened his ability to continue earning a living. Furthermore, a great deal of the equipment he'd acquired over years of doing hair had been destroyed or lost in the floods.

Another disaster that affected informal economies like Fat's during my fieldwork, linked to BP's operations, in 2010. While BP operated the Macondo Prospect, the rig involved was the *Deepwater Horizon*, which was owned and operated by Transocean. New Orleanians and Gulf Coast communities working directly in the food and fishing industry were impacted by the catastrophe; others, including workers in the tourism and service industries, found themselves once again kicked when they were down. Fat's clientele, mostly women working in the service industry, were unable to afford investments in self-care, and the economic chain that supported workers like Fat crumbled. While many people working in official service economies could, to some extent, make claims against BP, Fat and others like him would find such appeals lengthy and tedious, if not impossible. As usual, when these everyday dilemmas entered public discourse, they also shaped the narratives within bounce music. Before long,

I was hearing references to "getting that BP money" coming through the speakers at the club.

To some, working in Grandma's kitchen represents a move into a bottom location of regression and backwardness—sparsely decorated, old, of questionable sanitation, back door open to whoever wants to fly or walk in. In this way of thinking, Fat, the sissy—with his self-possessed "love me or hate me but you gonna pay me," "I'll lay your edges and shake in between, 'cause you got to give 'em a little extra" approach—is the figure of a familiar abject narrative about black pathology. But Fatman is also queering the dominant sexual division of labor—and Fat, his family, and his clients are collectively raising the bottom by culturally resisting the racialized and heteropatriarchal devaluation of black queer labor. This is where we find an epistemology of the bottom—communities inverting commonsense logics of race, class, and gender and reproducing relationships and spaces not meant to endure.

These alterable sites of black life—whether Grandma's kitchen or a bounce show's stage—are similar in that they express counterintuitive notions of power and community. However unproductive, underdeveloped, or regressive these places appear, they're key to thinking about hope and the future amid displacement. Spaces that present messy and "pathological" circumstances of blackness are remixed as significant to personal and communal development. Sissies become primary gatekeepers for these bottom relations and social holdings.

CATCH DAT BEAT

Years earlier, I'd observed another performance that centered sissy bounce and deployed a bottom epistemology—this time, a community play starring the iconic Big Freedia as a beautician and teacher.

Catch Dat Beat, a bounce musical produced and written by New Orleans native Lucky Johnson, premiered in the spring of 2009. Johnson, a well-known music producer, had decided to try his hand at theater after witnessing the success of fellow actor, producer, and New Orleans native Tyler Perry, whom Johnson also claimed as a cousin (Flaherty 2009). I thought it ironic that Johnson should cast Big Freedia, an openly gay black figure, as the central character of the play, considering Perry's own screen drag persona, Madea. Over the past twenty years, Perry's use of

1.2 *Catch Dat Beat* promotional poster. Lucky Johnson, https://www.luckyjohnson.com/.

drag has taken the black church community by storm while never directly bringing attention to the sexual and gendered politics of drag or queerness.

In *Catch Dat Beat*, Johnson directly engages queerness, bounce, and black culture as essential to notions of community in a post-Katrina New Orleans. Big Freedia's character serves as an icon of black heritage and as a member of a working-class black family who's expected to accept him.

I saw an early version of *Catch Dat Beat* at an Uptown high school auditorium. Months later, it reopened to sold-out audiences in larger venues throughout the city. I was happy to see the show in a space I imagined as more accessible to young people, for the cost of a movie pass. My friend and I arrived late; everyone else did too. When the play finally started, an hour and a half behind schedule, the auditorium had filled up. I noted all the different faces in the audience. The crowd numbered around two hundred people, mostly black families. Many seemed related to cast members; most were women and children. There were just a few seniors but plenty of thirty- and fortysomethings, teen boys and girls, younger kids, and babies.

While the production quality suggested a low-budget do-it-yourself high school play, with continuous technical difficulties and thrown-together props, a lot of effort had clearly gone into the music and casting. Each scene included guest appearances from different bounce rappers and skilled dancers. Over the show's run, the cast featured popular bounce performers like 10th Ward Buck, Katey Red, Sissy Nobby, Ms. Tee, and Gotty Boi Chris.

The play begins with Papa, the family patriarch (Johnson), sweeping the floor of the family hair salon. Papa lives above the salon with his grandson (Freedia), who runs the shop. As Papa sweeps, he shares a genealogy of bounce music. Each time he recounts a new phase in the genre's progression, the house DJ plays a song exemplifying that historical moment and Papa launches into a comical version of the complementary dance, making the crowd laugh. Soon, Freedia arrives from upstairs to the pleasure of the audience and goes about preparing for the day.

The plot follows Freedia, his customers, his family members, and the local pimp, a *Super Fly*–like character also played by Johnson. Freedia's customers, mostly women, come to get their hair done; while waiting, they recount their own experiences with bounce while lambasting each other over hair, style, and whom Freedia will work on next. As it's a musical, at times everyone onstage takes to singing and dancing and extolling the pleasures of "catchin' dat beat!" To "ride" and "catch" the beat are continually remarked on; doing these things, it's implied, can transcend mundanity and connect you with an ever-present but elusive spirit in bounce's rhythm. Catching the beat, the characters' dialogue suggests, represents a culturally specific knowledge; though it's illegible to outsiders, it can be imparted. According to the group onstage, Freedia is capable of transmitting this knowledge.

Freedia's cousin (and Papa's grandniece) Michelle arrives, making a surprise visit from Detroit. Because she doesn't understand the local expressions of dance, music, and style that are Freedia's expertise, Papa encourages Freedia and friends to explain bounce's importance as a part of New Orleans's cultural heritage. A rich point occurs at this moment: One of the salon's customers criticizes Michelle's style of dress and asks her if she likes boys, and before Michelle can respond, Freedia interjects with a great big "I do!" The crowd laughs, children and all, as Freedia's grandfather, caught off guard, feigns a heart attack. Freedia simply replies, "What? I thought you knew." Papa shakes his head and excuses himself to lie down, saying, "Sorry, y'all—I just found out my grandson plays tambourine." "Yeah, both of 'em," Freedia shamelessly replies, shaking both hands and arms in a wide welcoming gesture. For those unfamiliar, playing tambourine and the active hand movements involved are a euphemism for being gay.

Freedia and fellow bounce performer 10th Ward Buck begin planning a block party in honor of Michelle so she can learn the meaning of bounce and its significance to the community. During the intermission, the set is transformed into a block party at a public park; Freedia and Buck have organized it through their network of friends and family. While promoting the play, Johnson explained this plot point: "'Growing up in less fortunate neighborhoods, your parents would have card games, or suppers,' explains Lucky. 'Say Miss Carol across the street's light bill was due. Miss Carol would have a supper. Everyone in the neighborhood would buy a plate to help her pay the light bill.' In other words, continued Lucky, the block party comes from this tradition and is ultimately about 'how a people are able to come together in a time of need'" (Flaherty 2009). The staged block party and Johnson's interview express the importance of mutual aid among black people in New Orleans—a moral economy that sees through poverty and depression to account for each person's unique role in the community.

I'm not arguing that *Catch Dat Beat* is radically inclusive and without respectability politics. Advertisements for the play included a disclaimer saying there would be no profanity or lewd body gestures, a tough order considering bounce's signature twerking and face-down, ass-up moves. Whenever the DJ played bounce and the cast broke into dance scenes, they faced the crowd, limiting the usual focus on the butt. The play does offer an implicit framing of how one should live in this community, although I would also say it prescribes an inclusivity that expresses a bottom aesthetic and epistemological practice. It's also significant that the only white person in the play is the pimp's girlfriend, and she has no lines—bringing attention to misogyny, but perhaps also Johnson and the audience's complicity with what may seem like a just redirection of racialized power.

The block party is interrupted by the arrival of the police, who attempt to shut down the unpermitted gathering. The black actors playing the cops walk and talk with a comical affect black performers often reserve for self-important white men. When they threaten to make arrests, Freedia encourages them to enjoy the community and dance, and with some persuasion they falter and begin to do so. At this point, the music reaches a new high and the characters dance to a mix of bounce songs; the actual rappers who perform them make guest appearances, each running onstage to present their trademark dance and lyrical delivery. A couple dance troupes of young men perform flips, choreographed drills, and the most well-known bounce moves. Despite general attempts to "clean up" the dancing, once these performers hit the stage the real shaking and wobbling got started, and people were out of their seats, trying to join in. The crowd went especially wild when Sissy Nobby, whom Freedia often refers to as his daughter, made an appearance.

Toward the end of the play Papa joins the gathering and praises Freedia for showing his grandniece Michelle the importance of bounce music, inclusion, and local community. Papa goes on to say that he loves Freedia and that everyone should accept his sexuality—and accept others like him because they are family. At this point, I found myself observing the audience; there was applause, audible sighs of appreciation, and no apparent disagreement.

Years later, *Catch Dat Beat* still stands out as an embodiment of the post-Katrina reconstruction anxieties and hopes black New Orleanians brought back to the city after their mass displacement. To some, casting a sissy figure in a family space, and a school at that, might be surprising. But it's a surprise only because normative life has been oriented toward particular interpretations of black history and space that exclude black queer and trans individuals.

How and why do Big Freedia, as a person so *different*, situated in a space so marginal, and bounce, a music so "meaningless," come to represent the general feelings of estrangement felt throughout that audience—the poor and working-class, black youth, black women, old folks, disabled people, et cetera? Because the trinity of associations in which space, subject, and sound coalesce produces a frame in which everyone sees themselves, living. These archetypes of racialized alienation are only alien for those who do not hear home and kinship in the arrangement.

KINSHIP, CARE, AND RENEWAL

Taking in the daily conditions in which community members navigated crises, I saw how performances of care onstage dovetailed with practices that sustained many people through their evacuation and efforts to return home after Katrina.

In the back of Club Fusions, I listened as Legacy, a former backup dancer in the Cru, described her days and weeks following Katrina:

> When I first came back [to New Orleans], actually I had to adjust myself for the simple fact that during Hurricane Katrina I stayed . . . I stayed and I didn't evacuate. I stayed where I was in New Orleans East. And there—it was like twenty feet of water, and I actually stayed through it all. I was at a friend's house, a group of my friends. We really didn't pay attention to the storm and didn't think the storm was going to be as bad as it was . . . I mean, actually, it wasn't the hurricane. It was like, we stood, and the wind blew . . . it was the aftereffect, when down here in New Orleans the levee busted. And we were right by the levee. And if we was to peep our head out the window you could see the water just rushing and just hitting houses and stuff. It was like the movie Titanic—and when the ship was sinking the water was just hitting through everything.

Legacy's recognition of the breaking levees, and not the hurricane itself, as the source of "titanic" devastation is significant. It implicates a structure of the state as the cause of this unnatural disaster:

> [Three days later] there were people riding 'round on boats, basically telling you to get what you need to survive. . . . Whatever we could get out of the store we took and brought back to this hotel. . . . Everybody broke the windows. The whole hotel was full . . . and then after that we wound up finding a truck, and they brought the truck back to the hotel where we were. And they loaded the truck with not just us—they picked up other people and tried to help other people. [It was] actually a Heineken truck, and there was twenty-seven of us . . . so they picked up other people. Even one person had a dog. They had like maybe five or six kids, two older people—one had an oxygen tank and one was older. And we just left there, and we tried to drive and head toward Baton Rouge.

As Legacy, a trans woman who grew up in the bounce scene, shared her memories of evacuation and displacement, her account revealed the importance of black queer community ties. Legacy's relationship with her friends was defined by a preexisting network of black queer kinship, created through involvement in sissy bounce. These ties—onstage and off, in and outside the club scene—cohered relationships and offered a source of mutual aid in times of crisis.

The kind of solidarity, kinship, and caretaking these networks could offer exceeded the capacities of dominant social institutions like the church or state.[5] Because they occur outside dominant social institutions, survival tactics like the ones Legacy and her friends undertook tend to be marked as dangerous and subjected to discipline and regulation. This is evident in Legacy and her friends' attempts to evacuate:

> *When we got into Saint Charles Parish, they tried to make a turn with the truck and [it] caused traffic. . . . The police stopped the truck and all twenty-seven of us were arrested for looting, and we were on the Channel Four news. . . . Of course, the cops were like, "This is a bunch of gay people," and basically laughing and clowning about it. They tried handling us badly—pushing some of us, guns to our faces—'cause we were "looting." That's what they said, when we were trying to survive.*

Legacy and her friends were criminalized as looters and treated as sissies—two overlapping bottom positions made one.[6]

The narratives that circulated in the days following Hurricane Katrina often represented white families as survivors, "finding" bare necessities. Blacks, people on the other hand, were portrayed as ethnic savages and "looters" (Grey 2008, 132). The confluence of media representations and political rhetoric describing these "criminal activities" was used to justify FEMA's negligence, and to authorize local and federal agents to shoot to kill (Marable and Clarke 2008; Agid 2007).

Notions of cultural pathology were used to justify a militarized response and denial of aid to black people during Katrina—a pattern increasingly affecting disaster victims globally. Journalist and Katrina evacuee Jordan Flaherty states this clearly: "[New Orleans] has been demonized just as Reagan had demonized 'welfare queens' twenty years earlier, as part of an overall strategy to attack poor people" (Flaherty 2008, 44). The neoconservative dismantling of regulatory agencies like FEMA stems from Reagan-era assumptions about black families; as Roderick Ferguson explains, "The pathologizing of black mothers as nonheteronormative provided the discursive origins for the dismantling of welfare as part of the fulfillment of global capital" (2004, 124). Since Katrina, disasters have accelerated due to the impact of global warming; at the same time, conservative rhetoric has increasingly represented at-risk communities as blameworthy and undeserving of public aid. The most vulnerable and at-risk become scapegoats—devils that emerge from bottom locations and become a means of deflecting corporate and governmental accountability.

A web of private and public interests caused the crisis of Katrina, and it did so in the name of market development. The levee failures represent the vagaries of capitalism—particularly, its debasement of surplus populations in the interest of oil companies that contributed to the devastation of land. Other culprits include the multinational companies that depended on cheaply paid labor; the federal government agencies that neglected infrastructure; and the media and state, which reproduced an all-too-familiar narrative of deviant blackness to rationalize a slew of exclusionary interventions—part of the legacy of the welfare queen and her like, sissies and punks.

Legacy's lived experience is just one example of how these representations of deviance affected people as they fought for their lives. It also reveals a general approach to black evacuees throughout the region:

> We sat in jail for two weeks. . . . They took the children and sent them away from their parents. They sent the children to some kind of childcare. They didn't keep the children at the jail. They took all of us, the older people, and put us all in orange. . . . When we got to court the judge couldn't believe that those cops had arrested us for looting when we had to do what we had to do to survive. And the judge was like, "This is stupid. I had to steal a boat to ride my family from one place to another. Get all of these people out of my courtroom. All of these people are free to go."

While Legacy's story sheds light on systems of oppression at work, it also expresses a critique and a sense of coalition. Her group attempted to organize an escape and save lives across lines of difference including age, gender, sex, and species. Their efforts reveal a sense of defiance and solidarity that counters the state's criminalization and heteropatriarchal devaluing of "a bunch of gay people." The affinities and circumstances that brought together those twenty-seven people were determined by physical possibilities set within a terrain of scarcity. Their shared experiences of trauma and crisis provoked action and exchange in ways that defied the state's organizing principles:

> ALIX: What happened after you got out?
>
> LEGACY: Well, first my grandmother died. Then my mother got sick. Then I came home, and I took care of her. I'm the only child, so I had to come home to basically be with my mom every step of the way—'cause she has no brothers or sisters, I have no brothers or sisters, so I have no aunts or uncles on her side. So I had to be there for her. . . . I lost my grandmother; she was old and basically her body shut down on her . . . right after Katrina happened in August. And she died in September.
>
> ALIX: When did you get to see your friends again?
>
> LEGACY: I went to Houston, and this is when I got to see everybody. [In] clubs . . . this is maybe a month after the storm, a month or two—all my friends got together. . . . I was the one that was separated from them. . . . It was touching, because I wasn't around them for maybe a month or so—knowing that I was with them when I was in jail, and I couldn't see them all when I was in jail either. But I got to really see everybody, hug everybody when I saw them. And I mean, we all were teary-eyed. We all just cut up and had fun. . . . It was a gay club, yeah. I mean, that was easy. When we went there, we were all together. . . . When I got back home to New Orleans [after being evacuated to Texas], I started entertaining more and competing in pageants. It was a Sunday afternoon, and I was talking to my mother. And I told her, "I wanna basically just become a woman," and my mama was like, "If you gonna be a woman, you need to be the best at whatever you be." And she told me, "I'm behind you a hundred percent."

There is a sense of power in Legacy's memories that cannot be subsumed by dominant notions of black liberation, since those narratives of freedom have so often been tied to masculine ascendance, gender binaries, and capitalist liberal individualism.

The concepts of personhood, agency, and choice are slippery for those whose lives are subject to antiblack and heteronormative narratives.

Darieck Scott elaborates: "Notions of personhood underpinning our concept of choice are not necessarily in operation. Under such conditions agency is criminality and consent is constraint, thus problematizing and revealing the racial, economic, and social determinants of such putatively universal concepts as agency and consent" (2010, 156).

The bottom position in which Legacy labors, finds herself, and creates relationships is fugitive. The criminalized sissy is an image held up to Legacy—a figure deployed to confirm her low status in hierarchies of power. The sissy archetype is similar to the polarizing representations of the welfare queen and the black thug, in that these controlling images affect the daily lives and self-understandings of real people. Legacy's sense of freedom lies outside dominant notions of agency and personhood—and her capacity to invest in an alternative culture of redress and association points to an alternative notion of the future.

THE BOTTOM OF THE BOTTOM

During my first trip back to New Orleans after Katrina in the fall of 2006, the feeling of loss I had been left with was complemented by a profound sense of disorientation. Beyond the FEMA trailer parks, the military occupation that conveyed more threat than safety, and the eight- to twelve-foot-high flood marks left behind, there was an overwhelming sense of dystopia. A historical narrative about racial trauma, conveyed to me throughout my youth, ran beneath the self-evident character of the landscape. This was the bottom of the bottom. In the context of this "natural disaster," I couldn't get over my unnatural feelings of placelessness. I felt unmoored, as if that bowl of a city were floating out to sea—as if the continent had literally untethered it to float away from the national body.

Through struggles I experienced alongside my coperformers, I became more aware of the constraints defining their daily lives and the strategies helping to sustain them against processes of dispossession. I increasingly found myself, and my research, subject to the conditions and circumstances my informants regularly experienced. Conducting two years of fieldwork proved a financial struggle, especially in a city already economically depressed and under reconstruction. It was difficult to maintain a job, healthcare, and transportation while keeping up with my coperformers. My own relatives in the area had been displaced to Kansas; their home in the Gentilly neighborhood was completely destroyed.

I relied on a bicycle as my primary transportation, biking through heat and occasional flash floods to get to events and interviews, or just to, as the locals said, "make groceries." In my first experience trying to rent a small, affordable room added on to the back of a house, locally referred to as a camelback, I came to find that the kitchen sink drained into the backyard. I thought I could make the most of it until the next-door neighbor suggested I check the rest of the plumbing; I discovered that the toilet flushed and flowed right to my front door. Nothing says welcome home like the smell of your own shit.

I took up various odd jobs to support myself while allowing enough flexibility to continue my research. I applied for jobs in the service industry, which felt like a litmus test of my capacity to fulfill racialized and classed expectations. The Cru assured me I'd have no problem finding a job; as they reminded me, I was accustomed to speaking to white people and "boujee" folks. Black youth I met in the service industry, mostly other nonlocals, told me there were specific places I could work if I were light-skinned, others if I were nonlocal, and still others if I could speak without an accent. Despite the size of New Orleans's black population before and after the floods, few mid-range or high-end cafés, restaurants, or bars would hire black people, or men who for whatever reason might be seen as too aggressive, as frontline staff. In places where I did find employment, I was often treated as exceptional despite my lack of server experience. My employers and managers always mentioned the quality of my voice, mannerisms, and appearance as reason enough for my employment.

Without external funding to support my research, I supplemented my server income by offering piano and voice lessons, occasionally DJing, and art modeling. After my first attempt at leasing my own place and a subsequent confrontation with the slumlord who tried to withhold my security deposit and first month's rent, I realized few protections or tenant rights were available to renters. I resigned to live with a group of friends, mostly activists, in a Mid-City house that had been a sanctuary to many organizers, students, and artists. I rented what was most likely meant to be a large closet for $250 a month. Never again would I try to look for my own place; I realized there was safety in numbers, and I needed to make the most of what social networks I had available. Without health insurance, I treated my asthma, chronic bronchitis, and other issues through a musician's clinic at a nearby church and a network of friends working as first responders. On one occasion, I sprained my foot on my way into work. Within an hour, a friend in massage school had come to my job, diagnosed the issue, and treated me; they had to do so in my moments between waiting tables because my employer wouldn't excuse me. Given the pervasiveness of labor exploitation in formal service economies, my coperformers saw my efforts working in them as both naive and novel. Our dialogue, dancing, and music suffused my daily life as I moved between positions of insider and outsider, observer and observed.

Despite my lack of knowledge and skill in bounce performance, few audiences questioned my status as a black dancing body. On the other hand, ubiquitous racialized and classed assumptions made many people find my role as a researcher contradictory, if not wholly incredible. One acquaintance I'd known throughout my fieldwork finally told me they thought I was lying about being a graduate student. My attempts to approach my work as a professional scholar and conduct anthropological business often failed. This was productive in that even from the vantage point of the stage, I found myself subject to stereotypes and narratives of racial and sexual difference that brought me and my coperformers together. Even if my own identity as a black queer hadn't allowed me access to the group, the way we all were treated and the shared conflicts we experienced informed our relationships and mutual aid. My fieldwork proved anthropology to be the ambivalent "home" in which I struggled to live; because I couldn't assume that my commitment to the discipline was a stable site of privilege, my "performance" of ethnography necessitated a break with the prescribed methods of participant observation and anthropological discourse. At times, I had to consider that my research had failed—that I was not in the field, and that this was just life. I became a sissy from a bottom somewhere.

The above oral histories and autoethnography repeatedly reveal social wealth and empowerment in the most marginal of spaces, even when agency is precarious at best. These vignettes reveal important examples of the networks that sissy bounce and the party scene produce in the face of displacement, crisis, and the narratives accompanying them. These stories also reveal that black queer ideas and strategies are essential to a broader social justice movement: Ideologies like these expand the conditions of possibility for black people as they negotiate and move past crises, images, and narratives that limit their choices to criminality or constraint.

The time I spent with Vockah and the Cru cannot be understood separately from the conditions of displacement and instability brought about by Hurricane Katrina and enduring structural racism. The communal pleasure found in each show, informal gathering, and ephemeral moment passing a familiar face on the street was heightened by the dispossessive force of Katrina and the ongoing erosion of black New Orleans.[7] I never knew if a hello or a goodbye was more appropriate—if each encounter was a promise of the future or a trace of something that had passed and would never fully return.

Feminist scholars have shown that reproduction isn't simply a matter of biology and giving birth; it also includes the social and cultural practices that nurture people and produce the institutions of home and family (Lewis 2017; Lorber 2018). Social reproduction—whether preparing food, cleaning, educating, or providing myriad other social and cultural forms of care—are marked by gendered divisions of labor; they're also understood as the cornerstone of the nation-state.

Black queer cultural production constitutes a significant part of this reproductive work. Black queer contributions to community and black political struggle should be recognized—not only as responses to our everyday lives, but as strategies for navigating acute moments of crisis and furthering the ongoing project of black liberation. Without an epistemology of the bottom—as cultural labor that's formed in and through bottom locations, conditions, and identities—there is no future.

The Morrison quote that opens this chapter describes a power to describe and explain how and why we came to be (in the Bottom). In our performances, we pointed to a comedic yet hidden truth each time we cheered, "Face down!" and the audience screamed, "Ass up!" In dominant thinking, the bottom, in terms of anality, suggests practices that fail to contribute to dominant notions of liberation and growth. But black queer performances create and sustain spaces and social networks that counter such bioreductive notions. Audre Lorde (1984) described the erotic as an inner state of joy; while it's generally devalued, vilified, misused, and reduced to sex, it offers a profound force of connection and protective power. Raising the bottom requires a similar understanding of erotic energies—ones that are most certainly in the body, but that also spread out to inform a larger worldview. The power of black queer performances may hide just beneath the surface, fertile ground on which intersectional and antiassimilative futures are born.

CHAPTER TWO

GET IT HOW YOU LIVE TWERKING FOR SURVIVAL

> I'm a punk under pressure
> When we finish put my money on the dresser
> *The dresser, dresser, dresser*
> *The dresser, dresser, dresser*
>
> **KATEY RED** | "Punk Under Pressure"

Redbone was thirty-seven and from New Orleans. He'd started stripping in the French Quarter. On occasion, he'd go to New York to dance at black gay clubs like Chi Chiz and La Escuelita. He also organized strip shows for Black Gay Pride events in DC and Atlanta.

We crossed paths at a Rampart Street bar called The Page in November 2009. Fatman had once referred to the bar as Old Spice, jokingly referring to the bar's older black gay patrons.

Stripping up north was very different, Redbone told me: "People don't care to see you take off your clothes in New Orleans. They want ass and dick from the get-go." In other places, he explained, "they're not allowed to touch you very much beyond tipping, unless you invite them to a back room for an extra fee. But here people will give you a dollar, grab your dick, and try to put they finger up your booty hole. For a dollar!" He said I could make a good stripper with my body, adding that he could get me work in DC or New Orleans.

Redbone cared deeply about pleasing his customers. When people complained about a performer he'd brought on, he'd have to make a serious decision between the dancer, who was quite often a friend, and patron satisfaction. In New York, it was especially tough. Customers wouldn't spare your feelings: "You could be right on stage, and they'd get on the mic and talk shit about you." He didn't strip much anymore, but he knew he still could: "I still look good, and I'm not fat. You know, when I started stripping in the French Quarter, I didn't know what to do, and all I really had going for myself was a big dick." He'd slowly learned, though, with the help of someone he called his gay mother.

His boyfriend sat beside him at the bar, nursing a cocktail and occasionally nodding in agreement. Together, they ran a sex party on the West Bank. It had happened every Friday night for years. They invited me and said the best time to come was Bayou Classic weekend, which takes place the Saturday after Thanksgiving and serves as both a football event and a homecoming of sorts. I went on listening, sipping my Jack and Ginger. Then a man walked by, and Redbone rolled his eyes and made a comment about sissies and punks, adding, "I don't like it when they're too public."

In this brief moment, Redbone spoke to a contradiction I'd observed throughout the black queer club scene, as well as among Vockah and the Cru. It was ironic to me that we sat in what was, for all intents and purposes, a black gay bar; to anybody walking by, we ourselves were a bunch of black punks and sissies. We were talking about sex work and hustling, in a city historically and famously known for its libidinal economies.[1] To many, the context would be a primary example of a sexual, racialized, and economic bottom. Even here, though, a hierarchy of value and exclusivity could be found, based around masculine norms, the private/public divide, and freedom via capitalist enterprise.[2]

Sula, published in 1973 amid the dynamic social movements of the 1960s and '70s, is a tale directed at black people's desires to assimilate, integrate, and move up and out of bottom positions.[3] In the novel, upward social mobility is imagined through burying the imagination, managing one's physical comportment, and regulating nonheteronormative community members—in this case, whores and "broken" men, both of whom I see as relatives to the sissy.[4] In 1965, amid civil rights–era changes, young blacks people attempt to move away from the Bottom; Morrison uses this time period to warn readers about notions of racial uplift that polarize communities in exchange for inclusion in a society that's never quite civil. The bottom, she implies, cannot truly be left behind. Through sacrifice and shame, its pleasure and perils can only be "tucked away" through attempts to erase or make private what's dissonant in the community and the self.

The lives of the men of Morrison's Bottom, the story arc of *Sula*'s virtuous Nel Wright, and the moment I found myself in with Redbone—they all resonate with one another. Even in and among black queer communities, it's common to reproduce normativity by upholding, policing, and compelling others to conform to dominant notions of gender, sex, and family.[5] Does Redbone really gain anything when friendships and other unions are sacrificed in hopes of moving up and out of the bottom?

To circle back to Katey Red's "Punk Under Pressure" lyrics, for trans women, sex workers, and other queer subjects who don't conform to notions of belonging informed by the nuclear family, freedom from life's pressures is often defined through narratives of capitalist gain. In the lives of sissy bounce artists, there's a double bind produced by the demands of capitalist individualism and queer respectability—contradictory forces that "mold, immobilize, and reduce" our choices.[6] The artists I worked with didn't have a critique of capital per se, but on some level they knew success and money would require sacrifices, even when so much had already been lost.

This chapter considers some of the limits the Cru faced in attempting to use sissy bounce to promote more freedom in their lives. A focused interview with a former Cru member also suggests ways of rising above these ideological and material binds.

BETWEEN RESPECT AND SHAME

"You know a whore is an open book," Moe said, and Vockah replied, "... and that's why I can read you!" Everyone laughed in the back of the green room as we joked and bantered in a style reminiscent of the dozens, fashioning some defensive sarcasm should the inevitable day come when you need to exchange sincere blows.[7] There was an ongoing debate about how petty this or that performer could be. Fingers had been pointed at straight bounce artists' homophobia and transphobia, but arguably there was plenty of shade and violence happening in and among the queer community (Miller and Thomas 2007).

That night, we were preparing for a show benefiting an HIV/AIDS clinic in New Orleans's West Bank. The performance was at a popular club in the French Quarter, with a predominantly white audience in attendance. Billed as a sissy bounce event, the lineup included the Cru, Katey Red and Dem Hoes, and an up-and-coming artist named Nicky da B. I'd been asked to cue each act's music and DJ between sets to keep the audience moving.

Before the show started, the white host and organizer of the event, a doctor from the clinic, asked if these black queer and trans performers would come to the stage between acts to demonstrate taking an HIV/AIDS rapid test for the audience—after which they, along with audience members who wanted to get tested, could receive their confidential results from clinic volunteers in the foyer of the club. I was glad to see that the organizer was partnering with a black-led community-based organization (CBO) that regularly worked in the club scene, but ambivalent about the way sissy figures were deployed to "educate" audience members about risk and prevention. On-site testing was a common prevention and awareness strategy, but I'd never witnessed black bodies participating in a public health demonstration for a white and mostly heterosexual spectatorship in this way. It served as another example of sissy figures filling a pedagogic role in a preexisting narrative—one about personal responsibility versus pathological, unhealthy behavior.[8]

Randi, a public health volunteer and close friend of Vockah and the Cru, was working the event. "I knew Vockah from dancing in parades," he told me. "He was an iconic figure in high school and during Mardi Gras. A mutual friend introduced us on the corner of Bourbon and Saint Ann, and he liked me, so I got thrown into the group." We discussed his work as an HIV/AIDS outreach and prevention specialist with a black-led CBO, and he shared how those experiences related to the bounce club scene:

> RANDI: In my experience, because New Orleans is one small community, the gay community is small. The degrees of separation are even closer. The ratio of risk is increased because you're in such close proximity with people.... We go to clubs and we go to these other venues because we know no one else would host our population. We want to be able to not just identify negatives but also identify positives. Our goal

in identifying positives is that people know their status. You nip it in the bud: You can get healthcare, case management, and all these things.... Because we are a part of the population, we're relative to the community.... I know that in the state, New Orleans is currently number two—Baton Rouge being number one.... [In] New Orleans, out of all of the new diagnosed cases, 60 percent of them were African American men who have sex with other men; 80 percent of all new HIV/AIDS cases were men as a whole. I find that very interesting.

ALIX: Do you provide services to women?

RANDI: We're predominantly known for dealing with MSM [men who have sex with men] communities. There are other agencies in the city that cater to women.... That's actually one of my goals as I learn more about women—not just heterosexual women, but also women who have sex with other women. Trichomoniasis is on the rise—a venereal disease—and it's on the rise through lesbian contact, and it's very common. I really want to get out to the lesbian community, or even the heterosexual community. I do believe that women are more at risk for HIV.

Randi explained his passion for outreach: "Some people barely have food to eat, let alone the time and transportation to get a checkup." Although I'd seen testing happen in the predominantly black queer club scene, I had yet to see on-site testing in a predominantly white space with a spotlight on black queer and trans people, the proverbial "vulnerable and at risk." This event didn't situate the larger context in which black locals have historically had differential access to healthcare and education through structural oppression; it seemed less about creating awareness among audience members through reeducation and solidarity building, and more about engaging in a narrative of cultural poverty in which HIV/AIDS rates are a matter of black people's irresponsible and risky behaviors—a problem that can only be resolved through charity and outside intervention.[9] Randi spoke to this gap when he added, "One of my pet peeves as a taxpayer is that they don't even teach sex ed in schools anymore. Even for schools that have on-site clinics, they can't carry the condoms. They can test the kids for HIV or give them pregnancy tests, but there's no preventative measures in place. So with that, there's a certain amount of ignorance out there."

The access and resource deficits created by policymakers and the erosion of public education are often turned into a narrative where black people are simply careless, and thus funding such programming is a waste. I could see this narrative play out as Vockah and the Cru were asked to take the stage and be tested in front of the audience. When Fatman and the others went to check in with the clinicians for their results, Fat whispered to me, "I don't think some of these people want to know their results."

That you might fulfill the racialized, sexualized narratives embodied in the figure of the sissy and bottom tropes of bounce is a tough pill to swallow. So yes, you may not want to know your results or be questioned about your existing health status in and among an audience who've called on you to participate in a narrative they arrived with and came for. In this case, the stigma of HIV/AIDS signifies the queer excesses of sissies and the toxicity of the black working class. Although well-intentioned, charitable philanthropy often obscures the history in which those with the means to give have the power to because of ongoing disinvestment in public resources and a focus on the privatization of education and healthcare.

For Vockah, subjects like HIV/AIDS brought up painful and unresolved feelings that reinforced the need to capitalize on the commercial value of sissy bounce as a means of gaining monetary freedom. At the same time, a liberal individualist sense of freedom disrupted the sense of belonging and kinship the group had built among themselves. In an ongoing double bind, the Cru had to confront the constraints and difficulties of being family and community members while using the commodification of their identities as sissy bounce artists to take care of themselves and bring money home. Over the years, I watched as the Cru's performances pushed their audiences toward a more expansive notion of blackness and desire. I also observed how the narratives they boldly challenged onstage affected their interpersonal relationships in mundane life.

I encountered Randi on another occasion. The whole group visited the clinic for a film night in which attendees could meet with clinicians to get tested during a movie screening. That evening, almost everyone from the Cru got together for the film, with plans to go clubbing in the French Quarter afterward. When we arrived, Vockah shared that when he was younger, he'd volunteered with the organization and spent a lot of time there. As the leader of the Cru, and as the gay dad of two Cru members, Moe and Tader, Vockah was often referred to by group members as "Father" despite an age gap of no more than ten years. He frequently encouraged everybody to get tested; he often mentioned a close friend and former group member who'd died from complications of HIV/AIDS. He'd nursed them through their last days. We regularly performed a song dedicated to that friend.

One by one, we went in to meet with Randi, and later we received our results. After the event, we all piled into a car and went out. Over drinks, the subject of our results came up. Vockah started talking about who he'd last had sex with. "If there had been a problem, I know who I would have had to talk to," he said. "But I wasn't too worried. I topped him"—pointing out that the receptive partner, "the bottom," is generally considered more vulnerable to infection.

When men bottom, even in and among the queer community, they're often viewed as sources of toxicity and shame in ways that parallel the heteromasculinist misogyny directed at cis and trans women.[10] Bottoms get punked, not tops. One could feel the rim of a limit. You would think that the group's performances of twerk and lyrics that focused on the physical bottom as a personal and communal object of ecstasy would extend to sex itself. And perhaps in a more private setting this would be the case—but to say it out loud in our group, as Redbone said, would be "too public." Moreover, the merger of anal receptivity with meanings of toxicity and feminization dovetailed with racial and class discourses. Being treated as deviant because you lived in economic bottoms mirrored bottoming as a sexual position and moment of perceived debasement—circling back to the ghetto as a space defined by deficit and loss of self.[11] The construction of these positions—sexual receptivity, space, and subjectivity—are analogous.

Group members often assessed STI risk levels based on existing narratives of desire, gender expression, and whether people "looked good." The Cru's self-understandings produced a discourse about what kinds of behaviors and identities were indicative of being a sissy and thus assumed to be a bottom—someone considered more vulnerable. These observations were particularly strange to hear coming from Vockah, though, given that everyone saw him as a gender revolutionary and the most marginalized queer and trans youth gathered around him.

Vockah's reputation was partly due to his own past. He firmly identified as a man and a father to both his chosen kin and his blood kin, his young daughter. But almost everyone I spoke to who knew him from his early days, as a popular marching band dancer and teenage bounce artist, stated that when they met Vockah, he was a girl. Even Fatman said that was what had attracted him to Vockah back in high school, reminiscing, "Things have changed, because back in the day Vockah had colorful hair extensions and looked like a girl!" Chev off da Ave, another bounce artist, friend, and collaborator, explained that as Vockah became more popular as a bounce artist, doing studio sessions with nationally recognized rappers like Juvenile, he'd encountered pressure to masculinize himself. "I told him, 'There's no way you can make it big as a girl,'" Chev said. "I taught him how to dress like a boy." Friends like Randi would often push Vockah to assert his legacy, arguing that Vockah, rather than his peer and sometimes-competitor Katey Red, was the original trans bounce artist and thus the first "sissy" of bounce. But Vockah refused. When I asked him about what his close friends were saying, he denied it: "Yes, I liked wearing girls' clothes and wigs and hair extensions. But I never thought I was a girl. That's just what people said about me." Big Freedia, similarly, differentiated herself in this way. Freedia was often assumed to be a trans woman, but Freedia didn't identify as such, while Katey did.

Vockah said that at a young age, he'd begun dancing through a community program that included African dance, tap, and hip-hop. Like many kids in the New Orleans public school system, he tried out for the drill team and marching band early on. At ten, going through tryouts with the other boys, he started to improvise during the marching steps with choreography from his dance classes, emulating one of his icons, Michael Jackson: "The other boys began to move away from me and make fun of me, but I just kept doing my dance. The girls were enjoying it and started to come closer and follow me, and that was the beginning. Before long, I was leading dance squads in parades, surrounded by all the girls. Some people would throw food at me, but I didn't care."[12]

It was clear that Vockah wasn't just well known in the bounce scene; he was a trailblazer in terms of parading culture in the city. It was rare to go anywhere in New Orleans with him and not watch him be greeted by local black folks, young and old. I had to consider Vockah's influence on current parades during annual carnival festivities. I often saw numerous black gender-nonconforming youth dancing; group members noted that this was part of Vockah's legacy.

I took Vockah at his word about his own gender identity, but I also often listened to him express regret. I don't know how many times I heard him longingly say, "If I was a girl . . ." or express concern about his past and current life and what it would mean for his daughter when she grew up. When I asked him if he was ashamed of his past, he adamantly said,

"No!" declaring that nobody was going to define him. This was the struggle with sissy bounce, being from New Orleans, and coming from the projects. So many narratives aimed to define who you were, and you had to leverage those tropes toward survival while not letting them overdetermine your sense of self.

TWERKIN' ON TOUR

Everyone in the Cru was skilled at performing strength, power, and vulnerability, with fluidity in dance and style. They surrounded themselves with others who could too. This was key to each group member's status. During a two-week road tour up and down the East Coast, the boundaries between performing sissy bounce and rejecting stereotypes that accompanied those performances became clearer. Seven of us packed into a minivan in the middle of the winter and drove to shows scheduled in Asheville, DC, Baltimore, Philadelphia, New York, Providence, Boston, Cambridge, and Portland (Maine). It was ambitious to think we could travel the length of the Northeast and Mid-Atlantic while feeding ourselves on food stamps, paying for gas and accommodations with show money, and sleeping on floors or couch surfing with fans.

Each member of the group set out with differing hopes and dreams. Tader and Moe, the youngest members, wanted to see more of the world while supporting Vockah. Fatman was also deeply committed to backing up Vockah, but he hoped that greater recognition of his performing skills would change his economic circumstances. He often remarked that he was tired of being a beautician; he wanted to work as a personal stylist and perform full-time. For Vockah, the economic stakes were high: he felt the weight of supporting himself as well as family members who depended on him. Over the course of the tour, glaring divisions started to appear. It was often difficult telling whether concerns over a group member's health and safety were sincere or simply intended to cast deliberate shade regarding their "flaws." Despite the cold outside, our interactions grew increasingly heated.

By the time we reached New York, where we'd booked a week of shows, Moe and Tader's public behavior and hygiene had become the subject of passive-aggressive jokes. In New Orleans, I'd come to know both of them as typical young, vibrant dancers, on and off stage. Moe was only nineteen when he'd started dancing in the group; Tader was a few years older. Both loved the spotlight. Vockah almost always encouraged them. "I just want them to have fun," he once said. "I might be Daddy, but I'm not gonna try to control them." I'd watched Vockah gently guide them toward practical goals like getting jobs, returning to school, and obtaining valid IDs (by whatever means, possibly—Vockah told me he got his first driver's license in exchange for autographed CDs from a DMV official). After a year of doing fieldwork with the group, I had no doubts Vockah had touched their lives and inspired them; he'd done so for me. But even for him, there was a respectable limit. Within a public context far from the comfort of home, tropes and stereotypes that constructed our bodies as problematic and in need of discipline came out among the group. Moe and Tader's public exhibitionism, style of dress, and general loudness had turned into an annoyance.

On one of our few days off, the group wanted to visit the set of the live show *106 and Park*, produced by BET (Black Entertainment Television). Not a regular viewer of the show, I'd become more familiar with it through the Cru. Members saw it as the premier venue for up-and-coming hip-hop acts and trends. It was what everyone was tuned in to back in New Orleans, and the opportunity to be on the set in New York was an exciting prospect.

In an interview with Randi a year prior, he'd referred to the show as an example of the media's influence on black youth's wayward culture and values:

> I think media plays a significant part in what we see, and the music is totally changing . . . 106 and Park on BET—*it's a teen show, it's pretty much catered to kids up until twenty-three, maybe fifteen to twenty-three—these are the things they're getting. They're not getting Toni Braxton and "Love Shoulda Brought You Home"—they're getting* Get Rich or Die Tryin' *and "Get It How You Live." And the kids have adopted this mentality. It's almost like an invisible mentality: It's not gonna happen to me, but if it does, I'm okay with it, 'cause it's the norm. My boy is dead. That's how it happens. You gotta die some way.*

Get it how you live is a phrase that recurs throughout 1990s and early 2000s hip-hop. One of the earliest recordings making the reference is a 1997 album from New Orleans's own Hot Boys, released by Cash Money Records. I heard this statement often at the clubs, pointing to a notion of surviving by making the most out of whatever was at hand—making a way, even if others got hurt.

Before heading to the *106 and Park* set, everyone worried over their look—especially Moe, who talked and laughed into the mirror and at the thought of anyone who might say he didn't look good. He remarked, "I wish a bitch would," and "Bitch, you could never!" As I looked at his sagging skinny jeans, tank top, and button-down, I reminded everyone, "Hey, remember this isn't the South. You might want to sacrifice showing some ass and put a few extra layers on." For most of the group, it was their first time in New York or even traveling outside Louisiana and Texas.

Then we set out for the show. I'll never forget the excitement in Moe's face the first time he walked into a subway station and did what he would do any other time: He danced. The group found seats for the long ride through Manhattan. It was a moderately busy time of day. Moe shouted, twerked, and wobbled to the music in his head; he grabbed the pole in the subway car, and his pants began to sag more and more. The Cru, and everyone else on the subway, had become his audience. Vockah, noticing other passengers looking at our group as well as Moe, said, "Son, you doing too much." Moe noted this and continued enjoying himself. Having spent time riding the trains over the years, I told Vockah I thought it was okay—that I'd seen performances in which people did flips and tricks for tips, and what Moe was doing was tame by comparison. Vockah was unconvinced, but he avoided an outright confrontation. The others joined him in looking on and cringing.

We arrived early at CBS studios on West Fifty-Seventh Street, the home of BET. It was too cold to wait outside. All of us needed to use the bathroom. As the wind picked up, we got a bit more desperate for shelter. The dancers had been depending on tips from shows to pay for food and drinks, and everyone was running short. Throughout the day, one by one, we'd become exposed to a public sphere without public resources. We were in another economic bottom, looking for some way to turn things upside down.

I suggested we go into a diner; I ordered coffee while people took turns using the bathroom. By this time, everybody was frustrated, wishing they had more clothes on. New York was simply expensive, and organizing transportation and food wasn't easy. Fatman looked the other customers up and down and joked about turning tricks in the bathroom, saying, "Sir, would you like five for twenty?" Hustling was always joked about as an ever-present way out of no way. To my knowledge, only Vockah and I had experience as go-go dancers; no one else had ever admitted to anything more in terms of sex work. It was another reminder that we were indeed *punks under pressure*, and that you just might have to *get it how you live*. Fatman commented, "I don't know, y'all . . . I might have to sell these cakes and pies." We kept waiting, joking around to take up the time and distract us from our hunger and chilly circumstances. Once again, we were deploying an epistemology of the bottom through comedy and wit, cultivated on and off stage to redirect the impact of our negative circumstances into togetherness.

Over the course of the tour I'd watched the group get increasingly lean from exerting themselves with little money for food. I'd used the last of my food stamps so we wouldn't have to eat out every day in New York. Fatman had worked overtime doing hair to pull together money for merchandise to sell at shows. Despite our attempts at mutual aid, the tour was rough going, and this only added to the idea that we ourselves looked rough. As we walked from the restaurant back to the studio, Fatman looked at Tader, shook his head, and muttered under his breath, "She looks homeless!"

We joined a long line of audience members for an hour outside the studio, huddling together for warmth. When we entered, we stood along a wall. Security personnel, in black suits with walkie-talkies, stood before us. Moe commented, "Hey, we made it to the White House!" The level of security was, indeed, surprising. The guards directed us to remove our hats, open our bags, and not enter with any weapons or cameras. Moe went through a metal detector before me. When I passed through, the security guard looked at him, then told me, "Make sure his pants stay up," as if I were responsible for him.

We were led to a waiting room, where we stayed for another hour. The room was full of about sixty young black and brown women and men, excited to be on the set of one of their favorite programs. We passed the time watching videos on the many TVs around us until a manager entered. Sternly pacing the room, he presented us with a long list of rules and responsibilities, mostly focusing on our physical appearance and behavior. If anyone threw gang signs or danced inappropriately, he said, security would escort them out of the building. This confused and disoriented me. What dancing was inappropriate for a show based on commodifying and circulating black youth culture?

We were then led in small groups to the *106 and Park* set. Our group was directed toward a section of bleachers with someone who acted as a hype man, continuously encouraging us to have a good time within the confines of our seating. Each commercial break turned into a short dance-off. A house DJ and MC would call up members of the crowd, and they'd take to the stage and show their moves. The MC told a group of young women to "drop it like it's hot," then laughed, adding, "Hey yo, but I don't wanna see any dudes tryin' that!" Fatman heard this and balked, saying it was homophobic. During the next break, Tader was led to the dance floor, and all of us cheered him on. He'd come on tour for his vogueing and twerking skills. We could tell right away that he was nervous; he held back from his usual moves. As the music reached its peak, though, he finished with a few hand gestures and some shaking, truer to his abilities. Later on, everyone critiqued his performance, saying he'd essentially "butched it up" for the camera—at least until the end, when he'd relaxed. Fatman commented, "That was a dead giveaway." I found the moment and the whole process of entering the space incredibly awkward. In such a short amount of time, the pressure to assimilate and tuck away our real selves was taken up, into our bodies. It was like we were in chains, unable to move as we usually would.

The day had been full of contradictions and ironies. Over the years, I'd noticed a litmus test emerge in the group around the microcosm of dance. Some members were seen as too stiff and rigid to twerk effectively; on the other hand, an inability to perform choreographed, "structured" movements like eight-count routines or vogueing could also lead to criticism. Although Fatman's critique was in part an assessment of Tader's gendered performance, it was relative to the criticism of Tader and Moe's comportment throughout the day. It was commonly understood that twerking and putting the bottom on display was powerful and pleasurable, but it was also a given that everyone should know the limit, lest they truly become a sissy. These moments proved that the bottom as a part of the body was a personal, communal site of identification and antagonism that connected to larger notions of belonging and individual freedom. Our desires to achieve monetary and symbolic capital, outside the social wealth we'd already cultivated, could siphon the joy right out of us. Performance was so central to making ends meet that we sometimes forgot that the act was a fiction and not who we really were.

By the end of that two-week winter tour, everyone was tired of each other. Fatman commented on Tader's breath and body odor, suggesting they might be signs he was HIV positive and getting sick. Vockah referenced the death of his old friend, mentioning symptoms like swollen lymph nodes. Tader got into an argument with Fatman, and Fat shot back, "I don't know what's worse: your fart or your breath." The real joke was that all our lives were "open books" in which no pretense toward privacy or cleanliness could change dirty facts, statistics, or life chances. Four years later, after a short hospital stay and a silence surrounding the particulars of his condition, Tader died.

OSCAR

The high-energy dancing, singing, and other theatrical elements that characterized each performance involved hours of sweating and intense endurance. J-setting routines—precise, athletic, expressive choreographed dances like those of Southern marching bands and drill teams—were incorporated into shows; so were voguing and twerking. Almost as soon as I was brought into impromptu group rehearsals, I began practicing these routines, only to find that they weren't as easy as I had imagined. Before every show, plans had to be made in case there was an emergency. With so much relying on physicality, it became clear that chronic illness and inadequate access to healthcare were recurring problems in the group.

During my very first show with the Cru, one member's sickle cell anemia led to an emergency room visit. I'd first met Oscar during rehearsal earlier that day. By the time of our performance, he'd become so exhausted that he had to sit out the show in the green room. The night was particularly high-energy; at one point, the actress Kate Hudson appeared and was escorted into the green room to rub shoulders with Vockah. In the craziness of everything, I lost track of Oscar. It wasn't until the end of the night that I realized how serious his condition was. His body, unable to supply oxygen to his muscles, began to cramp, leading to severe pain throughout his limbs and back. He was hardly able to speak or communicate.

The rest of the group, already aware of Oscar's condition, had learned to respond by securing prescription pain medication through informal economies, since the only other solution to an intense sickle cell crisis was a blood transfusion. Like many people without access to adequate healthcare, the Cru had come to rely on an informal drug economy as a preventive and sometimes primary source of healthcare. While group members went about contacting people for medication, I could see that Oscar's condition was worsening and that he needed to go to an ER immediately. The group gathered him and put him in the back of a vehicle

I'd borrowed for the night, and I drove him to the hospital, alone. The rest of the band, along with adoring fans, went to the Waffle House.

When we arrived at the hospital, Oscar was crying and nearly unconscious. I had to drag him out of the back of the car into a seat in the emergency room as onlookers stared. In Oscar's state, he couldn't have cared less about our appearance—we were both still wearing makeup and tight mesh costuming from the show—but I couldn't say the same for the hospital staff. When I explained what was happening, they blamed him for letting his condition get so bad. Every member of the medical staff, from the admissions desk to the doctor, scrutinized us as they asked why Oscar didn't have medical insurance or a primary care provider. Despite the pain he was in, everyone assumed that if he wasn't insured or enrolled in a program that would provide regular blood transfusions as treatment for his sickle cell, then he was obviously exploiting the system for access to pain medication. Essentially, they assumed he was a junkie, and maybe I was, too, and the doctor was threatening to withhold treatment.

I had just met Oscar and knew nothing about him. I couldn't even get him to say his last name. I was afraid they would let him die right there, so I started to threaten the staff back. "This has to be malpractice," I told them, "and if he dies right here, it's on you!" Once the doctor decided to help, he acted as if he were doing us a favor, a one-off that wouldn't happen again. After more than an hour, Oscar was admitted. As the pain medication began to take effect and his body was finally able to relax, he became lucid and jokingly exclaimed, "I make one hell of a first impression," and drifted to sleep.

Oscar maintained a busy schedule—working as a pianist and organist in churches in and around New Orleans, directing choirs, and producing bounce tracks. Just like Fatman, he was ridiculously skilled yet overextended and lacked the resources to make much of his own. Oscar's work didn't afford him private health insurance. Sickle cell anemia, a chronic disease, is often stigmatized because of its associations with and prevalence within black communities. Most of the group was uninsured, including myself. During my fieldwork, I'd resigned myself to eating garlic and praying. Some of us received limited healthcare via Medicaid. Each of us walked a fine line in our individual and collective attempts at securing work (usually of the precarious variety), preventive healthcare, and healthy food. Controlled substances like marijuana, pain medication, and other drugs were considered not so much "recreational" as an available means of wellness. As I got to know Oscar, I realized his busy schedule was partly a result of his need to keep moving between various contradictory or ambivalent spaces in which he didn't feel fully accepted—circumstances that, in turn, exacerbated his condition.

Like Oscar, other group members found that a "private" or autonomous personal life was hard to maintain because of the double marginalization they experienced in their employment, their family's homes, and other resources that might ensure their stability. Social networks, work, medication, and other resources they'd once had (if they had them in the first place) were already disappearing well before the Katrina disaster; these losses were compounded by additional displacements of resources, friends, and informal economies afterward. It was normal for personal transformations, good and bad, to occur via public spectacles such as Oscar's crisis in the club and our experience in the emergency room. These circumstances were brought about by historical and ideological systems that existed far before us—and yet they seemed to bystanders (like the medical staff that evening) to fulfill a familiar and predictable narrative in which black queer bodies signify irresponsibility, liability, and messiness. True to discourses of cultural poverty, we sissies and punks become the producers of our own vulnerability and risky behaviors—as opposed to victims of oppressive systems that go unaccounted for.

That first performance (and all the other Cru shows) would have been tough to pull off without Oscar, dancing or not, because he was the only one with the production skills to put together the show disc (the custom audio mix that structured the entire performance). Despite this, other members of the group seemed unconcerned by Oscar's emergency. This was partly because it had happened so many times before. When I asked members of the group why they weren't there for Oscar when he needed them, I was told that while they hadn't been able to help in this particular situation, they had done so on numerous previous occasions, and in ways I most likely could not. Fatman even criticized Oscar for trying to dance and enjoy himself, saying he should have known better.

This experience highlighted a common theme connecting the various contexts I've shared. In each situation, dialogue between the group and me was deepened by our shared attempts at responding to crisis and misrepresentation. In each case, I expected my coperformers to respond to crisis in what I saw as a display of agency; I wanted us to resist misrepresentations and defend each other in ways I assumed were politically correct and progressive. Performers, meanwhile, were disidentifying with violent events, trauma, and misnaming in order to continue performing and living.[13]

Resisting violence, death, or trauma, which many would deem appropriate, is not a choice everyone wants or can afford to make all the time. Within formal politics and intellectualism, agency and opposition have been historically defined by notions of resistance that privilege tangible, often heteromasculine articulations of power, as well as appropriate forms of "evidence."[14] But looking only toward these narrow forms of agency misses discrete and contextual struggles; it also reifies spaces and practices along gendered lines.

Situations like these aren't unique. They're part of a larger struggle with ideologies that compel normalization and assimilation into dominant structures of capital and nationalism as a way out of bottom locations. Even as sissy bounce forced audiences and group members to continuously rethink notions of shame and respectability, narratives of erotic autonomy and utopic transcendence often assumed overly simple romantic notions of community and choice.

Two years later, Oscar invited me to his new place in the New Orleans East neighborhood. He had secured subsidized housing through a healthcare program for people living with sickle cell. He'd never had his own place and was excited to host. He said I was welcome to visit anytime—that this was going to be a new stage in his life. Only a few months later, Oscar was directing a local choir practice when he began having another sickle cell crisis. Choir members rushed him to the hospital. From the narrative I received and my own past experience, I could well imagine the scene. This time, Oscar didn't make it. He died at the hospital at the age of twenty-seven.

So many people attended Oscar's funeral that a few of us had to stand in the foyer or outside as the rain drizzled. Parishioners from the many choirs and congregations he'd played for and directed gathered with the clubgoers who'd danced to his songs. The context made me think back to Alice Walker's book *The Color Purple* (2011), where the "sinful" blues singer Shug Avery leads an entire juke joint through the doors of her estranged minister father's church to the song "Maybe God Is Tryin' to Tell You Somethin'." I felt a similar sense of redemption and union, a coming together of the profane and the sacred. A pressure built in me as a minister took the pulpit and said, "There are some people that might criticize and point fingers for the ways other people choose to live their lives. But as Scripture says, let he that is without sin among you cast the first stone.... He [Oscar] was ours!"

GRASPING SENSE

Eddie was a shaker extraordinaire who'd been an active dancer in his youth. Now, in his mid-thirties, he was leading a quiet life as a professional in the suburban area of Metairie. He still occasionally took to the stage when the Cru needed backup.

Eddie kept to himself, for the most part, and rarely came out to shows. I was surprised the first time I saw him perform: His personality changed when he started dancing. He twerked and shook all over the place. The Cru and the audience members hailed Eddie's skill; twerking isn't a dance just anyone can excel at. When I asked Eddie about his background and how he got so good, he said, "What really got me—oh my god, meaning as far as to execute [the dance]? It was an escape, probably; it was a way to release all of the tension of dealing with all kinds of stuff within a day for me. It was my X factor ... my emotional outlet."

Eddie had danced for everybody before Katrina. He seemed to be one of the few performers who'd maintained friendships with everyone, despite infighting and gossip. He was friends with Vockah and Big Freedia; he said he was the "villain" of the bunch because as teenagers they were all about church, and he was the first to go to clubs and dance.

He had grown up on Josephine Street, not too far from Freedia, until he was sixteen: "My mom wanted to get out of there because it was rat-infested." He laughed. "I was living in what we call a scatter-site.... It was like a downsize of the projects, about eight apartment buildings, and everybody shared the same porch." His mom, he explained, worked hard: "It was basically public housing, but we were paying rent." Eddie had lost his dad to cancer at twelve years old, and his relationship with his mom was tense. By fifteen, he was going to bounce clubs and bars.

> Me and my mom went through our differences. We had issues in times when she could not understand why I was involved in some of the things and people I was involved in, my friends ... I find great importance in alternative kinds of family, in the life. Sometime blood family just don't understand. But most of all, when you're going through the process of identity crisis—I guess, trying to come to terms with who you are—you need people that are going to accept

you in addition to your flaws, in addition to the things that don't really make grasping sense. . . . If I had some issues going on and my mama tripping, my family asking questions, I just get somewhere where I know they ain't gonna come, and shake the night away.

Eddie narrated his youth with matter-of-factness and amusement, discussing personal and familial tragedy and tension in ways that seemed to make light of what must have felt overwhelming at the time. He said that his mother couldn't understand why he wasn't like the other boys; she didn't get why he hung out with people like Freedia, who was seen as too flamboyant. But Eddie knew that Vockah and Freedia were true friends. They'd stayed close for years.

When I asked how he'd ended up dancing at a bounce club at fifteen, he covered his face in mock shame. "My grandmother—huh," Eddie looked up at the sky. "I'm sorry, Grandma!" Then he giggled. "My grandma was a dope dealer, okay?"

There was a club, and my grandmother was friends with a guy that owned the club. It was for adults, okay? But they would sneak me in the back. They use to like to see me dance with girls. They use to sneak me in the back and couldn't believe some of the things I'd be doing, and that I was doing as a boy— so I would tell 'em, "Just get me in and I'ma steal the show." Then one time the owner found out I was in there, and he went and got my mom while I was in there dancing, and they got me out right in time. They snuck me out of the back. They said, "Your mom is here, your mom is here!" and I hurried up and ran out of there. But I couldn't leave the music. So I went in the alley behind the club, and I finished dancing. And they were looking through the back door, shaking their heads, like, "That's a shame."

I laughed with Eddie as he recalled his youthful audacity, his self-described villainy, and his flagrant embrace of what he understood to be his flaws. There remained a vague recognition of what those flaws were all about: not acting like the other boys; disregard for the crisis of death and absence of his dad; dancing with the girls; Grandma's connects . . . and Freedia? To what narrative of black freedom and desire does this coming-of-age belong? Without knowing her, I also felt for Eddie's mother. "There's no way I could have done something like that in the small towns I'm from," I told him. "I didn't even know black people outside of my family, school, and the church." Then again, it was interesting that Eddie had entered the club scene in part because of his grandma's network of friends and possible clients.

In Eddie's narration, I saw a particular kind of engagement with the bottom. In it, hierarchical ideologies about regression, shame, and sin—whether in himself or in his family—weren't denied or sublimated, but were instead treated as fertile grounds for growth and expansion. For Eddie, twerking to the rhythms of bounce was more than fun; it was an act against regulation and conformity. His investment in dance played a central role in undermining assimilative pressures of class, status quo masculinity, and respectability:

> ALIX: How did dancing make you feel?
>
> EDDIE: It made me accept who I was and the things that came along—the characteristics that came along with me. If I'm different, and talk different, and happen to bend over and shake like a woman, it's beautiful, I love it! I'm gonna keep doing it. And they like it. They obviously like it. They keep wanting me to keep doing it. It made me feel like it's all right to be funny and shake while I do it.

Eddie described the ways dance allowed him to cultivate an antiassimilationist and intersectional sense of self. His memories of his past seemed to reproduce a stereotype: the crisis of the urban black family and the consequent devaluation of black boys and men into an emasculated site of abjection. Yet his memories didn't then rationalize a passive-aggressive hatred of black women, on whom stereotypes would place blame; or a longing for masculinized domination; or capitalist individualism as recourse to his supposed flaws. Instead, he engaged in raising the bottom as he learned to redirect assumptions about himself and his identity while staying in community.

Within a narrative of cultural pathology, Eddie is an example of black emasculation, fulfilling negative tropes of the sissy. From a culture-of-poverty perspective, the relationships between Eddie, his family, and the clubgoers produce the rat-infested home, drug economy, and bounce as expressions of vice and loose morals. But understanding culture as the source of social disorganization ignores capital's ongoing demand for surplus devalued labor, and the fact that labor still relies on the exploitation of black bodies. Ignoring the systemic effects of capital and dominant ideologies at work in narratives of cultural pathology leads to the scapegoating of single working-class black women as welfare queens, and their children as social pariahs.[15] These scapegoated people then become indispensable yet disavowed parts of capitalist expansion, providing the rationale for various forms of development, containment, and dispossession.

Eddie's story isn't invested in a blackness or queerness that defines freedom through heteropatriarchal constraints or liberal individualism. Instead, he embodies an epistemology of the bottom: He engages in performances that lead to productive forms of personal and communal growth, developing a blackness that doesn't normalize the status quo—that is, patriarchal, capitalist, or individualist notions of success or freedom.

....

When followers of Sissy Nobby's work decided to begin labeling all black queer performances "sissy bounce," no one knew the term would stick around. Many of the genre's artists went back and forth about claiming words like *punk*, *sissy*, and *ho* for themselves and their groups. The terms themselves veered between insult and endearment. No matter sissy bounce's popularity, we all knew being a sissy was something rooted in homophobic, misogynist attempts to name experiences characterized by shame and debasement. As Tavia Nyong'o writes, "The core meaning of getting 'put down,' 'flipped,' 'ripped off,' or 'punked'—from at least the late 1950s to the early 2000s—appears to be getting scapegoated within an erotic and masculinized economy of scarcity. In this economy, another's pleasure comes at the cost of your pain. Ass fucking serves as a 'prime symbol' of this economy" (2005, 22).

Sometimes being a sissy represented one's descent into these sexualized and gendered economies—a type of dehumanization that can't be anticipated or recuperated through any act of will. For the Cru to acknowledge their "vulnerabilities," they would also have to acknowledge their own inability to circumvent the broader systemic conditions that affect everyone. Revealing your inner life also meant revealing your inability to protect yourself or others from forces at home and in public.

There are limits in raising the bottom. The regulation of erotic autonomy, in the name of conformity, erodes social wealth in marginalized communities. Insidious culture-of-poverty narratives stifle black queer agency. The double bind persists: In one capitalist narrative, queers and trans people can *free themselves* from the normalizing structures of nationalism, belonging, and assimilation. And on the other side, a cultural nationalist perspective argues that pathological archetypes like sissies and ghettoized cultural objects like bounce represent the pathologies of capital, distorting the black family and true liberation by enabling people to break the norm. Attempting to navigate these constraints, sissy bounce artists revealed fundamental incoherence within narratives of capital and nationalism; however glaring, such incoherence was not unique but represented "the general estrangements of African American culture" (Ferguson 2004, 2).

The success of sissy bounce was hugely promising for the artists I worked with. Quite possibly it presented opportunities they will never see again. As much as Vockah Redu and the Cru attempted to make the most of the moment, the moment also demanded substantial blood, sweat, and tears. Struggling inside acute public moments of ideological dissonance, they were revealed to themselves as always and already outside dominant narratives of freedom and belonging. Their predicament suggested that choice might be an illusion, and that rights and opportunities assumed to be universal are only the property of a few.

Engaging in an epistemology of the bottom doesn't imply a universal concept of agency, personhood, or autonomy. It proposes a contingent notion of power, often registering as ephemeral and liminal points of encounter that are performative and must be reconstituted through praxis rather than determined by a priori notions of community. We cannot assume when and where people find the capacity and strength to reach down, within themselves and each other, and mobilize this intersectional and antiassimilationist potential. I don't want to suggest a romantic or utopian notion of community is at work; I do want to suggest that unity is produced through its enactment, rather than presupposed. What Vockah Redu and the Cru expressed was a capacity to act, feel, critique, and coalesce that shifted in appearance and character relative to the context in which we found ourselves.

CHAPTER THREE

BACK OF TOWN
A BOTTOM GEOGRAPHY

"I got a new boy, and that nigga trade / And he back of town, Callio, driveway!" This lyric, frequently sampled by DJs, had become the signature chant of bounce rapper Magnolia Shorty. Shorty was a household name in New Orleans; her songs were in high rotation on the radio, with tracks like "Smoking Gun," "My Boy" (with Kourtney Heart), and "Monkey on tha D$ck" in the queue at every party. She was one of a number of well-known women in bounce, among them Lady Red, Ms. Tee, Cheeky Blakk, Deja Vu, and Crowd Mova Crystal.[1]

Shorty, Renetta Yemika Lowe-Bridgewater, had begun her career in the mid-1990s as a teenager, voicing a reality shaped by New Orleans's public housing projects. She'd grown up in the Magnolia projects with Vockah and other members of the Cru. I met her only once, at a promotional photo shoot for *Where They At*—a 2010 gallery exhibit of photography, music, and biographies of bounce performers. I arrived with Vockah and the rest of the Cru, and the event turned into an impromptu reunion. Many of the performers hadn't seen each other since before Katrina. The disaster had brought about much of the city's displacement; many working-class black residents from public housing projects had

3.1 Magnolia Shorty photographed for the 2010 *Where They At* bounce music exhibition. Photo by Aubrey Edwards.

permanently lost their homes and communities. Even before Katrina, though, dispossession had already begun, through the welfare reforms of the 1990s.

When I introduced myself to Shorty, I wasn't sure what to expect. Her quiet, composed manner was a stark contrast to the persona her music expressed. Shorty had drawn comparisons to Lil' Kim, a New York–based artist whose highly sexual songs had emerged on the national airwaves around the time Shorty began rapping locally. Vockah told me he'd gotten into bounce because of Shorty—that she'd passed him the mic.

In both Shorty and Vockah's songs, *back of town* was a familiar refrain that held deep meaning for audiences. Bounce performers in their generation often used the term to refer to the Callio projects, a back-of-town location that was itself divided into a front of town and back of town. Historically, though, "back of town" more generally represented geographic bottoms—land that was often flood-prone and less habitable where black and poor communities had been pushed. This designation existed in contrast to "front of town"—spaces that typically existed on higher, more valued ground.[2]

The original colony of New Orleans was situated in what would eventually become the French Quarter. Referred to as the Crescent City, it hugged the higher ground close to the river. Before receiving the name Faubourg Tremé, the area just beyond the French Quarter—one of the city's earliest free black communities—was commonly referred to as "back of town," a term that described its position relative to the French Quarter, the city's colonial core. Congo Square was also located back of town; there, under French and Spanish colonial rule, enslaved Africans from West Africa and the Caribbean (and African Americans who'd already lived in New Orleans for generations) gathered on Sunday afternoons to sing and dance, performing and producing culture within the confines of the plantocracy.[3] Later, a portion of the Tremé would become Storyville, a hub of both sexual vice and music within the South.

There's a vast communal investment in both the concept of "back of town" and the memories it evokes. The phrase pops up across descriptions of black New Orleans over two hundred years, appearing in colonial historical accounts, mid-twentieth-century blues and jazz, bounce, and mainstream hip-hop. As a trope, back of town transcends any specific location. It has long served as a poetics of landscape, returning communities to bottom geographies—locations defined by racial, economic, and sexualized difference.[4] Music and performance can be understood as related ways of imagining these locations—as can literature, as Toni Morrison describes in her essay "The Site of Memory":

> You know, they straightened out the Mississippi River in places, to make room for houses and livable acreage. Occasionally the river floods these places. "Floods" is the word they use, but in fact it is not flooding; it is remembering. Remembering where it used to be. All water has a perfect memory and is forever trying to get back to where it was. Writers are like that: remembering where we were, what valley we ran through, what the banks were like, the light that was there and the route back to our original place. It is emotional memory—what the nerves and the skin remember as well as how it appeared. And a rush of imagination is our "flooding." (1990, 98–99)

Bounce's efficacy is partly defined by the ways it collectively remembers, in a flood that returns the listener to particular sites.[5] A site isn't simply a location; it also incorporates memories, images, or other qualities that take you there. For locals, bounce provides a collective pathway to back of town as a primary site of blackness.

In a culture-of-poverty framework, community norms and personal actions allegedly produce broken homes, immorality, and the material conditions in which people find themselves—as opposed to, for example, the systemic and structural forces behind adverse shifts in housing. In contrast, the poetic framework behind "back of town"—a locale similar to Morrison's fictional neighborhood, the Bottom—is designed to redirect reductive, pathologizing ideas about home and domesticity in places of chronic fragmentation and dispossession.

Back of town is also a way to talk about shared longing, functioning as a catchall for geographic bottoms that are locations of desire. Regardless of whether people understand the systemic conditions of white supremacy and capitalism that produce back of town, local music provides a medium where identifications and antagonisms around black space can be felt, shared, and collectively processed.

The gallery turned out to be my only opportunity to meet and speak to Shorty in person. Less than a year later, I learned through a Facebook post about her violent and untimely death. Moments later, the popular radio show host Wild Wayne confirmed that Shorty had been killed—shot twenty-six times in a bloody drive-by shooting. The papers, radio, and local gossip all speculated about how she'd come to be caught in what appeared to be the contract killing of the friend in whose car she was a passenger. Quiet as it was kept, the implied acceptance of such violence normalized certain black bodies and black spaces as permanently doomed.

Magnolia Shorty's lyric is more than a simple reference to back of town. She conjures and expresses shared desire through a poetics of landscape. It's not just that her new boy is a "nigga" or black, or that he's "trade," or that back of town is simply an imagined space—Shorty, and the DJs who emphasize this chant through the repetition of their samples, create the sense that their desires for those imaginaries are one.[6] In bounce at large, the force and arrangement of songs imagine and memorialize wards, schools, and specific streets defined by blackness, poverty, and displacement—places that in many cases no longer physically exist. They are commemorated as locations of desire for an idealized romance, whether fleeting encounter or enduring love. Cultural expressions like this affect memory and awareness of space by enlivening the way it's spoken about; on local terms, they chronicle the changing face of oppression and resistance.[7]

Bounce rappers and DJs often evoke the projects, wards, schools, and other cultural sites they come from. In "Smoking Gun," Shorty creatively pairs the Twelfth Ward neighborhood and the Magnolia, Melpomene, and Calliope projects with imagined figments of desire, calling the listener to go there:

> And if a nigga is a soulja and he out that Magnolia, heller, heller
> And that boy don't need no help, he out that muthafuckin' Melph, heller, heller
> My nigga dick stay hard 'cause he out that Twelfth Ward, heller, heller
> And you already know he out that fuckin' Callio, heller, heller
> Let's go!

One of Vockah Redu and the Cru's biggest hits, "Roll Call," represents specific community members, along with the projects and neighborhoods they hailed from. The group takes the listener on a call-and-response tour of different projects, schools, and neighborhood centers:

> [Vockah:] Who, who they wanna see? . . . A-V-E . . .
> [Cru:] Ooh! Gee ah! You not gonna stick that dick in my mouth!
> *Y'all hoes stole our shit, but other hoes still ain't got it . . .*
>
> You see him at the club, that's your boy, that's your trade
> They want them hot boys, back of town, Rocheblave . . .
> *Callio! Callio! . . .*
>
> Front of town, back of town, by the tree, Coco, Nutty, and PeeWee
> *Broussard! Rabouin! . . .*
> Melpho, Mel, Mel Melpho, Melpho
> *(mene, mene, mene, me mene mene!) . . .*
>
> Coming back (*hard!*), coming back (*hard!*)
> Coming back (*hard!*), coming back (*hard!*)
> Franklin (*Yard!*), Franklin (*Yard!*), Franklin (*Yard!*), Franklin (*Yard!*) . . .
>
> Mimmy (*yeah!*), Trell (*yeah!*), Teddy (*yeah!*), Herb (*yeah!*)
> Go in Clara Court and get that fire-ass herb (*oh yeah!*)

Will (*yeah!*), Larry (*yeah!*), Randi (*yeah!*), Tonto (*yeah!*)
This is for my (*H-oes*), I'm down for my (*hoes!*)

Rock, rock, rock and roll
Gert Town, P Town, Hollygrove
This is for my (*H-oes*), I'm down with my (*hoes!*) . . .
Vock, Vock, Vockah! Gra, Grahonda! Joi, Joi, Jadah! Ta, Ta, Tasha! Ya, Ya, Yatty! Ni, Ni, Ninny! Ni, Ni, Nikki!

As the title implies, the song takes us back to the classroom and offers a lesson about spaces, people, and desires. The listener is compelled to remember and recognize them. Vockah's calls receive responses from the Cru, which at the time was made up of his teenage friends (whom he also called the Ave Girls). At the end of the track, all their names are shouted out.

Bounce is an inherently social form—a dialogue and relationship between artists, DJs, and audiences that allow them to produce and memorialize spaces, places, and community through song. The songs represent itineraries and geographies in a manner that's akin to other local performances of parading and procession, avoiding the reductive ways that identity and place appear in dominant mappings of a city defined by tourism.

Many bounce recordings reproduce the energy of a live performance, where call-and-response is a standard way to create crowd participation. When we performed "Roll Call," our calls and responses weren't only a means of building energy and connection; they also made people feel represented and proud of where they came from. Call-and-response certainly isn't specific to bounce music—but bounce's use of the form to focus on places and people that in some cases no longer exist animates a process of memory-making and strengthens those representations' capacity to generate feelings of home. The communal deployment of tropes like back of town circulates a counternarrative that pushes back against dominant ideas of communities as nothing but poor black ghettos. For members of those communities, the music is a catalyst for finding meaning in the past and a guide for reconstituting home in new and provocative ways.

Like Magnolia Shorty, who took her name from the housing development she grew up in, others claimed New Orleans's street and project names as their own. The Ave Girls, the group of young women who were the original Cru, articulated self and community in ways that often intersected with black transgender and gay male narratives: They talked about the issues between themselves and controlling men, the police, or their homes. These queer and femme dialogues and expressions of desire helped shape a contemporary, intersectional, antiassimilative back of town—in this case, a place defined by tensions with heteropatriarchal notions of community.

A sense of ownership, intimacy, kinship, sex, and self-possession runs throughout "Roll Call." It would be easy to assume that Vockah, Magnolia Shorty, and the Ave Girls' provocative lyrics are simply a matter of sex, but a closer listen makes clear their intention to take up space and declare their communal ties. The Ave Girls' replies, and Shorty's lyrics, are evidence of black women's efforts to claim space beyond the traditional domestic sphere; they assert themselves in the bounce scene and throughout the community.

When I asked Vockah about the women members of the Cru, the Ave Girls, and Shorty's group of friends (who called themselves the Magnolia hoes), he said, "They were go-getters. When we were young, we went to the same schools. They were self-built women, fashionistas, and entrepreneurs. And most of all, they survived it. The Ave Girls made up the Cru in the beginning, but then they started seeing boys and having babies. They would still come into the studio to do recordings, but that's when I started performing with boys."

ALIX: How did you get to know Shorty?

VOCKAH: In elementary. She used to come by my house and eat breakfast, and I used to do her hair. In middle school, she was going to [Alcée] Fortier [High School], and I was trying to get in [to that school], but I ended up at Rabouin. By 1997, she dropped the song "Monkey on tha D$ck," and it was blowing up.

She was still coming over, and she inspired me to rap. They were having a block party one day and a DJ was playing. I was in the shower, and she came and hollered at my back window, and she said, "Vockah, come on!" I went out and got on the mic, and this was my first time. When I got on the mic my heart was beating really fast. She was rocking it, singing "Monkey on tha D$ck" ... when she gave me the mic, the drop hit, and I said, "Jump high to the sky, fall down in a splits, and monkey on a Magnolia dick." After that, I went home and I recorded myself, and I started passing out tapes.

Magnolia Shorty and the Ave Girls formed a circle of care and empowerment: Whether doing each other's hair, taking over the streets, or expressing shared desires and antagonisms, they collectively worked toward survival for as long as they could. Magnolia Shorty's violent death was a shock to us all. When I called Vockah to offer condolences, he was barely able to speak. Through tears, he said that he wouldn't be where he was, doing what he was doing, if she hadn't passed him the mic.

Vockah was one of the first black queer artists preceding the wave of bounce that represented straight men. He was following in Shorty's footsteps. Their relationship to each other and the community they grew up in had been threatened by private economic development and attacks on social welfare. Through bounce, both artists could express themselves as racialized, classed, and differently feminized bodies, voicing resistance to their marginalization and solidifying their centrality to their communities.

Magnolia Shorty's untimely death was followed by a number of impactful community losses. In the days following, I heard and experienced a mixture of responses that, once again, rationalized black premature death through dominant narratives about violence and space. Newspapers, local gossip, blogs, and social media sites like Facebook and YouTube speculated about Shorty's demise, concluding that she was associating with the wrong people and existing in the wrong place. Although she was shot twenty-six times in an apartment complex parking lot in the middle of the day, the details of what happened somehow remained unclear. Nobody knew enough to share an informed story; a narrative of black criminality remained the dominant explanation for why a twenty-eight-year-old black woman from the Magnolia should die. Like black people the world over, Shorty was also often victim-blamed, as if merely living and being black meant consenting to one's own violation.

THE DISPLACEMENT OF THE PROJECTS

The last fifty years of liberal and conservative political debate have produced divergent opinions about private versus public (government) solutions to public welfare and housing. These debates don't question which communities get to define the public good, nor do they include the voices of those whose lives are on the line. In New Orleans, resources were funneled out of public housing, transportation, and the levees themselves. The process of residential segregation first paired large, racialized geographies (e.g., back of town) with neglected infrastructure. Then, disaster, encroachment, and the displacement of black communities allowed investors to pursue opportunities for "renewal" and reconstruction.

Beginning in the mid-1970s, long before Katrina, city planners focused on a problematizing narrative that centered blighted housing, broken infrastructure, and ideas of black deviance. This narrative focused on ways to remove low-income communities, using federal and state public resources to partner with private business; the goal was a market-driven response to public housing. The market-driven responses to urban governance that emerged in the Nixon era have since become commonplace. Urban historian Megan French-Marcelin outlines the process by which, starting in 1974, "mayors across the nation abandoned redistributive antipoverty projects in order to enable broad private-sector urban revitalization":

> In New Orleans, as in cities across the country, local officials deployed new federal urban aid in ways that provided private-sector developers with the insularity necessary to conduct development in ways that excluded low-income residents from a share in the city's economic future.... The new [federal Community Development Block Grant, or CDBG,] program gave mayors autonomy over a broad range of physical development activities, while narrowing redistributive programs and cutting more comprehensive antipoverty programs....
>
> Though leadership of the nascent public-private partnership insisted that growth of the area would benefit all residents, the omission of low-income neighborhoods (and the opinions of their residents) from the growth zone ensured that redevelopment and redistribution would not be coterminous.... Rather, the exclusion hinged on boundaries wherein a predominantly black, low-income labor force denied unionization was also criminalized in those spaces when not operating as labor. Therein, growth was maintained by making certain spaces, places, and people subject to the threat of a police state....
>
> Though CDBG was a program conceived to benefit low- and moderate-income areas, the ambiguous language within the legislation actually facilitated the proposed diversion of aid. The legislation's rhetoric, which replaced poverty with blight as the central

enemy of cities, was deployed throughout the act without definitional clarity.... If seemingly innocuous, the shift in vocabulary reinforced the notion that addressing economic inequality was no longer critical to the survival of cities so much as the restoration of a physical environment reflective of a consumer class.... Blight could be anywhere. Thus, city community development plans defined their project scope in language that ranged from environmental and physical to sociopsychological and pathogen-like. (2019, 242–46)

In New Orleans, representations of blighted housing, uninhabitable space, and broken infrastructure were paired with ideas of pathological black deviance—a combination traceable to a political economy of exclusion that's spread across major cities. The assumption that market-driven development could respond to poverty better than federal urban aid was part of a narrative that also blamed low-income black communities for not securing middle-class status in the wake of civil rights legislation. This backlash to the gains of the civil rights era was also a means of scapegoating marginalized communities for an ongoing fiscal crisis while compelling communities of color into a growing culture of militarism and policing at home and abroad.

Although the rise of neoliberal policy is often associated with Reaganism, these forms of legislation (along with the racial discourse that facilitated them) can be traced to earlier administrations. Policymakers at the national and local level have, over decades, employed stereotypes of deadbeat dads, welfare queens, queers, and sex workers; these stereotypes (many of which attribute excessive desires to black bodies) have overwhelmingly shaped a national narrative about the nuclear family, gender expression, and class.

Vockah and most of his friends grew up walking the streets—rather than riding in family vehicles or on an efficient transit system—in part due to the same conditions by which many black people found themselves trapped during and after the levees broke and the city was flooded. The black urban population was strategically immobilized over time through processes of structural segregation from white middle-class neighborhoods and ensuing disinvestment in other infrastructure, such as public transportation and emergency evacuation response systems.

Multiple forms of benign neglect have resulted in patterns of immobility followed by displacement in New Orleans. This neglect also informed ongoing, everyday forms of isolation and movement that defined social practices as simple as getting around town. My interviews with Vockah suggested that black displacement after Katrina wasn't an exceptional moment of crisis, but the continuation of racist practices in urban planning.

I asked Vockah if he'd left New Orleans because of Katrina, and he responded in the following way:

> No. We received notice that the [Magnolia] project was being torn down. Everybody received notice they were tearing it down to rebuild it, and they made people an offer to move back. They were taking it down to rebuild it—but we knew it was the government and how they wanted to make the area white, soon. Even though they've rebuilt it up nice, people are still waiting and don't have a home. Some went to Houston. Houston messed up a lot of people's lives after Katrina. Some people still don't have a place to stay. If you couldn't fulfill your lease and you were on Section 8 and the lease was broke, you'd have no place to stay. They wanted Washington Avenue from Saint Charles all the way to Claiborne to be white. I knew I was going to miss everybody. We had to travel to see each other. It was crazy—those were my girls, we grew up together. But by that time, I felt like the world was about to change.

Vockah describes the multiple displacements of project tenants in New Orleans, done via changes in public housing policy during the 1990s and after Hurricane Katrina.[8] He also recalls those displacements' influence on the close relationships he had as a young gay black man with black women.

The compounded forces of social welfare reform, disaster, and displacement—not to mention the spread of HIV/AIDS—have shaped the black community along lines that crosscut sexuality and gender. Political scientist Cathy J. Cohen asks, "How do we use the relative degrees of ostracism that all sexual/cultural 'deviants' experience to build a basis of unity for broader coalition and movement work?" (2005, 38). In many popular sissy bounce recordings, black queer men, trans folks, and cisgender women chant and call out together. Black women, particularly black lesbians or studs (butch women or trans men), managed clubs, bartended, and showed up as regular audience members. Leaning on Cohen's inquiry, I ask, How can we use bounce performance and back-of-town narratives to situate potential forms of autonomy and coalition for the future?

Everyone I spoke to for this research project had at some point been displaced from New Orleans, for periods ranging from a few months to a few years, after they were evacuated or detained. Some are still on the move. Those who could return to the city experienced a continuing displacement through the loss and reduction of life-sustaining resources, social networks, and employment. For many others, moving back to New Orleans was not an option. When the city and federal authorities took the displacement of public housing occupants as an opportunity to quickly dismantle the black community, they did so knowing no alternative housing was available; as a result, many were forced to stay where they were, outside the city. Violence was yet another reason many chose not to return, knowing fewer community resources would lead to increased tensions. Vockah, like Magnolia Shorty, lived between Houston and New Orleans, making regular trips home to visit and perform. When Shorty was killed, reports said she'd only just arrived in New Orleans from her Houston home.

Bounce performances embody the struggles between dominant narratives and counternarratives about black space. Magnolia Shorty's songs represent a set of social relationships defined by nostalgia, ambivalence, and desire for a specific self and community. Intimate desires and affinities are juxtaposed against a backdrop of infrastructural neglect, residential segregation, and tropes of the ghetto. Home, both as memory and as social knowledge, is caught between these conflicting notions—a place one misses, yet not a place one necessarily wants to go back to (even if that were possible). Home's power, as a place that can only be communally imagined, contributes to the proliferation of its meaning and the relationships it sustains.

Back of town is a place where deviance, transgression, and sex are thought to preoccupy all inhabitants; it's where the juke joint used to be, and where blackness was appreciated without having to conform to dominant standards. It represents places produced through oppression, where people nonetheless make the best of a bad situation and hold on to what they have. The Magnolia and New Orleans generally may not be places people can fully possess, but they can be actively imagined and reconceived wherever one finds oneself. This seemed to be true for Vockah when I questioned him in 2010 about his displacement:

ALIX: How did you find people? I know it was hard . . . and this was before Facebook.

VOCKAH: I really didn't see anybody. I started a new life. Not until last year—I started seeing people. . . . Uptown was more, like, bougie, but still hood. . . . The schools uptown were better. You'll have to talk to somebody downtown, and they'll be like, "Oh, Uptown, it's poo!" Everybody's gonna feel this way about their hood. . . . The Magnolia was happening. Look at who's all from there: me, Juvenile, Lil Wayne. Everybody is Uptown.

Vockah discussed life in the Magnolia and growing up in New Orleans's Uptown in fairly idyllic terms. He often referenced hip-hop royalty Lil Wayne and Juvenile alongside the black women he'd worked with as peers before mentioning that he'd been tapped to be "the first sissy of Cash Money [Records]," even though he objected to the term:

ALIX: And what happened?

VOCKAH: Oh, nothing. I was on the under label from them. They weren't ready for that yet. They kept me hidden. We used to use the same studio: me, Juvenile—he use to be his big-lipped self up in there. . . . Yeah, they know me. Ask them 'bout me when you interview them. Ask 'em 'bout me, baby.

Vockah paints a picture of the Magnolia as not only a pleasant place, but also a place to be proud of, despite the conditions that produced it. In his hindsight, the struggles of growing up as a "sissy" in the black community take a back seat to positive representations and memories of home. Vockah provides a narrative in which blackness, sexuality, and place are remembered for their positive value, rather than their negative aspects.

COLONIALITY, SOUND, AND SPACE

Throughout my research, I lived on the boundary of two downtown neighborhoods and two adjacent streets distinctly marked by race and class. My street was mostly made up of recent incoming white homeowners, who at times went out of their way to inform us they owned their homes and we—an assortment of mostly black and brown students and activists—were renters. This was in contrast to the street parallel to us and directly beyond our backyard, Gentilly Boulevard.

Many people know Gentilly the boulevard (as opposed to Gentilly the neighborhood) for its racetrack and casino, along with the fact that it hosts the annual New Orleans Jazz and Heritage Festival. The street is less well-known for Stallings Playground, a public park that provides leisure and entertainment to locals throughout the year. At Stallings, the basketball court was active all day. Young kids and adults played for an audience of friends, passersby, and any neighbors who cared to step onto their porch for a distraction. In the summer, the park's pool offered an oasis from the oppressive heat. Old men regularly gathered to play dominoes and chess, and parents brought their children to a gated jungle gym that provided safety from the busy road, where traffic ran between Mid-City and the Gentilly neighborhood a few miles downriver. The rhythm of life at the park and on the boulevard itself greeted me daily as I biked back and forth across town to work. What also greeted me was the marked disparity among my street, the boulevard, and the park.

Not long after I moved to New Orleans, the contrasts among these spaces became clearer. I was washing and hanging clothes in my backyard among the banana trees, bougainvillea, and creeping cat's claw vines that threatened to bring down the side of our house. Sounds of life came from the park and the street, just beyond the houses adjacent to my yard. Sometimes I could feel the earth and our house shake from passing traffic; the loose, moist soil made almost all roads frail and riddled with potholes. I'd become accustomed to the jarring shakes, car horns, and shouts; to me, they were just part of the ambience. But as I hung my clothes out to dry that day, I wasn't prepared for the middle-aged, casually dressed white woman who walked into my yard from the side entrance, her hand resting on a holstered gun. She scanned the yard before acknowledging me to ask, "Did you hear that noise? I thought I heard shots fired." Shocked, I could only shake my head no. "It must have come from back there, from Gentilly," she responded, and without another word, she backed away to leave the yard.

This was how I met the cop who lived across the street. The entitlement that led her to enter our yard with a gun, in some off-duty effort to protect and serve herself and the rest of the block in the face of the danger she assumed to emanate from either our house or Gentilly Boulevard, rested on the same conflation of blackness, violence, and property relations that led people throughout the city to deem streets like ours essentially safe and others violent (Manalansan 2005; Hanhardt 2013).[9] In addition, it's significant that in contexts of privilege—around class, race, gender, sexuality, and domesticity—perceptions of danger and threat are frequently marked by "hearing things."[10]

The structures of feeling that inform fears of racial difference are interwoven with anxieties about environmental threat. These anxieties are less about natural disaster than they are about the inevitable results of settler colonialism's effects on modern infrastructural expansion. Although settler-colonial and infrastructural forces have intensified "disaster" in the lives of white working-class and poor communities, the worst forms of violence are experienced by black people, who are simultaneously conflated with and blamed for the destabilization of domestic life. Ideas about black people overflowing ghettos have an interplay with the imagined danger of a wild natural landscape that might overwhelm civic life—and both scenarios produce similar feelings of crisis in the minds of people like the neighborhood cop (Hage 2016).[11] Why do these spatial imaginaries persist, and what function do they serve?

The face of a particular desired community comes into view through negating the ways life is lived (or unlivable) somewhere *back, behind, and below*—in this case, spaces where blackness hasn't yet been transformed by the type of development and uplift that's presumed necessary to ensure progress. Settler colonial ideas about space conflate geographies and racial bodies, using development narratives that normalize benign neglect in the lives of black people (Klein 2007; Woods 2017). Amid this normalization, black culture is more than arbitrary: It's an essential means of navigating life in social and environmental bottoms.

Among both colonists and urban planners, black bodies, black culture, and black spaces were historically imagined into "back of town," an uninhabitable geographic nexus antithetical to civic life. In New Orleans, this designation originated as a settler colonial response to the ecological conditions of building a city in marshes and attempting to channel the Mississippi River's flow with levees and pump systems. In this setting, black bodies and their difference became conflated with uninhabitability in a colony encroached on by water.

In New Orleans, black residents—and anyone excluded from white civic belonging—were relegated to low-lying, flood-prone areas outside the colonial core. What had once been known simply as "back of town" took on a new identity as the Faubourg Tremé, becoming one of the nation's first communities of free black people. This geography of marginalization also gave rise to spaces of cultural resistance and creativity, most famously Congo Square, where African diasporic peoples—both

3.2 *The Bamboula*, circa 1886, depicting a dance ritual in Place Congo. Sketch by Edward Winsor Kemble. Hogan Jazz Archive, Tulane University.

enslaved and free—gathered on Sundays to sustain and reinvent traditions of music, dance, and communal expression.

On February 21, 1819, Benjamin Henry Latrobe, the influential Anglo-American architect whose designs were used as the basis for New Orleans waterworks, went for a stroll, crossing the boundary of the French Quarter into Congo Square or, as it was referred to at the time, Place Congo. His diaries and sketches provide some of the fullest accounts of the performances that occurred there:

> In going up St. Peters Street and approaching the common I heard a most extraordinary noise, which I supposed to proceed from some horse Mill, the horses trampling on a wooden floor. I found however on emerging from the houses, onto the common, that it proceeded from a croud [*sic*] of five or six hundred persons assembled in an open space or public square.
>
> I went to the spot and crouded near enough to see the performance. All those who were engaged in the business seemed to be *blacks*. . . . They made an incredible noise. . . . A man sung an uncouth song to the dancing . . . and the Women screamed a detestable burthen on one single note. . . . I have never seen any thing more brutally savage, and at the same time dull and stupid than this whole exhibition. (Sublette 2008, 275–76)

Latrobe's conflation of blackness with nonhuman sounds, savageness, excess, and brutality—and his awareness of a geography of race—are key to the relations I see in New Orleans today. Latrobe died of yellow fever before he could see the completion of his work in the city, but his designs would contribute to the 150 years of urban expansion. As New Orleans grew, Congo Square was integrated within the city limits—but as performance studies scholar and historian Joseph Roach notes, "The liminal character of the old market remained" (1996, 64).[12] Latrobe's designs, in which groundwater was pumped out of swamps and floodplains, allowed the Crescent City to expand and civic life to flourish. However, the downside of pumping and drainage is anthropogenic subsidence. The human-assisted sinking and compaction of mud and soil over time has produced what we now know as the "bottom of the bowl."

New Orleans's geographic order has been discussed as a regime of racial segregation that's still closely related to plantation structures, in which slave quarters were built in proximity to the master's house (Lewis 1976). Local environmental racism and this spatial regime have pushed blacks people into the bottom of the bowl—the devalued land more prone to flooding (Colten 2005).

According to geographer Richard Campanella, New Orleans was once mostly above sea level, albeit covered in swamps: "Native peoples generally adapted to this fluidity, shoring up the land or moving to higher ground as floodwaters rose. But then European imperialists came to colonize. Colonization meant permanency, and permanency meant imposing engineering rigidity on this soft, wet landscape: levees to keep water out, canals to dry soil, and in time, pumps to push and lift water out of canals lined with floodwalls" (2018).

Subsidence, flooding, and urban development and population stress are part of a slow-moving crisis caught in a downward trajectory—and blackness has, again and again, been positioned at the bottom of these processes. In New Orleans, as the city increased access to dry topography and its population grew over the twentieth century, white flight and suburban growth characterized the former swamps and new dewatered frontiers. As Campanella explains, "The white middle class, eager to flee crumbling old *faubourgs*, moved into the new 'lakefront' neighborhoods en masse, to the point of excluding black families through racist deed covenants" (2018).

Cultural preservation is a bedrock of New Orleans, but the city's marginalized communities and cultural sites have repeatedly succumbed to

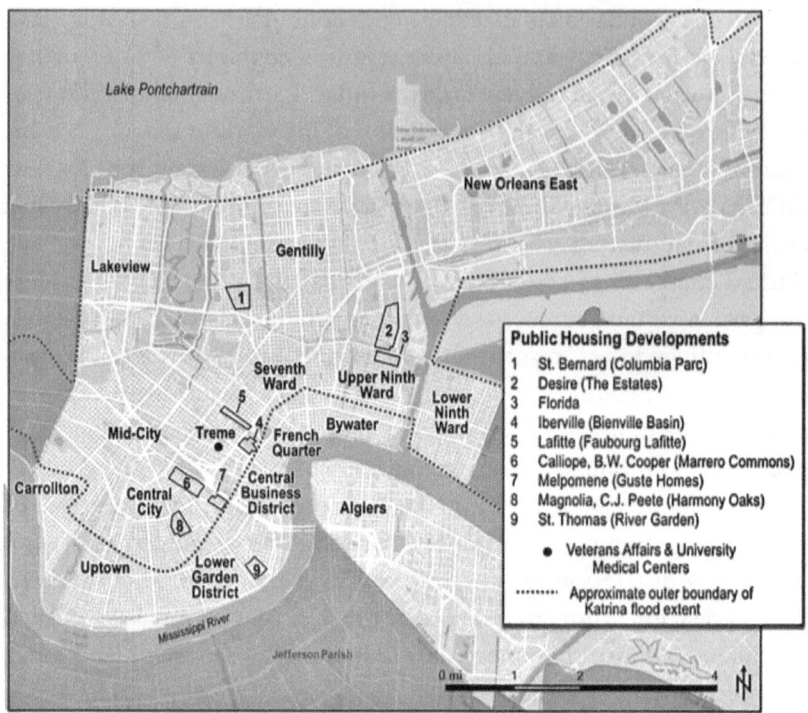

3.3 Map of public housing developments throughout Orleans Parish. Source: Brand and Baxter, "Post-Disaster Development Dilemmas," 220.

the effects of life in the bottom of the bowl. Despite what looks like a flat topography to outsiders, higher ground is in short supply and thus often inaccessible to residents on lower ground. Communities in the bowl are hit hardest by hurricanes and floods: Despite Hurricane Katrina not hitting the city directly, some of these neighborhoods experienced as much as twelve feet of saltwater flooding (Campanella 2018).

The city's nuanced topography is easily overlooked unless you've lived in it. Many tourists experience the city only within the elevated boundaries of the French Quarter, or on raised boulevards such as Esplanade Avenue, Saint Charles Avenue, Napoleon Avenue, and Magazine Street. When travelers enjoy the beauty of the old plantation houses, they're unaware that the neighborhoods just beyond them, once filled with slave quarters, are still marked as black and/or low income. If a flash flood warning were to be called, everyone in these low-lying areas would promptly move their cars to the major boulevards, where their vehicles, if

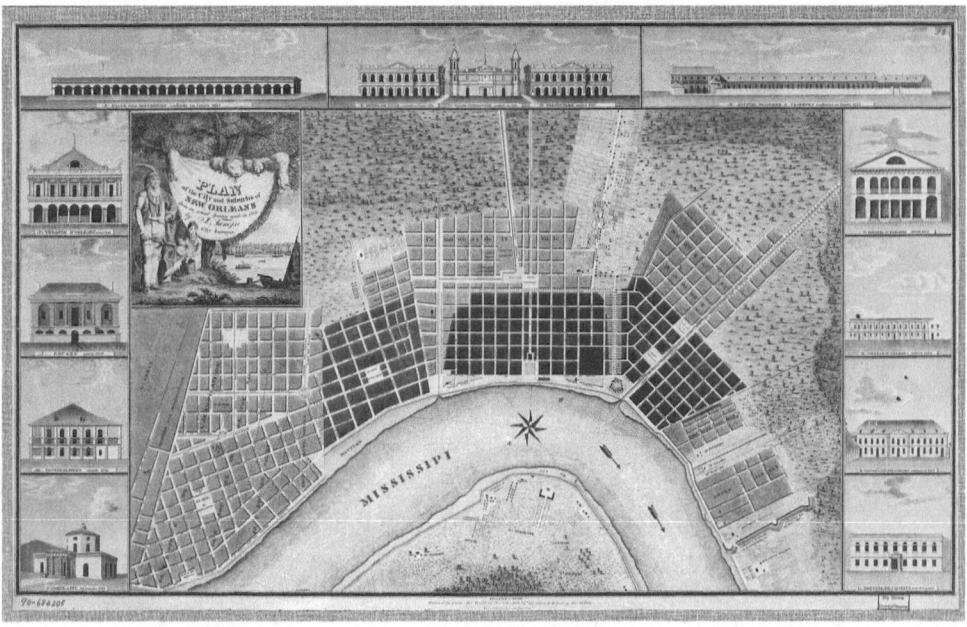

3.4 Plan of the original city, suburbs, and marshland of New Orleans, created by I. Tanasse, city surveyor, in 1815. Source: World Maps Online.

not their bodies and the rest of their possessions, might make it through the storm.

The Lower Ninth Ward is a prime example of the merger of blackness, centuries-old environmental segregation, infrastructural neglect, and subsiding land. Before Hurricane Katrina and the breaking of the levees, this area was home to the largest population of black homeowners in the United States. The entire area was also below sea level. Hurricane Betsy in 1965, Katrina, and numerous other disasters led to waves of displaced and dispossessed black families.[13]

"Hearing things" prompted Latrobe's passage from the city proper to the back of town, a place where his European colonial self might succumb to the wilds of blackness and the environmental conditions of the swamp (which did eventually happen—yellow fever, a mosquito-borne illness, thrived in the dense, humid city).

Sound studies scholar Ana María Ochoa Gautier writes, "The presence or absence of sound ... stands as the very mediator of the presence or absence of life, showing us how myths (or cosmologies) can tie events into structures. But the acknowledgment of such a relation—based as it is on admitting the agentive acoustic dimensions of nonhuman entities in the affairs of humans—is largely based on an understanding of the relations between humans and nonhumans that unsettles the historically constructed boundaries between nature and culture, the human and the nonhuman, in Western modernity" (2016, 139).

Latrobe crosses what he imagines as a threshold between humanity and the nonhuman wild, prompted by his perceiving something outside Western notions of legibility and civility. According to architectural historian Dell Upton, Latrobe's experience spoke to pervasive anxieties about the influence of black music and urban governance in the city:

> Structure and harmony, measure and control, as well as content coherence, were indispensable signs of musicality and of humanity itself. By implication, black music threatened to undermine socialization and morality. (Black dance demonstrated the reality of that threat.) Indeed, to white authorities all black vocal expression was noise that disturbed citizens, undermined order, and needed to be regulated. In limiting the right of slaves to gather and be heard in New Orleans in 1817, the council also forbade "whooping or hallooing any where in the city or suburbs, or . . . making any clamorous noise, or . . . singing aloud any indecent song." (2007, 27)

These historical tensions reveal sound and music as intangible markers of life and death, humanity and nonhumanity, in the expansion of urban space. Given past and present efforts to discipline black bodies along these lines, it's vital to consider the stakes in reproducing black sound against efforts to silence them.

Efforts to regulate black expressions of culture and desire were not simply a matter of public life, but a struggle over the normalization of race, sexuality, and gender in the private sphere. Ghettoized, subsided land is often conflated with the black bodies that exist in them, and bottom spaces and inhabitants are seen as active threats to civic life. Black music and performance—whether in Congo Square, New Orleans blues, or Magnolia Shorty and Vockah Redu's work—are creative mediations of systemically produced bottoms. These cultural forms are strategies born out of the geographic and ecological circumstances of being positioned as nonhuman property, "objects" that are part of the environment.

Anthropologist Ghassan Hage states, "We are witnessing what is now a well-known and well-researched process: the increasing inability of industry and government to control, manage, and recycle the by-products of the exploitation and transformation of natural resources" (2016, 45). Although Latrobe died of yellow fever after submitting his designs for the drainage and water systems that would eventually become a part of the expansion of the city, his and other colonial ideas of race and space still inform our lived relation to black sociability and black expressive culture. Bottom geographies are everywhere, their locations shifting and changing in relation to white supremacist and capitalist development.

FROM BLUES TO BOUNCE

In his 1966 song "Back o' Town Blues," Louis Armstrong sings:

> I had a woman, livin' way back o' town
> Yeah, she treated me right, never let me down
> But I wasn't satisfied—I had to run around

The New Orleans native and jazz icon identifies "back of town" as a location of desire, where his woman stays. He also admits that her good love just wasn't enough. This recognition of an imagined space alongside ambivalence toward figures within its bounds connects to contemporary tropes in both bounce and mainstream hip-hop.

Louis Armstrong called the Faubourg Tremé, the historical back of town, home through a great deal of his life. Indeed, Louis Armstrong Park is the location of Congo Square—and also an area where, during the federal expansion of interstates in the 1960s, five hundred homes were razed to build Interstate 10, demolishing Armstrong's residence and displacing a thriving black business district along Claiborne Avenue.

The thoroughfare was once lined with live oak trees, resembling other affluent parts of the city, but by the 1970s, it had become a concrete jungle. Despite the displacement of black families from single tenement homes into public housing projects, black New Orleans has maintained a strong relationship to this area through legacies of procession and parading; Mardi Gras krewes and second-line parades regularly occupy the space. These legacies of black sociability cannot be understood separately from exclusionary and exploitative infrastructural development.

For over two hundred years, back of town has signified a relationship between two sets of experiences: on one hand, colonial ways of thinking, rooted in the prospect of being besieged by the wilderness; and on the other hand (for the "savage"), a generative cultural setting produced by violently dispossessive urban planning. For Latrobe, crossing over is to pass from a space of white civility to savagery—whereas Armstrong describes the (im)possibility of a space that can fulfill interpersonal desires amid the precarity of black life. The two men are not alone in this complicated relationship.

Decades after the death of Latrobe and the end of Sunday gatherings at Congo Square, back of town became the home of Storyville—the red-light district where sex work, blues, and jazz flourished. It's not happenstance that a red-light district on the periphery of Victorian notions of family and home was situated within the racialized geographic bottom.

As historian Clyde Woods explains in *Development Drowned and Reborn*, "One of the defining features of the new urban segregation movement was the organized removal of 'white vice' from white districts and its imposition in Black neighborhoods. An international seaport and the most open city in the fundamentalist South, New Orleans used an 1897 ordinance to push adult prostitution, child prostitution, gambling, drug trafficking, drug abuse, and other 'white vices' out of the central business district and into the Storyville District adjacent to the historic African American neighborhood of Tremé" (2017, 86).

The organized relocation of white vice into black neighborhoods "demonstrate[s] that racial-sexual domination is an ongoing spatial project" (McKittrick 2006, 121). Throughout the late nineteenth and early twentieth centuries, New Orleans's bottom geography was also a persistent site of premature death due to overcrowded subpar housing, persistent flooding, and standing water that allowed mosquitoes to spread yellow fever. To add to this, mortality rates in post–Civil War New Orleans were made worse by an active anti-Reconstruction movement that successfully prevented black people from receiving federal aid in healthcare and education. Positioning illicit sexual economies near black neighborhoods imbues both sets of spaces with a shared representational field of excess, sin, and self-loss. This symbolic merger of a racial and sexual bottom formed a trope that's been used to define black New Orleans to this day.

By the time of Armstrong's birth in 1901, the promises and hopes attached to Reconstruction had dissolved. *Plessy v. Ferguson* upheld the legality of segregation in a city that previously knew a more complex system of racial stratification than other parts of the South. Music and performance would become one of the few avenues of social mobility for black residents like Armstrong. Growing up in these geographic bottoms meant experiencing a mixture of pleasure and pain, still audible in Armstrong's music as well as in bounce. In the blues, this duality is represented as a crossroads—a point at which the possibilities of black individuality, community, and kinship meet ongoing reproductions of blackness as the antithesis of humanity ("horses trampling on a wooden floor").[14] This duality also resonates within the hard-hitting, bass-driven music of Magnolia Shorty and Vockah Redu and the Cru. Back of town is no longer attached to any specific geography; much like the legacy of blues and jazz, it circulates and moves with black people.

BACK OF TOWN TILL INFINITY

Eight years after Magnolia Shorty's death, her influence entered the mainstream. Her sampled vocals from "Smoking Gun" appeared throughout Canadian rapper Drake's 2018 hip-hop single "In My Feelings," a hit that topped the *Billboard* Hot 100 chart for ten weeks.

Drake's successful song also put back of town in the limelight. The video, shot in New Orleans, opens with a *Romeo and Juliet*–like vignette. The rapper arrives at the stately balconied home of his love interest, KeKe (La La Anthony) and throws rocks at her upstairs window. When she opens it, irritated, he professes his need for her, saying, "I'm trying to come to you like a man." Soon after, they're interrupted by KeKe's mother (played by Phylicia Rashad). "Carry your ass on home, now," Rashad admonishes Drake, "and don't forget to go when you leave." Rashad's casting and performance draw strongly on her iconic portrayal of Claire Huxtable in *The Cosby Show*, a sitcom that emphasized the domesticated nuclear family.

One of the song's producers was bounce artist Adam "BlaqNmilD" Pigott; alongside Shorty's sampled vocals, "In My Feelings" features uncredited vocals from the women of Miami-based rap duo City Girls. Bounce star Big Freedia and the City Girls' Caresha "Yung Miami" Brownlee also cameo in the "In My Feelings" video. (Interestingly, one of Drake's earlier hits is called "Started from the Bottom.")

Although KeKe's home is quite far from the material conditions of public housing, the video for "In My Feelings" draws on all the primary qualities of back of town, depicting a geographic bottom filled with excess, pleasure, and blight. Like Armstrong's back of town, it's also imagined as the location of ambivalent desires. An assembly of black women, sissy figures, and bounce performers populate the video as Drake dreams of romantic, and perhaps domestic, love. But never fear: At the end of the video Drake wakes up and realizes he'd lost himself in a strange dream. "Nobody would stop. It was terrible," he says.

By imagining back of town, the geographic bottom, as full of ratchet characters, Drake unknowingly participates in an enduring narrative that echoes Latrobe's fears of black savagery and reflects the historical merging of vice with black neighborhoods. His video's narrative also, significantly, associates self-loss with these particular spaces and New Orleans as a whole.

Drake's characterization of the "terrible" dream world of New Orleans mirrors the experiences of the black men who attempt to escape the Bottom in *Sula*. Instead of seeing the counterintuitive power, coalition, and pleasure uniquely available to them, they only perceive impediments to modern, masculine individuality.[15] These men's narratives are contrasted against those who find pleasure staying in the Bottom. Morrison seems to caution that black men who try to surpass bottom geographies' economic and geographic limits, or who denounce bottom communities and pleasures in a desire to affirm hegemonic masculinity, often find themselves disillusioned and alone. The consequence of breaking with social bonds found in bottom geographies is the loss of a kind of wealth and power that cannot be easily replaced by monetary or other outside symbolic capital.

The wealth Magnolia Shorty and Vockah found in passing the mic was part of a longer genealogy of black performance. In lifting up the imagined and real relations that exist back of town, their music redirects and repurposes pathologizing narratives to create alternative visions of home and belonging. This iteration of a bottom way of knowing continues similar traditions in blues, jazz, and African diasporic performance in Congo Square. New Orleans's devalued black geographies are in tension with dominant notions of space that define black locales—streets, wards, and projects—as places most travelers should avoid. The commercial and residential sites that have traditionally been the face of the city—Bourbon Street, the French Quarter, Frenchman Street, Saint Charles Avenue—are rarely referred to in the poetics of life back of town. Bounce obscures these sites and instead encourages audiences to reevaluate—and thereby value—ghettoized spaces.

Sissy bounce, and bounce at large, maintains focus on sites and social relationships that are being continuously eroded. Attempts to render racist institutional and cultural practices invisible had, for the most part, been successful in New Orleans—and throughout the nation—until the lack of emergency response to Katrina broke through the dominant narrative of a postracial city and society by clearly displaying the marginality of black populations. Despite this, back of town—an abject space produced and maintained by the effort to sustain sites of "real" value—will always have a future because geographic bottoms exist everywhere and in every time. In another two hundred years, we shouldn't be surprised if someone, somewhere, is waxing poetic about the same collection of meanings, whether as an object of desire or a contradictory home.

CHAPTER FOUR

TOUCHING THE RIM: GENTRIFICATION, POPULAR CULTURE, AND THE COLLECTIVE ASSHOLE

In *Killers of the Dream*, white lesbian and civil rights activist Lillian Smith wrote (of education and the color line in the segregated South), "Not only Negroes but everything dark, dangerous, evil must be pushed to the rim of one's life" ([1949] 1994, 75).

Black sexualities and the black body itself have been ghettoized; conversely, black neighborhoods, streets, and other social formations have been persistently associated with the body's own bottom. Sissy bounce played a cultural role in the creation of a new New Orleans, while inspiring a global interest in the bottom's power. But as sissy bounce ascended toward the mainstream, new audiences used the genre to engage in taboo pleasures while failing to invest in the counterintuitive, coalitional politics of bottom epistemologies.[1] This partial engagement reinforced, rather than redirected or resisted, racial and economic stratification. Playing with black queer culture became, effectively, akin to rimming a personal and collective asshole.

Sissy bounce's "moment" was connected to New Orleans's contemporary urban shifts. As the music and artists began moving from local stages to national and global popularity in the 2010s, the cross-cultural contexts of race and class were on vivid display (though largely neglected in media coverage). Observing what new post-Katrina demographics saw in sissy bounce reveals the limits of a bottom epistemology once again. Bounce's coalitional potential was further undermined when two interrelated bottom objects—in this case, black neighborhoods and twerk dancing—were turned into what black feminist scholar Jennifer Nash refers to as "representational passageways . . . through which viewers are allowed access to racially marked spaces" (2014, 448). These passageways made racially marked spaces more visible—and more materially and economically accessible—through forms of disaster capitalism and neoliberal gentrification.

THE HOT NEW THING

The first time I met the chosen family that was the Cru, I was invited to Fatman's house in the Bywater. I was surprised at the location, wondering how Fatman could afford to live there; in Katrina's aftermath, the downtown neighborhood was quickly earning a reputation as one of the most gentrified areas of the city. High rents had made it impossible for many of the longstanding black residents to return. The only other neighborhood residents I knew were part of a new post-Katrina demographic of mostly white, nonlocal transplants, most of whom had arrived in the city as volunteers.

Before long, I met Fat's roommate Paris, a twenty-six-year-old white woman from Idaho. In time, Paris and I would get to know each other; we would take on similar roles managing and performing with Vockah and the Cru. Over the years, I would come to understand Paris and sissy bounce's growing nonlocal, nonblack audience as a microcosm of larger macropolitical changes.

Paris and Fatman's close friendship had developed out of the precarity following Katrina's impact. They'd met each other and bonded during the turbulent aftermath, shaped by black displacement, an influx of nonlocal volunteers, and a deepening housing crisis.

FIELD NOTES, DECEMBER 10, 2009

Fatman and his boyfriend Reginald live with Fat's friend Paris, who's been in New Orleans for a few years since she came to do relief work. She says Fatman and his family were her neighbors, and he and his family took her in. I'm not clear how long the three have been living together, but they share a two-bedroom shotgun in the Bywater.

I told Paris about my project and my studies in race and sexuality. She became defensive and started explaining why she, a white woman, was close friends and living with gay black men. She said she didn't really like hanging around white people and didn't like white men, for the most part. She said she comes from a culture in which being a heavyset woman is unattractive. She also said she's an assertive person who doesn't fit into passive-aggressive notions of womanhood or whiteness. Paris says she's attracted to black men, and she likes the way black men approach her. She also says she's a bit of a "fag hag."

When I mentioned transplants and how it was interesting how predominantly white audiences were fascinated with and possessive of Big Freedia, she sought to distinguish herself from them, saying she'd rather sit around the house with Fatman and Vockah than run the streets partying with white people, who she said are inauthentic. Over the next few nights, Paris directly asked me if I thought she was like the other transplants who try so hard to be near black queers in town.

Issues like gentrification and cultural appropriation were hotly debated throughout New Orleans at the time; in the context of sissy bounce performances, they were common topics. Paris's self-description—of someone who resisted notions of sex and gender informed by whiteness and patriarchy—was consistent with other narratives I heard from the growing transplant audience. This new demographic was made up of people who came to New Orleans to volunteer in the reconstruction and renewal of the city; many of them decided to stay and live there.

I asked Paris to reflect on her relationships with the Cru:

ALIX: Can you tell me about how you met Fatman and the rest of the Cru?

PARIS: I was living uptown in a part of New Orleans called Pigeon Town, and my neighbors were two young black gay men, Fatman and his boyfriend Reginald. I was just living my life, and every single day I would walk past this house, and these two young, beautiful, energetic men would just be blasting bounce music, dancing their asses off on their porch, just hanging out. They were my neighbors . . . and I was, like, immediately attracted to them. . . .

Things started moving very quickly after the initial introduction. I mean, at one point, Fatman told me he'd never had a white friend—like, straight up just told me that.

He was like, *Okay; I'm going to show you my world.* We would get in my old beat-up Mercedes and drive into the French Quarter. We'd go to Bourbon Street. They would braid my hair. At the time, I was honored and just, like, flabbergasted. He was the most entertaining person I had ever met. Like, I only wanted to hang out with him.

They got kicked out of their house in Pigeon Town. Some out-of-state guy bought the house and everybody had to leave. Fatman didn't want to live with his grandma. And so, at that point, I was like, *Well, let's just move in together.* I found a place in the Bywater, and I got a lease, and they moved in.

ALIX: How did you end up in the Cru?

PARIS: I was familiar with bounce music. I'd lived in New Orleans long enough. This would have been 2008. As I did more uncovering of bounce music in New Orleans, . . . [its] artists and [their] connections to Cash Money. I was, like, researching all of this, and I was really into Lil Wayne, of course. Fatman was just a vault and encyclopedia of knowledge around all these different people. But Vockah was his thing. That was his people because that's who he danced for back in the day.

I remember the specific night that we met. I legitimately fell in love with every single one of them, and in a way that was hard to explain . . . I had never experienced it before. I just fell in love with this totally new, beautiful vibe that I'd never felt before.

When Reginald lost his job, Fatman found it hard to pay for their share of the rent and bills. Eventually Reginald had to move out, and Fatman decided to follow him. "We lived together for like six months, and then it all went down in a blaze of glory. And it was fine," Paris said. "They eventually moved out and I kept the house." If there'd been any drama around their living situation and Fatman's leaving, it all seemed to have come out in the wash. Even so, I noted a marked difference in our access to housing. I never knew Fatman to have a stable place to live for more than a few months. I too, struggled to find affordable housing.

We all began seeing each other more often as we worked together to build up Vockah Redu and the Cru. Paris was an undergraduate while I was a graduate student, and we both used the resources we had to start managing and booking shows. The group started performing regularly, and Paris's place was usually headquarters for planning and practices.

Paris expressed an optimism common in newer residents' discussions about living in New Orleans—a belief that the city and its unique culture offered an escape from US culture at large. A number of scholars have taken up this issue of New Orleans's presumed exceptionalism (Dupont 2004; Keeble 2016; Luft 2009; Adams and Sakakeeny 2019). In her 2019 essay "Neoliberal Futures: Post-Katrina New Orleans, Volunteers, and the Ongoing Allure of Exceptionalism," anthropologist Vincanne Adams describes how exceptionalist narratives surrounding the volunteer response to Katrina supported a neoliberal emphasis on a privatized safety net and an expanded private housing market, while gaps in governmental aid (from entities such as FEMA and the city's Road Home Program) grew. As the city's demographics shifted following Katrina, going out to dance and shake at sissy bounce shows became a pathway to the city's cultural distinctiveness.

As we've seen, black neighborhoods in New Orleans have long served as bottom geographies—viewed as inherently deviant and simultaneously acting as productive repositories for alternative ways of life, including forms of vice—that conflict with dominant notions of civic society, domesticity, and the nuclear family. In addition, black spaces, people, and culture have historically been treated as resources offering a pleasurable escape from dominant notions of whiteness and sexuality; this pattern is particularly pronounced around black musical traditions (which themselves form a foundational origin of rock and roll).[2]

These centuries-old patterns persisted within the context of sissy bounce, but took on new meanings in a post-Katrina New Orleans, where disaster capitalism proliferated (Klein 2017). Paris wasn't alone in her excitement and love of the Cru—her recognition of a larger community of transplants highly invested in sissy bounce (and in particular Big Freedia) reflected the broad buzz and energy of the time. Downtown New Orleans was ground zero for this community; many of them, like Paris, decided to make the area their indefinite home.

The growth of this new demographic paralleled the expansion of new infrastructures—including schools, hospitals, and the tourist industry—aiming to welcome and facilitate access and employment for a growing market base. In 2015, economist Ben Casselman described the postdisaster shifts in the city, drawing from the US Census Bureau's official estimates: "More than 175,000 black residents left New Orleans in the year after the storm; more than 75,000 never came back. Meanwhile, the non-Hispanic white population has nearly returned to its pre-storm total, and the Hispanic population, though still small compared with other Southern cities, has grown by more than 30 percent. Together, the trends have pushed the African-American share of the population down to 59 percent in 2013, from 66 percent in 2005."

Much of the city's post-Katrina reconstruction focused on the return and growth of middle-class white families.[3] What's been less discussed is how a younger demographic of predominantly white artists, queers, students, and volunteers also contributed to neoliberal urban expansion.

Paris described some of the motivations behind her relocation:

ALIX: What led to your move to New Orleans?

PARIS: I'm originally from Idaho—the Rocky Mountains. I grew up, you know, in a rural area—farm culture, cowboy culture, and neo-Nazi culture. I was queer as a youth, identified early as bisexual, and felt very uncomfortable. It was a very conservative red state. And so I left. I left, and I just started hitchhiking around. I went to college. Dropped out of college. Did the whole thing. I came to New Orleans initially to volunteer the October after Katrina. So that would have been October of 2005—and we started gutting houses, and just basically got down here . . . boots-to-the-ground kind of justice. That kind of started my love affair and my initial chapter with New Orleans. And then I just didn't leave again after that. I mean, I just became a resident at that point. I'm a New Orleans transplant.

I'd often heard black youth say that in New Orleans, the *N* and *O* stand for "no opportunity"—though this clearly wasn't the case for everyone. The narrative around New Orleans since Katrina has mostly focused on the mass displacement of locals, but Paris's memories reveal the desires that lead many people to the city; for them, it's a location where exceptional narratives and countercultural norms can be found.

Like Paris, many came to New Orleans to participate in the rebuilding and became familiar with New Orleans's bottom geographies through the representational passageway of sissy bounce. By deploying discourses of color blindness and multiculturalism, this new demographic could enjoy black culture while simultaneously deflecting criticism over their role in the displacement and disorientation of the black community.[4] People came to New Orleans to participate in a range of reconstruction projects; they found that despite its instability as a place affected by disaster, the city also held great possibilities. As sociologist Rachel Luft notes:

> Narratives of the storm, both those that emerged while the catastrophe was unfolding and those that have explored the ongoing aftermath, have frequently pointed to the glaring racial and economic inequality that contextualized the catastrophe. The emphasis has been a critical corrective to the pervasive racist colorblindness that helped produce such devastating consequences. Unfortunately, however, most of the discourse has also been limited by its neglect of substantive feminist, intersectional analysis. By intersectional I mean a gender- and race-conscious framework that exposes the way in which structural sexism and racism came together to produce the disaster and even the social justice response to it. (2016, 2)

Sissy bounce's growing mainstream popularity brought these disparities into stark contrast. Although bounce had been around for years, and producers from outside the area had attempted to work with artists toward mainstreaming it, the genre's crossover to the national and international stage was propelled by the dynamic urban shifts stemming from post-Katrina renewal.[5]

Paris herself felt conflicted about her own ties to this new demographic and her relationship to the Cru:

> *It was this hot new thing for a lot of the punks in the Bywater—a lot of the transplants, a lot of the hipsters that came after Katrina. It was this weird thing. I just felt like I was getting this, like, street cred because I was hanging*

with these black gays, and so that gave me leverage with the punks in this weird way too. It was like, Oh, she's fucking hella cool because she's, like, rolling with them. It was really uncomfortable. It's uncomfortable talking about it right now and being transparent about it.

It was like I got this street cred because I was a white girl hanging with them. With all the Bywater kids it was like, How does she know them [when she's] totally fucking white? . . . and Oh, well, I want to know her, because then I can know them. And so then I was thrust into this delicate gatekeeping situation, right, with other white people. . . . It was gross. The thing I had in my friendship with Fatman—it was really wholesome. We were neighbors, and it became this other thing that then came. The Bywater at that time . . . there were a lot of really delicate things happening at that point, racially. Now that I can look back at it and be like, Oh, that was problematic; I don't know how I feel about that—that makes me uncomfortable.

The hipster and punk, as Paris names them, are classed and racialized subjects that have a long history with and relationship to blackness. In his 2005 essay "Punk'd Theory," Tavia Nyong'o critiques the writings of Norman Mailer in "The White Negro: Superficial Reflections on the Hipster" ([1957] 1998). Nyong'o argues that Mailer's notion of the beatnik or white hipster approximates that of the queer and punk (and, I'll add, the sissy). In Mailer's homophobic perspective, the hipster or beatnik is vulnerable to becoming queer through a "situation beyond one's experience, impossible to anticipate" (225)—namely sodomy. This "impossible to anticipate" situation is the product not only of Mailer's homophobia, but also his racial anxieties about white people who reject dominant norms and *touch the rim* of "inferior" cultures—thereby becoming vulnerable to the degraded economic, sexual, and gendered bottom status both queers and blacks people are thought to occupy.

The various forms of cross-pollination between people moving in and out of the city helped start a buzz about sissy bounce that spread throughout the nation. Black queers had already been performing bounce for a decade, but the demographic makeup of the audience had changed. At shows featuring Big Freedia or other popular sissy bounce acts, you were now more likely to see white audiences. In 2010 Katey Red, the foremost trans woman in bounce, described the attendees of shows outside New Orleans as "pretty integrated" and as "mostly girls, mostly a bunch of nasty hos with they shorts up they ass, trying to shake like a dog" (Dee 2010). Sissy bounce became a gateway where ideas around violence, safety, and sex intersected discussions about where you lived and who you lived with and around.

In reporting that often employed color-blind framings, national news began representing sissy bounce as a sexually provocative yet safe form of hip-hop. The promotion of sissy bounce glossed over the demographic growth of whiteness in New Orleans, instead focusing on rhetoric around sexual expression. Few reports addressed the racial makeup of the audience, because doing so would have meant engaging debates about cultural appropriation in the context of racial and classed gentrification.

In a 2010 *New York Times Magazine* piece titled "New Orleans's Gender-Bending Rap," journalist Alison Fensterstock told the article's author, "There's like a safe-space thing happening. . . . When Freedia or Nobby's singing superaggressive, sexual lyrics about bad boyfriends or whatever, there's something about being able to be the 'I' in the sentence. That's not to say that women can't like the more misogynistic music too. I like it—some of it's good music. But it's tough to sing along about bitches and hos when you're a girl. When you identify with Freedia, you're the agent of all this aggressive sexuality instead of its object" (Dee 2010).

For many new fans, black queer culture seemed to offer the possibility of undermining oppressive notions of femininity and finding a pathway toward sexual liberation. When Fensterstock, not quite realizing her own power and authority in defining local culture, began using the label "sissy bounce" in her editorials, no one knew the term would overdetermine the larger genre of bounce.[6] Her above quote also fails to acknowledge that experiencing gendered or sexualized objectification in one context does not preclude possessing agency, even aggressively so, in another. While some audience members were experiencing sexual liberation, others (including the performers) were experiencing the inherent violence of disaster capitalism and gentrification.

There is a common history of black sexuality, black cultural forms, and black neighborhoods being objectified and used in unison toward the subjective and social formation of whiteness. Sissy bounce, and cultural aspects of the genre like twerking, could thereby easily be used as tools for helping nonblack personhood find its "I." Sissy figures (in particular Big Freedia), bounce, and cultural expressions like twerking—all persistently associated with bottom locations such as black neighborhoods—were treated as passageways toward "aggressive" yet "safe" notions and practices of sexuality and space-making.[7] This space-making extended beyond New Orleans's dance floors and contributed to the racial and economic gentrification of its communities.[8] Crucially, the feelings, opinions, well-being, or potential transformation of black queer people and the larger black community weren't topics of concern.

As Big Freedia gained popular appeal, a major subtext in media representations of sissy bounce was that the genre was inherently sexual but also a positive, safe, moral way for progressive audiences to engage in hip-hop music and dance. Twerking, shaking, and the overall focus on bottom pleasures harked back to 1990s hip-hop artists like Uncle Luke's 2 Live Crew, as well as songs like Sir Mix-a-Lot's "Baby Got Back" and Juvenile's "Back That Thang Up" (the latter released on Cash Money Records). But sissy bounce was considered an ethically sound alternative, one that could sidestep earlier works' and artists' issues of misogyny and homophobia. A 2011 show review in the *Washington Post* summed up the sentiment:

> With party chants equally obscene as Uncle Luke's best work, drum machine beats at the same tempos and a deification of the derriere in perpetual motion, Freedia worked the crowd into a frenzy for an hour. She conducted a form of carnal square-dancing, with call-and-response refrains, New Orleans neighborhood shoutouts and instructions for increasingly more athletic variations of the basic booty shake.
>
> But unlike Luke and rap at large, it's trickier to apply concerns about misogyny since in Freedia's case, a self-proclaimed "sissy" is exhorting crowds of mostly women to gyrate in adoration of her and for one another. And the explicit sexual lyrics are flipped in context when the rapper is openly gay. So everyone bounced with a clean conscience. . . . A magnanimous master of ceremonies, Freedia eventually drafted most of the audience into her stable of dancers. (Anderson 2011)

Sissy bounce didn't introduce ass-shaking to the world, but it made it appropriate for crossover appeal. Through the black queer figure of the sissy, audiences could more comfortably view, access, and perform bottom pleasures.

Blackness is associated with cultural objects that overrun the imagined boundaries of whiteness and womanhood. The increasing national conversation about bounce performances provoked concerns about how and why white people could access black cultural forms while still feeling clean and safe. Outsiders' perceptions of safe space within sissy bounce rested on certain presumptions: that misogyny was no longer a worry because heterosexual black men weren't present; and that there was no need to be concerned about violence or abuse among women or queer people.

Sidestepping concerns about misogyny, homophobia, and sexual violence practiced by women and queer people themselves, new sissy bounce audiences could express lingering fascination with (and anxiety about) whiteness meeting the bottom. The cleanliness, morality, or safety of black women or black queer people could remain vague because promoters and media sources sought to make sissy bounce a commodity for nonblack consumers. Sissies hadn't become the focal point of bounce because a radical coalition had formed in the wake of Katrina's disaster and trauma; they were instead a pleasurable means to bottom ends.

TWERK LESSONS

In my time with Vockah and the Cru, I learned that twerking was never a queer thing, or a woman thing, or specifically about sex. Like bounce itself, it was just part of being black and local. People twerked at children's birthday parties, weddings, and sweet sixteens as expressions of community and belonging. Black men across the spectrum were not afraid to twerk, as can be seen in DJ Jubilee's 1990s videos for "Stop Pause (Jubilee All)" and "Back That Azz Up" (Take It to the St. Thomas), the precursor to Juvenile's "Back That Azz Up."[9] Vockah and other local artists were aware of this past, but despite this, twerk was increasingly defined by people from outside the community as an inherently feminine, sexual performance. As twerk gained more and more popular appeal and circulated through social media, tensions between different performers and audiences led to more than a few claims of co-optation.

In 2009, Big Freedia began performing with backup dancers who were popular among the new demographic of nonlocals. One white backup dancer in particular went by the name Altercation. Whether intentional or not, regularly positioning white performers at the forefront of sissy bounce shows reflected and further influenced the makeup of the audience. Like Paris, Altercation embodied many of the racialized, gendered tensions circulating around sissy bounce. In Big Freedia's 2011 video for the song "Excuse," the dancer can be seen participating in the staged twerk class led by Freedia.

Ironically, in real life, Altercation would begin teaching twerk classes, giving interviews, and participating in lectures about sissy bounce. Presenting twerking as being "about bringing sex back to a positive place" in response to rampant sexual violence toward women, the dancer sometimes framed the form as a means for gendered (but racially neutral) subjects to access freedom—a way for women to cultivate body and sex positivity while removing their "American, puritanical chastity belt[s]" (Welch 2011). Once again, a passageway was created by engaging in bottom pleasures, where exceptions to the moral and perhaps religious strictures of American culture were thought to be found. For many new fans and participants, there was an optimism and joy in playing with the taboo bottom of black cultural expressions like twerking—but that optimism glossed over structural violences toward black neighborhoods, people, and communities, rather than redirecting taboo bottom associations toward coalition and caregiving.

Altercation implied that, instead of being a form of cultural appropriation, dancing and performing sissy bounce constituted a kind of cultural reciprocity—where "instead of just taking from this New Orleans bounce culture, you give something back to it" (Welch 2011). The dancer added that one such way of giving back was simply to dance "when Freedia tells you to." This definition suggested a political neutrality in which black culture, space, and bodies could freely be consumed in exchange for acts of performative allyship. No doubt, white performers monetizing teaching and sharing black cultural forms was a powerful role to play, but how it led to solidarity with (and resources for) black communities was unclear. Cultural reciprocity usually means there's mutual benefit between groups, and that groups who've experienced oppression benefit especially.

The Cru was frustrated with the authority claimed by someone outside the culture to address and define the significance of twerking and explain what giving back to the black community looked like. This kind of paternalism, in which outsiders to the culture spoke for a community already dealing with political silencing, had become more and more common. Fatman became particularly heated when he heard that Altercation was charging people to teach twerk classes. "I've been doing this my whole life and they're getting paid to do it?" he exclaimed. "What are they even teaching? There's no choreography!" The group began deliberately misnaming the dancer, calling them Appropriation.

It wasn't clear if Big Freedia's lineup had disgruntled others. But in 2013, after years of seeing Altercation at the forefront of Big Freedia's dance team, Freedia had her first nationally televised performance on *Jimmy Kimmel Live!*—and Altercation was positioned in the shadows, almost unrecognizable. Before long, Big Freedia began centering local and black dancers.

Despite Fatman and other Cru members' feelings regarding Altercation and other nonblack performers and promoters willing to take up the spotlight, there may have been some hypocrisy considering the makeup of the Cru. In the winter of 2010, we had our first tour in New York, and both Paris and I played important roles in the planning and performances.

FIELD NOTES, JANUARY 28, 2010

Paris and I met to continue the meeting from the night before on our own. For most of the meeting we stuck to the agenda—organizing merch, bookings, et cetera. She said that she wanted to talk to me about the tensions between the two of us and what she was feeling. She said that she had a close relationship with the others and that she felt like she couldn't be herself around me. She said she always felt as if she might do something wrong in my presence. Then she went on to say that as far as helping with the group, I don't do enough or that I'm not there for the Cru the way she is.

I told her that I don't like a lot of the aspects of her relationship with Vockah and Fatman and that I prefer to keep my boundaries. I repeated what I had already told the whole group—that I would never be their "Platinum Pussy" (one of their nicknames in the group for Paris). In the back of my mind, I thought they might as well say Platinum Mastercard because every time there's money needed, she volunteers to pay for things, despite claiming to be a struggling student. I told her that she needs to stop buying things and offering her time selflessly when she doesn't realize what she wants in return and then getting mad. I also said that part of it is a gendered dynamic in which [the Cru] are probably used to having women take care of them even though they're not straight.

I told her that I thought her anxieties over my presence were because I didn't need her. I wasn't dependent on her for money, transportation, or housing, and I wasn't looking to be saved. She responded that she and Fatman work together mutually toward their rent and utilities and that he always pays her back for everything. From what I can see, money is always precarious for Fatman, as it is for most of us, and Vockah said he doesn't believe this [i.e., that Fatman always pays her back]. She argued for her individuality and personal ability to transcend race and class dynamics. I told her these differences were present whether or not she wanted to acknowledge them.

I had to consider my own positionality in relationship to Paris, the Cru, and the larger community. Paris wasn't alone in her feelings toward me. Around Vockah and the rest of the Cru, I resisted talking about anything political, and there was a general sense that my concern with social justice and activism was just no fun. There were obvious tensions between me and other managers, promoters, and bookers. In this crowd, I found it okay to talk about the power dynamics of sex and gender, or even race and class, as long as it was about the past—as opposed to any contemporary conditions that might implicate us. But it was hard to keep my mouth shut when it came to the ins and outs of daily life, especially when it came to our shows. I had constant disagreements with various gatekeepers—in particular, Big Freedia's manager, a straight white man who, on more than one occasion, used his relationship to individual performers to dictate the meaning of black queer culture (even to me, an actual black queer person). I often encountered people who assumed that despite the number of existing racial, classed, and gendered hierarchies, and the conditions of gentrification, they could be morally neutral participants within the culture, able to transcend difference.

The difficulties of pulling off our first tour in New York would bring these issues out onstage. Everyone was given a role to play during performances. Fatman and a dancer named Dauphine Jody sang backup; they were the best twerkers in the group. Vockah was on the mic; he did some of everything, including leading the choreographed dances. Paris was most often offstage, managing and being a point person between the venue and the group.

I'd struggled with learning all the routines—especially twerking. I had what they called a "pretty boy shake," meaning I was too conservative, maybe even insufficient. I was fine with that, considering the effort and physical exertion I witnessed the rest of the group endure. Most often, I acted as a DJ, a comfortable role that allowed me to observe the stage and audience. I took on the job of cueing up music and acted as an audiovisual tech by default. There was still a learning curve, and I definitely was not invited back to one venue after blowing out their speakers.

Our first show was at a gallery exhibit on bounce on the Lower East Side.[10] There was a stark contrast between performing in a bright museum atrium and in smoky bars. Vockah started doing a few songs, and the Cru danced in the middle of a crowd that formed a circle around the group. I was outside the circle at the DJ booth with a view of the setting. Before the trip Fatman had started teaching Paris how to titty bop, a dance that was like twerking from the front—all the better if you had breasts to shake. When I cued up the right song, Paris went next to Vockah and did her dance. She'd even designed a shirt with a sparkly titty bop label to catch people's eyes.

Toward the end of the show, Vockah began introducing the dancers and thanking the organizers of the event. When he said, "And next we have Paris, our Platinum Pussy!" He hit the Ps with a bit of demand in his voice. Paris walked up beside Vockah, head high, ready for her moment. From where I stood, I could see that the whole crowd gasped at the name, looked to whom he was speaking, then let out a second gasp. Neither Vockah nor Paris noticed the crowd's shock. Later, when I told them what I'd seen, they both were somewhat pleased that they'd "pushed some buttons." In an interview I did with Paris later, she had this to say about the tour to New York:

> *It was done with so much, like, loving intent. I mean, looking back now I'm just like, Oh my god, that was ridiculous. But at the time, I was like—I kind of, you know, went for it. I was like, Okay, I'm going to be this character when we go onstage. When we travel or whatever, I'm just going to do it.*
>
> *That trip we took to New York . . . [and] other times that we would be like . . . going into a mall to get fucking clothes . . . and multiple times at restaurants and things like that . . . because of the fact that they were gay black men, they were so used to it, they were so used to the abuse, so used to the mistreatment, and so used to being fucked with. . . .*
>
> *Watching the mistreatment that [Fatman] endured on the daily, I mean, I literally felt like—and this is, again, this is really problematic. But at that time, I felt like I had to, like, protect him, and, like, help him. You know, like, I was like this white savior fucking person. And it's not good, and that's never going to end well. But at the time, it worked. It just worked.*

Between what happened onstage and in our daily lives, it could be difficult to tell where power lay. Even if members of the Cru had a problem with racial dynamics and paternalism occurring in Big Freedia's camp because of performers like Altercation, there was plenty of tension among ourselves. Paris's comment about the problem of becoming a white savior poses larger questions. Are all forms of caregiving equal? If individual acts of care aren't understood within a larger context of systemic white supremacy and capitalism, for example, the risk and vulnerability Paris recognizes among the Cru might only appear as similarly individually determined incidents, rather than systemic parts of a larger power structure. Relearning and rethinking care is critical to a bottom epistemology.

Most of the artists I performed with had fluid sexualities and gender expressions, making it difficult to conform to dominant LGBTQIA+ identities. Vockah, for example, had been in relationships with women, had a child, and shifted in his gender presentation throughout his life. Audience members constantly misgendered him, and he repeatedly said he identified as a man. Big Freedia was assumed to be a trans woman even though she identified as a gay man, used he/him as well as she/her pronouns, and explained that he preferred wearing women's accessories and wigs. Katey Red transitioned throughout this time and eventually began identifying as a woman. Although we had our differences, falling within the sissy label and performing dances like twerk led to a homogenizing of our individual identities and self-expressions. This was part of the reason many performers hated the label sissy bounce, a term more reflective of the emerging audience's perceptions than what was really simply bounce music.

Given our gendered indecipherability, many people decided that even if we weren't all gender-nonconforming, it was easier to think of us as an undifferentiated mass of sissies. Sissy bounce's commercial power also made resisting this homogenization difficult, because denying the assumptions could result in accusations of self-denial or craziness—or an artist could be deemed too aggressive or unprofessional to get bookings or preferred rates for shows. This all came to a head when the group felt pressure to please audiences, ensure payment, and further their careers. When performers chose to contest their treatment or insist that some things were not for public scrutiny, audiences and critics assumed they were embodying "down-low" stereotypes rather than attempting to maintain some autonomy or agency.

During interviews and conversations, inquiries about how to twerk would devolve into invasive questions about our sexual practices, gender status, and other things unseen—an interest Fatman pushed back against and questioned. There was almost always an assumption that if you could twerk (and twerk well), it was an indicator of your inner freak, and a marker of excess and deviance.

Vockah Redu and Cru were all for cultivating sex and body positivity, and audiences flocked to the music in large part because of its explicit resistance to and denouncement of male abuse. But we didn't always feel safe or comfortable at our own shows. Twerking was often mistaken for an invitation for audience members to cross boundaries, or to assume we had no boundaries at all. People would ask what our genitalia was like, suggest performers' bodies were modified, or equate twerking with a desire for sexual submission, which often led to dancers being grabbed without consent. Even while performing, we often needed to argue that our actions, words, or attire weren't an invitation. Paris and I would sometimes position ourselves between the stage and the crowd so the rest of the Cru could complete a choreographed routine without being grabbed and pulled on. Paris was tall and strong; I once watched her pick up another woman and threaten her if she overstepped one more time. Almost every night, someone would try to hump one of us onstage.

The idea that Vockah, Fatman, and other artists could make well-informed decisions for themselves and further their own careers was ironic, given the many obstacles around them. I often joked that anybody with a laptop could do my job, but even this simple role was complicated by race and class. The straight white guy who previously DJed for the Cru had used his ownership of a laptop, his other equipment, and his relationships with club owners to bargain for large percentages of the night's earnings—sometimes 50 percent—leaving the remainder to be divided among the numerous performers.

The Cru's past experience with exploitative people factored into their insistence on Paris or me taking on additional tasks—communicating their needs, making sure they got paid what they were supposed to, contacting clubs and venues about possible shows. I couldn't believe the paternalism many gatekeepers displayed. They made decisions about which news sources or journalists could interview artists, ensured they got their own sound bites into those interviews, and demanded production credits on recordings. When I questioned one promoter who booked a show and shortchanged the group, he said he would increase their pay once they proved their professionalism. Vockah and Fatman had been performing locally for over a decade, but transplants involved in the scene for only a year or two were dictating whether they could handle it. There was a clear assumption that black performers were more bodies than brains. At times, my multiple roles became confusing and contradictory. I was trying to help while simultaneously doing field research—all while attempting to avoid replicating paternalism, or acting as a savior and thereby treating the Cru as a vehicle for personal insight or access.

Paris and I worked on fundraising for our New York tour by creating an artist profile and informational packet to circulate by email. Aware of the problematic ways sissy bounce was being marketed, as well as the Cru's resistance to the label itself, I asked the group if I could request donations from queer organizations in New York and describe the group as made up of black queer people (using whatever language or terms we chose). Vockah immediately said no. This wasn't about the group's sexual identity, he explained; we were representing bounce and New Orleans. I understood his feelings, considering past experience, and conceded, saying the videos and images we shared would speak for themselves. In response, Vockah yelled, "We don't look like sissies!" After our second tour to New York, as I wrapped up my fieldwork and began letting people know I'd be leaving New Orleans to finish graduate school, Big Freedia's manager asked me, with all sincerity, "I wonder what will happen—how will they make it without us?"

As sissy bounce began shifting from local performances to national and global exposure on television and social media, its foundational conditions of race, class, space, and community were abstracted and obscured. Sissy bounce's movement into broader popular culture via the larger music industry also offered audiences an increasingly globalized passageway to bottom locations, with elements of the genre becoming increasingly dissociated from black queer performers and New Orleans.

WHO'S THE QUEEN?

Pop star Miley Cyrus's 2013 MTV Video Music Awards performance will go down, at least in mainstream memory, as the birth of twerk and the beginning of a decade of ass-centric popular culture. Cyrus enters the stage, performs her song "We Can't Stop," then transitions to join singer Robin Thicke for his song "Blurred Lines," eventually bending over and shaking in front of him.

How and why did Cyrus's dancing on Thicke and slapping a black woman's bottom on prime-time TV while singing "To my homegirls here with the big butts / Shaking it like we at a strip club" become primary examples of sex positivity—and the most recent version of an old sentiment, "Free your mind and your ass will follow"? Cyrus delivered her lyrics while attempting to twerk to the beat; the moment caught the eye of the nation, and quickly spread worldwide. When questioned about her performance, she proudly claimed she'd received more tweets than the Super Bowl, 306,000 per minute. Although she didn't perform to a bounce song, feature Big Freedia, or make any reference to New Orleans, viewers aware of the larger cultural context could see that Cyrus was in part riding the coattails of bounce artists (Fensterstock 2013).

It's likely Cyrus had direct contact with bounce music in late 2010, while filming a movie in New Orleans, and was aware of the genre's growing popularity. By 2013, desperate to break from her childhood Disney character, Hannah Montana, and disconnect from a career closely tied to her father, country musician Billy Ray Cyrus, the artist saw just what she needed in hip-hop; she would go on to produce music with rappers like Juicy J and Wiz Khalifa.

Cyrus wasn't the only pop star to clue in to sissy bounce and its embrace of the backside. Though straight bounce artists from New Orleans were finding it difficult to cross into the national spotlight taken up by their queer and trans counterparts, internationally recognized hip-hop artists were beginning to integrate elements of the culture into music that attracted huge audiences to twerk. Like Cyrus, they also turned sissy bounce into a passageway to their own empowerment.

At the time, Big Freedia, Katey Red, and Vockah Redu and the Cru were performing around the country, internationally, and in major music festivals like sxsw. As twerking workshops that resembled Freedia's Jazzercize-themed "Excuse" video popped up, I began hearing elements of bounce's repetitive hooks and visual representation in mainstream hits. In the video for Big Sean's 2011 "Dance (A$$) Remix," fellow rapper Nicki Minaj twerked to the beat while rhyming:

> I don't know, man, guess them ass shots were off!
> Bitches ain't poppin', Google my ass
> Only time you on the net is when you Google my ass

The energy and repetitiveness of the song gestured almost directly to Big Freedia's track "Azz Everywhere," released the year before. Nicki Minaj twerks for Big Sean and the camera as she raps about ass shots (or what some call pumping, in which silicone injections and other products are used to augment the glutes and thighs—also a means of accentuating twerking). Her lyrics point to the parallel and intersecting growth of the internet and social media along with the expanding preoccupation with ass (embodied in black cultural expressions like twerk) throughout the 2010s—when twerking made its way into mainstream conversation, alongside expressions derived from our collective experience of tech (LOL, LMFAO, selfie).

While popular musicians took advantage of sissy bounce and twerk's resonance as a safe, sex-positive form of hip-hop, Big Freedia and others continued to assert their centrality and influence. In a 2013 rebuttal to the media attention given to pop stars (and in preparation for Freedia's reality television show debut), the Fuse Network—a channel specializing in music programming, reality television, and lifestyle series—organized a *Guinness World Records* "twerk-off" in New York City's Herald Square. Three hundred fifty-eight dancers, ranging from eight to eighty years old, "ass-embled." Big Freedia explained that winning the record "would open a lot of doors and set history for bounce music and let the world know that we've been twerking for a long time," adding, "This is not new at all" (Fuse TV 2013). But despite Freedia's attempts to control the narrative and establish her own story, the spotlight would gradually shift away from her and sissy bounce in favor of more heterosexual and gender-normative representations.

Big Freedia doesn't appear in Beyoncé's 2015 video for the song "Formation," but the track includes a sample of Freedia's voice—and through that sound, another passageway was created.[11] Freedia booms, "I did not come to play with you hoes! / I came to slay, bitch! / I like cornbreads and collard greens, bitch! / Oh yes, you besta believe it!" The sample plays over two images that are particularly interesting in relation to notions of racial authenticity, and ideas about the black queer as passageway. First, we see the iconic image of a hatted Beyoncé standing in front of a plantation-esque doorway, framed by black men dressed like formal attendants. Second, we see the interior of a beauty supply store; rows of wigs frame three young black women, one stroking a wig on a mannequin head. This collection of sounds and images isn't arbitrary—it gestures toward a historical narrative that requires a broader viewpoint and careful listening.

As a black artist, Beyoncé employed sissy bounce—and Big Freedia in particular—in ways that differed from the cross-racial approaches of nonblack artists and audiences. "Formation" highlighted the lyrical pronouncements of a racial identity that was not simply Southern but rooted in a discourse of exceptionalism and authenticity. By featuring Freedia, Beyoncé situated herself alongside—while literally rendering invisible—a New Orleans figure whose popularity rode on their own realness. Given Freedia's nonnormative sexual and gender expressions, it's worth asking why Beyoncé didn't sample more recognizable or straight New Orleans artists, like Juvenile (or, given her feminist message, Mia X). Why were black queer figures the interlocutors through which Beyoncé presented her own sense of blackness?

As Big Freedia's voice is heard, the camera pans through the aisle of the beauty supply store—a marketplace where blackness isn't defined by static notions of gender but fashioned out of fluid, everyday cultural practice. In this site of possibility, black women and gender-nonconforming black people can imagine and resist essentialist notions of race and gender. Who is authentically black or femme, and who gets to decide? The focus on wigs and bundles of weave brings to light debates about who is and is not an authentic woman or femme—an especially relevant question when it comes to Freedia, a femme black gay man who enjoys wearing these accessories. The setting also nods toward accusations about how working-class people spend their money, and beliefs about the need to discipline their supposed excesses and wastefulness. True to form, the need to regulate ever-present criminal black bodies is signaled by a sign that hangs on the wall and reads, "WARNING—SHOPLIFTERS will be PROSECUTED." This assemblage of sounds and images implies that Beyoncé, like Freedia, will not be regulated. This allows Beyoncé to push back against notions of authenticity as a fixed essence that belongs to certain people, even local New Orleanians.

But there is some contradiction here. By framing herself with images of alienated blackness, does Beyoncé suggest her plight and Freedia's are the same in order to critique capitalism and heteronormativity? Or does sampling Big Freedia over the image of beauty supplies simply refer to the marketplace in which Beyoncé (despite her blackness and femmeness) comes not to play but to slay, as a liberal capitalist? If the latter is true, the narrative of racial freedom and desire in "Formation" is misleading in its usage of queerness, images of New Orleans, and the sound of Big Freedia as a representative of the working class.

Black capitalists reproduce enduring power structures when they annex working-class struggles toward agendas that don't benefit those at the bottom of political and economic hierarchies. This isn't unique in the history of New Orleans's black politics; according to political scientist and New Orleans native Adolph L. Reed Jr.:

> There is the ubiquitous discourse of racial/cultural authenticity that has become a key trope in local black politics.... Thus appeals to the rich African / Creole / African American heritage, neighborhoods, and practices as vital contributions to New Orleans's distinctive culture have long since become pro forma in debates over who gets what, when, and how.... In all those expressions, claims to the authentic constitute elements of a moral economy that hinges on a presumption that authenticity confers a sort of political standing, that on examination is generally familiar but incompatible with, if not antithetical to, a left-egalitarian politics. (2019, 308–9)

On second glance, the discursive realm in which Beyoncé frames her Negro-Creole-bama performance extends far beyond what we hear and see. If the video attempts a well-intentioned political solidarity that misses the mark in terms of local politics, if not or maybe the national context of race relations, it's not alone. Black elites' commodification of the plight of the black working class has often co-opted forms of culture in service of community development, in ways that have further exploited the most marginalized (French-Marcelin 2019). Claims of racial authenticity have often led those in power to advance their own integration into the political process while using white supremacy as the focus of reform—but also failing to acknowledge their complicity with capitalist logics that remain on the plantation. Effective racial solidarity is undermined by the competitive individualism capitalist development demands. In a bootstrap ideology, the performance of black culture is critical to individual notions of belonging—as opposed to the communal redistributive promises of post–civil rights era reconstruction. These shifts in culture and symbolism affect people's lived experiences and material conditions—as Big Freedia's future struggles demonstrate.

REPRESENTATION AND ITS MATERIAL CONSEQUENCES

By 2013, Big Freedia and sissy bounce were reaching audiences throughout and beyond the United States, thanks to increased television coverage. In 2010, Freedia landed her first national prime-time broadcast on an episode of *Last Call with Carson Daly*. In 2011, Freedia and Katey

Red both appeared on episodes of HBO's post-Katrina New Orleans dramatic series *Treme*, which was integrating bounce music into its second season.

It was becoming clear that bounce and black queer performance were not subcultures, but everyday parts of the city's rich cultural heritage and post-Katrina revival. The TV appearances added context to the years of editorials focusing on the genre. In all these depictions, including *Treme*, sissy figures were treated as bounce's primary representatives. In 2013, the reality TV series *Big Freedia: Queen of Bounce* began airing on the Fuse network; for many viewers, a show depicting a black gay gender-nonconforming person at the center of familial, communal, and loving relationships was a first.

Despite what Big Freedia and other bounce artists had accomplished, twerk's global popularity was (and is) generally attributed to Miley Cyrus. In many ways, this mirrors the association of vogueing with Madonna and her 1990 hit, rather than the black, brown, and queer ballroom scene from which the dance emerged. It's ironic that after Big Freedia spent years extolling the pleasures of bounce and twerk as a multicultural safe space, a white woman with no relationship to twerk's origins was ultimately recognized for this cultural expression.

Responding to Cyrus's MTV performance, Big Freedia said:

> They're just using anybody possible just to get that buzz since twerking is hot now. I'm still trying to wrap my head around this, though. I knew the twerking thing was really taking off, but I didn't know it would blow up like this. . . . I expected it would happen, but by me working so hard. I didn't think it would happen that way. That's why I'm working so hard—for it to happen on my end, not on the end of someone who's not even familiar with the culture. That's what's so offensive, when you've been doing it for so many years and then someone who just jumped off the porch tries to do it. (*Kpopstarz* 2013)

Others went further than simply pointing out appropriation: "Cyrus's twerk act gives minstrelsy a postmodern careerist spin," music critic Jody Rosen wrote (Demby 2013).

Of course, there was nothing new about this. Annexing blackness to signify white sexual excess is a long-standing means of identity formation that performers like Elvis Presley, Buddy Holly, and Madonna all benefited from. Arguably, it's challenging for any pop star to reach such heights without riding the coattails of black music and performance—or, alternatively, drawing sharp distinctions between themselves and blackness. Historically, the trauma of living through white heteronormativity's notions of personal and societal development sometimes leads people to blackness as a counteragent to hegemonic notions of personal and communal progress. Treating black sexualities as passages to bottom locations offers access to a playground of anal associations that include waste, excess, sin, and dirtiness.

In 2015, Big Freedia faced legal and financial setbacks after being found guilty of taking money from the US Department of Housing and Urban Development over a period of four years, when her income exceeded eligibility for subsidy. Welfare queen tropes emerged; after being found guilty, Freedia was made to pay $35,000 in restitution and serve three years of probation.[12] This incident affected Freedia's brand such that the title of her reality show, *Big Freedia: Queen of Bounce* was changed to *Big Freedia Bounces Back*.

Deflecting accusations that she was taking advantage of the welfare system, Freedia stated, "Housing vouchers are a vital lifeline for many people I know in New Orleans and around the country, including struggling artists. I truly believe there needs to be more programs for artists and musicians to teach basic financial literacy and planning. Coming from where I came from, I know that I could have used that kind of assistance. I'm exploring ways to be a part of the solution in this area and am looking forward to putting this matter behind me" (Mock 2016).

Fans took the violation seriously but also noted that in a city with deep housing insecurity—made worse by post-Katrina gentrification—precarity often affected black artists and musicians most of all. Big Freedia had managed to maintain a successful career while negotiating the ways deviance is attached to being black, queer, and from the hood. Criminalizing infractions like hers only added to the problems of housing insecurity and mass incarceration. In addition to these concerns, I felt that an opportunity was missed to push the discussion of welfare fraud into the realm of reparations for black communities victimized by state violence—through government redlining, neglect by design, and criminalization for profit.

In the decade following Katrina, the Bywater, where I first met Paris, would develop a housing crisis that paralleled the tourism industry's return (Gladstone and Préau 2008). Local resident and anthropologist Matt Sakakeeny reported:

> I now live in the epicenter of neighborhood change, in a mixed-use neighborhood called the Bywater that sits about a mile upriver from the French Quarter. Prior to Katrina, the Bywater was one of the city's most mixed neighborhoods in terms of race and class, but the black population decreased 64% between 2000 and 2010 and home prices have risen over 75% since the flood. Not coincidentally, the Bywater and adjoining Marigny and St. Roch neighborhoods are where the largest concentration of new transplants have settled, driving up rental prices at even higher rates than the rest of the city. (2015)

In many ways, the Bywater has proved to be the canary in the coal mine, illustrating the pitfalls and intersections of redevelopment and cultural tourism.

In post-Katrina New Orleans as well as far beyond the city, new audience demographics constructed sissy bounce as a "safe space" and passageway toward freedom—a place that allowed them to temporarily and literally shake off the disciplinary strictures of whiteness, heteropatriarchy, and capitalist individualism. Locally, this related to shifts stemming from post-Katrina reconstruction; nationally, the shifts were linked to an age of chronic economic and political precarity. Not unlike the role minstrelsy played in affirming racial divides during post–Civil War Reconstruction and throughout the Jim Crow era, sissy bounce insulated nonblack, heterosexual, and economically secure audiences from the tensions of post-Katrina racial and class relations. As a product of public housing projects and imagined ghettos, the genre provided a passage to black culture, through which the pressures of meritocracy and liberal individualism could be, for some, collectively relieved. Twerking and proximity to blackness also became synonymous with breaking taboos about sin and miscegenation; they offered hope in the wake of personal and communal social change.

Again, however, enjoying the "deviant" pleasures of bottom performances and cultural objects without focusing on coalition and caregiving reinforced rather than redirected racial and class stratifications and hierarchies. A lack of intersectionality and awareness extended from dance floors and into surrounding neighborhoods and broader urban geographies—reinforcing neoliberal economic trends like the displacement of low-income black communities, the growth of individualist notions of care, and the erasure of public resources.

These impediments to raising the bottom occurred through notions of class as well—notably, when black elites appropriated working-class plight and increasingly alienated notions of blackness. Beyoncé, Drake, and other black artists utilized visual representations of New Orleans while sampling elements of sissy bounce (Big Freedia in particular) to try to establish their own authenticity and signal resonance with the plight of the black and Southern working class. Did these representational dialogues constitute meaningful union and contribute to collective transformation?

The nonblack and heterosexual bodies that participated in these cultural expressions did not suffer the same material consequences that their black queer counterparts did. Although audiences could enjoy temporarily playing in and with the bottom, artists like Big Freedia often found that the taboo desires that led fans to momentarily enjoy *touching the rim* of black queer life affected performers in more inescapable ways. In New Orleans, forms of precarity I saw predominantly white audiences experience in their attempts to touch that rim were in stark contrast to the sustained, ongoing crisis that lay beyond that edge. All the while, social media and popular culture were widening the gap, making for a more distant gaze.

CHAPTER FIVE

RAISING THE BOTTOM
CHURCH GIRLS
AND SECULAR MUSIC

> The worshipful act—be it prayer or preaching, welcome or song—seems to mirror the whole in which it is embedded. Both act and service follow the same trajectory. Turn up the fire; let it sizzle; then turn it down. But never turn it down all the way. Never fully return to the last point of rest. Instead, keep raising the bottom, ever boosting the ambient energy, ever bringing the sustaining lows closer to the fiery peaks.
>
> **GLENN HINSON** | *Fire in My Bones*

In the spring of 2011, Vockah invited me to a "family and friends" gathering at an Uptown Baptist church where he'd grown up singing in the choir. It was the first time many congregation members had seen each other since Katrina. The service was full of testimonies. Congregants detailed hardships, described joyful reunions, and memorialized those who'd been lost. Big Freedia was also a member; he'd once served as a musical director, and he returned for this homecoming event and led the choir.

Ethnomusicologist Glenn Hinson observes that the structure of feeling in spiritual worship and gospel music often mirrors the joy of erotic pleasure. Describing black gospel mothers who laid the foundation for rock and roll, music journalist Ann Powers observes, "Women took the holy impulse inward and dwelled upon it as it ebbed and flowed. Their sense of eroticism's pleasure and need ... translated into a new, shockingly immediate and current framework for sanctified joy" (2017, 87–88). Black queer bounce performers navigate these same hierarchies and polarizations of body and soul, sacred and secular, spiritual and erotic—just as bounce music, like the church, incorporates notions of fellowship, sanctuary, and spirituality.

I sat in the pews with Cru members. One member, Rose, now performed only occasionally with us, but had been a key background singer before Katrina. While I'd met former members who identified as transgender or transsexual after their younger years in the Cru, Rose was the only trans woman who still actively participated in the group. We kept each other company, and she gave me some of the history of the church.

The service that day was also a revival, attended by a visiting congregation and minister. The home choir performed first, Freedia up front directing, Vockah in back with the tenors. Not surprisingly, Freedia's role as a bounce artist who could inspire and provoke audiences to act in response to specific calls informed his approach to the choir and congregation. His long arms moved like cranes, accentuating highs and lows as the choir followed. His hair was in a conservative bob cut and a more natural color, but he was no less a sight to behold. After the home choir finished and sat, the visiting choir sang, then their minister gave a sermon.

The presence of queer and trans people in the church was no surprise to me, but their degree of visibility was unique. The presence of multiple bounce artists—including Freedia, who was quickly becoming a rising star within and outside New Orleans—felt even more unusual. When the visiting minister took the stage, though, he made the surprising move of delivering one of the most queerphobic sermons I had ever heard, even going so far as to make a comment about Adam "marrying Eve and not Steve." I'd heard this kind of rhetoric all my life, but it was surprising to see a visiting pastor make this statement in this context—not just any Sunday, but a special reunion and fellowship event in the aftermath of Katrina. His rhetoric was even more unusual, Rose told me, because of the church's inclusive history: "He must not know where he is," she said, "because this church isn't about that." She and I spent most of his sermon chatting with each other and waiting for him to take a seat. Once he did, the lightness and feel-good vibe of the service returned. There was no "getting happy," as we used to say where I grew up—meaning no one was dancing passionately and running through the aisles, catching the spirit—but the togetherness and fellowship were strong. The experience made me consider the similarities of the church and the club scene where I'd met everyone. Both spaces, I realized, facilitated sanctuary and fellowship through the healing and connection collective song and movement create.[1]

BODY AND SOUL

The black church is the most powerful social institution within African America (Cole and Guy-Sheftall 2003). Like other dominant institutions, it plays a significant role in defining families and communities, as well as what constitutes appropriate or deviant citizenship within black culture. Even non-Christians and nonchurchgoers feel its impact. The church's confluence with other dominant institutions, like education and government, shapes a pervasive worldview.

European Enlightenment ideas—in particular, the polarization of the body (and the material world) versus the soul (and the spiritual plane)—have been naturalized in black church communities, affecting the broader community's relationship with bodies and sexuality. Black studies scholars have taken up this issue; in the 2001 essay "When You Divide Body and Soul, Problems Multiply," for example, scholar and Baptist minister Michael Eric Dyson discusses why some black Christian theologies have adopted European philosophical thought. He argues that black music might offer a solution to this paradox:

> There is a profound kinship between spirituality and sexuality.... Black Christians are reluctant to admit the connection because we continue to live in Cartesian captivity: the mind-body split thought up by philosopher Descartes flourishes in black theologies of sexuality. Except it is translated as the split between body and soul. Black Christians have taken sexual refuge in the sort of rigid segregation they sought to escape in the social realm—the body and soul in worship are kept [in] one place, the body and soul in heat are kept somewhere else.... Black culture, especially black music, has healed, indeed transcended, the split between mind and body inherited from Descartes and certain forms of Christian theology. The black church

has given a great deal to black culture, including the style and passion of much of black pop music. It is time the church accepted a gift in return: the union of body and soul. (317)

Dyson describes how this captivity has led to a sexual power structure in the black church where the heterosexual exploits of ministers are treated with ambivalence while women, queer people, and those living with HIV/AIDS are stigmatized and often alienated. Although many black communities in the United States and abroad treat queerness and black matriarchy as products of European influence in the African diaspora, ideas about the black body as inherently aggressive and heterosexual have been adopted partly due to European colonialism's instrumentalization of the church (Mogul et al. 2011).

Black queer studies scholars have gone further in describing the specific effects of these ideas. As Roderick Ferguson points out, the church has used the talents of black queer congregants while simultaneously scapegoating them for systemic issues such as the HIV/AIDS epidemic of the 1980s and 1990s. He speaks to black queer people's indispensable yet disavowed role via his childhood memories of a choir director named Edward: "Even as 'sissy' was a stigma akin to the mark of Cain, the men who folks referred to as such had qualities that everybody deemed attractive. Back then, they seemed to understand that, funny or not, Edward and men like him were part of us—little pieces in the mosaic that made up the neighborhood" (2007, 56).

Describing Edward's death in 1981 of what would later be recognized as HIV/AIDS and the rise of religious conservatism in the community, Ferguson explains that sissies "ceased to be peculiar men whose services were relied on" and instead "became pariahs who had to be identified and excluded" (2007, 57). We are demonized—but we're devils the congregation can still take pleasure in. One might say that in the context of the church, the representational passageway that becomes visible through the sissy isn't the ghetto as bottom, but hell itself.

Alongside its other practical forms, raising the bottom is also a practice of decolonizing spirituality toward the union of body and soul—destabilizing rigid notions of the sacred and secular in the name of ecstatic, healing collectivity.[2] Where church is concerned, applying an epistemology of the bottom means taking apart binary, hierarchical logics of good and evil, sacred and secular, spirit and flesh. Ministers are epistemological authorities within the church; how do bounce artists function as similar authorities within the alternative institution of the black queer bounce club? And if the church is defined by sacred and expressive "bodily" practices—fellowship, singing, catching the spirit—how do moments of collective joy like twerking and releasing ourselves to the rhythm also produce healing and catharsis?

FUSIONS

Between 2009 and 2015, three primary nightclubs regularly offered bounce music for the black queer community: Club Vibe, Orlando's Society Page (which became simply "The Page" after a change of ownership), and Club Fusions.

Club Vibe, a smaller venue on the edge of the Seventh Ward and Tremé neighborhoods, was originally owned by a black woman. Its initial patrons were mostly an older clientele of black lesbians. The sound system was big enough to make your teeth rattle. The small stage across from the bar had a large mirror, ground zero for twerk-offs and drag shows. Vockah gave me the impression that the club's gradual shift to a younger, more mixed bounce audience had something to do with him. He said that in the early 2000s, the owner and he had agreed to a weekly residency of sorts where he and the Cru would host and hone their skills. Hilariously, he claimed that VIBE stood for Vockah's International Bounce Entertainment.

The Page, offering a mix of bounce and R & B, was definitely the most visible venue catering to the black gay community, due to its Rampart Street address at the edge of the French Quarter. Originally, an older male crowd gathered there; to this day, passersby are likely to see a crowd of black men outside its doors, sometimes occupying the entire street.

Then there was Fusions, at the time the largest and most raucous of the three clubs. As a site of black queer fellowship and an alternative sacred space, Fusions deserves deeper examination. The venue's name points to its structure, its history, and the bottom knowledge cultivated within its walls. Established in the mid-'90s and located firmly in the Seventh Ward, the twenty-thousand-square-foot warehouse could hold hundreds of people. "Originally it was a 'straight and gay' club, you could say," an old-timer told me. "The straights partied downstairs, and the gays went upstairs. But you could go to either space. People would enter through separate entrances and start off in one or the other, but as the night went on and the party got going, people would mix." It wasn't clear when this mixing up of demographics stopped (or if it ever did), but eventually Fusions became known as primarily a black gay club.

At thirty-something years old, I was well traveled. I'd enjoyed nightclubs throughout the United States and partied extensively in New York, Los Angeles, London, and Berlin. None of that prepared me for Fusions. The first time Vockah and the Cru took me there, I stood in line outside what resembled a rundown hole in the wall, waiting to pay my ten dollars. When I heard how loud it was and sensed how many people were inside, the hair stood up on the back of my neck. Jitters of excitement mixed with nervousness. Inside, ascending the stairs to the upper ballroom, flashing lights bombarded my eyes. There was a smoke machine, but a good deal of the smoke in the air came from weed.

It was the most futuristic club scene I'd ever experienced. I stuck close to the Cru because it was almost impossible to find anyone through the crowd. Above me and to my side, a man twerked on top of the bar while bartenders served drinks between and around his legs. I almost fell over a woman in a green Day-Glo sundress and flip-flops who, face down and ass up, twerked with abandon on the floor. As we approached the room's center, a formation of marching J-setters appeared on our right, like a military formation. To my left, a group of men stomped in a line that snaked around the space. Before long, I realized they were part of a fraternity; in response to them, another line of both men and women started their own dances and hand gestures. My friend Randi pointed them out and explained, "That's an underground sorority—and the women initiate the guys into it."

Fusions definitely lived up to its namesake. On a separate occasion, Randi had discussed the club at length with me in an interview:

> Fusions is unlike other clubs you can go to in Atlanta [where] there's a plethora of options—you have lounges for gay men, you have specific club times for men of certain age brackets, you have certain racial groups who can go to certain ones; everyone assimilates in a kind of cafeteria style, all the cool kids here at this club, all the lesbians at this club . . . they're all so gay and unified in their own respective cultural groups. But here, with Fusions, from the age of eighteen till fifty, that's it. . . .

> *I would be more of a square if I hadn't gone through Fusions. It's like the boot camp for gay kids. If you can go through Fusions, you're cool. If you can make friends in there, you're cool. If you can stick up for yourself, you're cool. If you can learn how to dance . . . It's a one-stop shop for community, and that's what it is. You meet other races in there, the lesbians, the old and young—but it's interesting because all of this is around bounce music, and there's a certain amount of personality that bounce has that kind of fosters this culture. . . . People call New Orleans this gumbo. It's kind of like the gumbo is in the music. It's, like, in the dance.*
>
> *You're not going to dance like that in church. But you can do that in your secret society. . . . I feel like Fusions was really that place, to really fellowship.*

True to Randi's experience, the place offered a kind of fellowship I'd never experienced elsewhere. I'd never seen so many queer women and men party together. Over the years, I met and interviewed many people from Fusions—some as young as eighteen, some in their sixties.

Fusions supported a different level of visibility and inclusion among gay and trans clubgoers. Discussing his early days in the club scene, Randi had this to say about the mix of gay and trans people:

> *I didn't really hit the scene going out till I was twenty-one, at least twenty, 'cause I was very scared. I dated this one guy named George, and he had a transgender friend, and it totally freaked me out. I was like,* Oh my god, she is a freak . . . everything about her is crazy. *. . . I knew they were close friends, but I just couldn't identify why someone who was gay would want to hang with someone who had breasts and a penis, and at the time it just caused such a glitch in my relationship. But then he was so adamant about it, and just pro-trans. He was like, "Man, she's a really cool person. She's smart and intelligent. She has a job. And she's not some crazy freak." I just couldn't wrap my head around the concept and the connection between the two. . . .*
>
> *I wanted to be identified with just being gay, 'cause I was attracted to men, not because of what people assume gay people to be like—the glitter, the drag, and all that. I just wanted to be gay because I knew that I appreciated men. . . . When I found the gay scene and the things I saw at Fusions, there'd be violence and all this crazy stuff and I was like,* I'm not one of those kids *. . . but as it related to the transgender girl, I thought about it more and more. You know, trans women are really misunderstood—and gay men, too, in a sense, but there's a lot more respect for being gay. . . . To be trans and just walk out in the*

street in broad daylight with a wig on, or go to the store to pick up cigarettes or a soft drink, can be brutal. So I kind of thought of these things and was like, Man, must be a really, really difficult life—[especially] *after really knowing George and getting accustomed to the club scene.*

As I got to know [George's friend], she was a really sweet person. And I think that she pretty much shaped my passion toward transgender women now. And Rose was actually the first who I actually met and became comfortable with as a friend. I don't know if she knows it—yeah, but Rose was actually the very first person I met and got accustomed to being around, and to get an idea what it was like to mentally be trans and how to live that life. And I found so much positivity in Rose. And I was like, Okay, she's not a freak; she feels this way. *I just learned that through her. . . .*

But last year, . . . I just kind of did research, and it's interesting to me 'cause a lot of my friends now are trans. I have trans men and trans women friends. I highly respect them. I don't think it's something I could do—it's not my feeling. . . . I don't personally exude that amount of confidence.

It's, like, superficial on another level, but you know, [Fusions is] where I met more girls. . . . It's like, they tell you "certain types of music make you smarter," or "rap music makes you feel a little more violent." Bounce gives you that feel like, Just have fun and meet people. *Because when you see people dance the way that we do, it's like you walk up and [think],* Well, I wanna know her just because of the way her ass jiggles!

Counter to the black gay club scenes Randi had experienced in other cities, where community members assimilated into respective tribes, Fusions and the bounce scene in general encouraged pleasure, hybridity, friendship, and coalition across gay, trans, and even straight identities. After hearing Randi's story of growth I recalled my time with the members of the Cru at church and wondered if the inclusivity I'd seen that day had been cultivated in the church or in the "gumbo" bounce and the club scene produced—or if these institutions had all worked together through a shared ethic of care.

The radical fellowship I observed at Fusions was complemented by shows that were as sincere and formal as official rituals. Mondays and Saturdays were the main nights to go. The beginning of the week always featured a drag production with multiple performers, followed by a bounce set; on the weekend, it was bounce from open to close. A raised stage with a mirror reflected the room, functioning as a pulpit and choir stand all at once. One of the most common drag acts featured staged wedding acts performed by drag kings—often studs (trans men or masculine-presenting women) lip-syncing bounce versions of R & B songs like Jagged Edge's "Let's Get Married" (whose impassioned chorus begins, "Meet me at the altar in your white dress"). The "grooms" would enter the stage, dressed in tuxedos and suits, and serenade the crowd. The "bride" would then make a dramatic entrance, sometimes accompanied by a wedding party. You never knew who was going to step out and be unveiled, but the performance never got old. On a few occasions, the weddings were so dramatically heartfelt I wondered if an actual marriage had occurred.

These performances frustrated the line between the church's supposed monopoly on sacred practice; they revealed the club as more than a site of secular entertainment, a space where profound unions were made before the community. Ironically, one of the old-school emcees who facilitated Fusions' shows (in similar fashion to Big Freedia's choir direction) was named Priest. He would introduce different performers; when the drag show ended, he'd call out chants and direct the dancers. One after another, he would call movements and the shakers would take turns. All the while, he acknowledged community members in the crowd, giving them their praise.

Sadly, Fusions burned down on the tenth anniversary of Hurricane Katrina in 2015. Thankfully the building was closed at the time, and no one was hurt. It was rumored that the fire was the result of arson, perhaps the work of a disgruntled patron.

The club's owner of twenty years, Tyronne Williams, told an interviewer, "For this community itself, it's going to be very devastating. It's a loss to them because this is one of the biggest gay clubs in the city of New Orleans, and we have patrons who come from all over on Saturdays and Mondays to come out and enjoy theyself, so now it's basically like there's nowhere for them to go" (Ermac 2015).

Perhaps because so few venues were willing to host black queer and trans people, or perhaps because of the economic conditions that limited people's options, Fusions was where you could get your life. This is not to say it was utopia. Randi often expressed his dislike of the frequent fighting. People who'd never been to Fusions often joked about going and getting shot or stabbed. To outsiders, there was a general assumption that it was a site of inherent violence and a breeding ground for public health concerns and a source of stigmatized associations with HIV/AIDS—

despite the frequency of more serious violence, even murder, in the commercial districts of Bourbon Street and the French Quarter. Katey Red acknowledged the issue in a nuanced way: she once told *Vice* that when her out-of-town white friends said, "I want to hang out with some black people, I wanna see where you hang at," she took them to Club Fusions. "It's a lot of bounce going on in there," she explained. "My fan base is real, real high in there. They may have a fight in there, but there's no gunplay" (Ermac 2015). Like Red and Randi, I regularly witnessed brawls inside and outside—in the parking lot—but relative to the amount of joy and transcendence possible within the club, I still found it worthwhile.

In its sensory excess, Fusions fulfilled all the primary associations of a bottom location. Every time I pulled up to the venue, I noticed the stark contrast of the inside goings-on relative to the surrounding neighborhood. After Katrina, the Seventh Ward and Saint Bernard Avenue were sparsely inhabited; at night, it felt like the setting of a dystopic film. You could still see the high-water marks from the 2005 flood. But to enter Fusions was to be inundated with life—life so abundant and overflowing that at times it seemed the whole building was getting high and taking off. Whenever I meet anyone else who experienced Fusions, an unspoken recognition (and often an excited "You were there!") is exchanged. The connections fostered in the venue embody French sociologist Émile Durkheim's ([1912] 2016) concept of collective effervescence—a unifying excitement, born out of joyful shared experiences, that secures social bonds and provides a foundation for empowerment.[3]

CHURCH GIRLS

Just as Club Fusions remixed ideas about the sacred and secular, certain bounce rappers have become alternative authorities who use bounce as a tool to catch the spirit. Big Freedia's remarkable rise as the genre's most well-known performer is primarily due to his incredible work ethic—but also his deep faith and commitment to the community, first learned through the church. Freedia has never been shy about expressing these things, even onstage. By revealing the sacred capacities of black queer culture and bounce, Freedia has raised the bottom in ways that still influence debates about spirituality and popular culture.

Watching Big Freedia direct the choir at his church was one of only a few times we'd seen each other in my two years of fieldwork. As his career took off and my coperforming with Vockah and the Cru developed, it was difficult to stay in touch. But not long after that Sunday service, I had the opportunity to ask him about his history with the church:

> ALIX: How have you dealt with your role in the church and being a bounce artist?
>
> BIG FREEDIA: It was very difficult—'cause there was bounce at night, then having to get up and go to church and do the different things I was into, like being the choir director. Having to get up and teach the choir on Saturday morning, going to clubs at night on Friday night. . . . I wasn't hiding it, and then the word just started buzzing even more—*Y'all choir director is Big Freedia!*—and it just became crazy. Certain people started trying to push me away in the church home when they shouldn't have. And God say, "Accept everybody for who they are." I kind of just backed up and kind of . . . yeah, like, left the church. I didn't do it immediately—just over time. But I slowly did it. And I was still directing the choir.
>
> I still go back now and direct the choir when there's reunions. But it was a very challenging experience to go through that transformation, from being a choir director to a bounce artist. It was very difficult. . . .
>
> It's like, that really bothers me when the pastor get up . . . they'll talk to you like they want you to do all these different things. But when it's time for the sermon, there's always a gay topic or something pertaining, and it's thrown directly at you. A lot of people, they'll give it away once church is over—you know, say different things to you and try to make you feel better. . . . I was always the strong one. I always believe in God. And I always had God first in my life and still have God in my life, even though I'm not in a church home. I still pray all the time. And I still do what I can do for my church home—be there when I can. But, like, things totally changed for my life, way back.

Big Freedia's complicated experience of being useful to the church's goals while also shamed through the pulpit echoes the experience of many queer people who've experienced "church hurt"—the sadness and pain of being alienated from and losing trust in a church home. Nonetheless, as Freedia says, those difficult experiences haven't stopped him from continuing to pray and give back to the church community. In a 2019 interview with *Nylon*, when asked how he'd made it so far, he said, "First and foremost, keeping God first. In everything I do, no matter what it is—a performance, waking up in the morning, going to sleep, something successful happening in my career—thanking the being that's making it happen. Everything else falls in line. And just being humble, staying true to myself, and staying connected with my family, my friends, the fans. I'm just trying to balance it all, and the only way to do that is prayer. Prayer is a big part of it, for me and my whole team" (Ramirez 2019).

Despite his home church experiences, Freedia hasn't allowed others to define his relationship to God. He sees no contradiction between his artistic life and his spirituality; his daily life and his life onstage are undergirded by an attention to balance, connection, and prayer. Freedia's artistry and spirituality feel mutually constituted in a way that brings to mind Audre Lorde's explanation of the erotic as power. For Lorde, the erotic isn't simply about our sexual lives—it's also a deeply felt sense of joy that infuses our whole life with intentionality and purpose.

Debates about the spiritual erotic can be traced throughout the history of black cultural expression—in particular, the intimate entanglements surrounding gospel, spirituals, blues, R & B, and hip-hop (Powers 2017). Generations of soul singers have walked the fine line of infusing secular performances with church-honed elements of sacred practice. Notable artists like Aretha Franklin, Nina Simone, Donny Hathaway, and James Brown used vocal, instrumental, movement, and dance forms and techniques of the black church in order to tap into collective desires. Meanwhile, both modern and historic gospel artists, such as Sister Rosetta Tharpe and Mahalia Jackson, have walked a tightrope and faced criticism for "worldly" expressions of desire, materialism, and work created with secular peers. (Little do people know the most successful gospel artist of the last ten years is Kanye West—as of 2023, he'd claimed *Billboard*'s year-end Top Gospel Artist title for three years running.) It's in this long tradition of cross-pollination that Big Freedia and other bounce artists speak to both the needs of the flesh and the collective need for healing from trauma and alienation.

One song that captures this spirit and articulates it through bounce is Big Freedia's "Explode":

> I'm 'bout to explode, take off this load
> Unleash my belt and make it go
> I'm 'bout to explode, take off this load
> Bend it, bus' it open, won't ya make it go

The lyrics might seem solely sexual at first—but as Freedia notes, he's also expressing desire for a different kind of release. In an interview with *Access Hollywood*, he discussed the song's meaning:

> When I recorded "Explode" . . . it was releasing all of these different things, these different energies, and putting them, you know, out of my mind, when it's time to get to the stage. You know, a lot of these things that you deal with in your everyday life, you know, sometimes they become overwhelming. They make you want to explode. . . . When I get on stage, I flip a switch and I let all those things that I'm going through . . . I let them go and go into my safe space, which is the stage. (Evans 2022)

The safe space Freedia and audiences seek through bounce may represent a more egalitarian, expansive sphere of connection than formal religious institutions can offer. Jafari S. Allen, exploring the spiritual capacity of black queer clubs in the house music scene, writes, "Classic house/club refrains implore the dancer to 'free your body,' 'move your body,' 'give it up,' and 'let yourself go' which may be interpreted as sexual innuendo, and is also understood in the space of the dance club as an exhortation to a deeper psychic and spiritual freeing that only takes place through the pleasures of the body. . . . The transformation takes place through collective effervescence evoked by the music, the people and the safe*r* [*sic*] space for spinning and spiraling" (2009, 318). Like house music, "Explode" and other bounce songs perform a cultural labor that's certainly sexual at times, but also often discounted for the ways they use dance and song to express pleasure—and perhaps love—outside of dyadic, heteronormative conceptions.

Freedia's work has exported the "freeing" potential of bounce far beyond New Orleans—particularly through his dialogue with global pop star Beyoncé. In her 2022 song "Break My Soul," Beyoncé samples "Explode." The song came out in June 2022, during ongoing pandemic-related recovery and economic instability. Freedia's sampled lyrics encourage listeners to "release" not only their wiggle but any and all constraints—their anger, their mind, their job, their trade, their stress. To this Beyoncé adds that she's building her own "new foundation" and finding a "new salvation." "Break My Soul" became an anthem of sorts, capturing the spirit of discontent at a time of global crisis. Described as an ode to the Great Resignation—a trend in which workers quit their jobs in response to poor conditions, remote work, fear of exposure to CO-VID-19, and general dissatisfaction with the status of the US economy—the song struck many listeners as encouragement to participate in a mass "release" of capitalism.

This reading of "Break My Soul" is in part true, and critics could use this theme to point to the contradictions of Beyoncé, a multimillionaire, encouraging fans to quit working. But the song and album's mixture of black queer cultural forms and emphasis on "looking for something that lives inside me" gestures toward redefining value in terms of spiritual wealth, rather than money. (The inclusion of Big Freedia, a bounce artist, on a house music track might initially seem odd, but it becomes less so in light of Freedia's church background and house music's history of sampling gospel.)

Beyoncé remixes the binary, hierarchical structures of sacred and secular expressions elsewhere as well: "Church Girl," also from her *Renaissance* album, addresses the duality of sacred and secular longing, moving even further toward destabilizing the secular/sacred divide. The song opens with a sample from the phenomenal gospel group the Clark Sisters and their 1981 song "Center of Thy Will." Dorinda Clark-Cole's voice opens the song: "Lord, place me—I wanna be centered," she sings. "I wanna be centered in thy will." A bounce-like, twerk-worthy rhythm follows, playing on bounce's rhythm without quite replicating it.

I grew up listening to the Clark Sisters, and I've sometimes felt they were my only connection to the black church as I negotiated my own feelings of alienation and church hurt. Over the years, I've heard other black queer people express the same sentiment. It was deeply meaningful to hear "Church Girl" open with a sample that taps those feelings of loss and desire to remain centered in a relationship to god.

The song caused no small amount of controversy in pulpits around the country. Its lyrics consider the capacity to be happy through collective joy and dancing "without a man," a clear contestation of patriarchal hierarchies and judgment. The relatable protagonist "shake[s] that ass and them pretty tig ol' bitties" while "doin' God's work" and getting to "church in the morning." The song's placement on an album that celebrates black queer people also makes us wonder who this church girl is: Is she a gay man like Big Freedia, who uses he and she pronouns; a lesbian; a trans woman or man; or a woman who's straight but doesn't conform to religious heteronormative ideals (an unmarried mother, for instance)? What does it mean for any of these church girls to stay centered in god's will?

In its plea to god to meet us where we're at, in the flesh and in the world, rather than endure living death toward a potential freedom in heaven, "Church Girl" recalls Thomas Dorsey's early twentieth-century gospel great "Take My Hand, Precious Lord." "I am tired, I am weak, I am worn," Dorsey's lyrics implore. "Take my hand, precious Lord / Lead me home." Dorsey's songwriting was radical in its day, breaking from the convention of spirituals that emphasized freedom in the heavenly ever after. By asking god to meet him in the here and now—to take his hand, his flesh—Dorsey shook up binary oppositions of Western religious thought that polarize body and spirit and precipitate secular and sacred divides (Powers 2017). The progenitors of Beyoncé's "Church Girl," Big Freedia's "Explode," and perhaps a broader black aesthetic tradition all fit firmly within an epistemology of the bottom.

Through my time coperforming with Vockah Redu and the Cru, going to Club Fusions, and enjoying the fellowship of black queer community, I learned a deeper love of my body, one that acknowledges it as much more than a site of vulnerability and risk. Some might take offense to an emcee like Vockah or Big Freedia telling us to "touch it like a dog," but I don't assume they infer the violent history where a black body is more animal or dirt than human; I hear them directing me toward a primal embrace of the flesh. We should actively learn to love our bodies—not as distant metaphorical temples, but within the everyday beauty of the flora and fauna we're situated within.

Toni Morrison conveys this imperative well through Baby Suggs's character in *Beloved*. The elder woman and "unchurched" preacher leads a community of freedmen in the post–Civil War era; she offers this sermon in a wooded clearing:

> "Here," she said, "in this here place, we flesh; flesh that weeps, laughs; flesh that dances on bare feet in the grass. Love it. Love it hard. Yonder they do not love your flesh. They despise it. They don't love your

eyes; they'd just as soon pick em out. No more do they love the skin on your back. Yonder they flay it. And O my people they do not love your hands. Those they only use, tie, bind, chop off and leave empty. Love your hands! Love them. Raise them up and kiss them. Touch others with them, pat them together, stroke them on your face 'cause they don't love that either. You got to love it, you! And no, they ain't in love with your mouth. Yonder, out there, they will see it broken and break it again. What you say out of it they will not heed. What you scream from it they do not hear. What you put into it to nourish your body they will snatch away and give you leavins instead. No, they don't love your mouth. You got to love it. This is flesh I'm talking about here. Flesh that needs to be loved. Feet that need to rest and to dance; backs that need support; shoulders that need arms, strong arms I'm telling you. And O my people, out yonder, hear me, they do not love your neck unnoosed and straight. So love your neck; put a hand on it, grace it, stroke it, and hold it up. And all your inside parts that they'd just as soon slop for hogs, you got to love them. The dark, dark liver—love it, love it, and the beat and beating heart, love that too. More than eyes or feet. More than lungs that have yet to draw free air. More than your life-holding womb and your life-giving private parts, hear me now, love your heart. For this is the prize." Saying no more, she stood up then and danced with her twisted hip the rest of what her heart had to say while the others opened their mouths and gave her the music. Long notes held until the four-part harmony was perfect enough for their deeply loved flesh. ([1987] 2004, 102)

Baby Suggs speaks to a theme that has followed black expressive culture since the postslavery period—the importance of the body, and of taking pleasure in the body, after the long shadow of enslavement. The ability to self-determine what we do with our bodies in the realm of sex, gendered expressivity, comportment, and dance is no small matter. We cannot underscore enough the importance of loving our flesh as a practice of preserving ourselves, building communal ties, and following a pathway to the sacred.

Church girls come in all shapes and sizes, come in all bodies and genders. They may be hetero, queer, or trans. And perhaps they call fellowship by a different name, like the "kiki," "the lime," or just a party. Or maybe the space is not called a church, but a ballroom, "the house," the club, or the stage. If they call god by a different name, say "the divine" or "the sacred," I doubt the naming will go unheard and unrecognized. Rarely is power experienced in a vacuum. The question is, What do you do with it?

TWERK TO THE GRAVE

Many people passed away prematurely during my time in New Orleans—and over the subsequent years, a pattern of precarious illness and premature death followed the Cru and their community. I couldn't imagine the weight Vockah carried with him. In the summer of 2020, Fatman died from an asthma attack at age thirty-eight. Oscar and Tader never made it to thirty. Vockah's mother, whom he'd worried about losing in his efforts to escape his life circumstances, was killed in a hit-and-run in broad daylight. Numerous other people who contributed to this research—many of whom had become close friends—either died or left the city in search of stability and safety.

Fatman had always struggled with severe asthma. Sometimes during our shows, particularly ones in cold northeastern winters, he'd have to sit out, resting and using his inhaler. His father had asthma as well; after one particularly bad period, Fat called his doctor's office to request a particular inhaler his father used that he'd found relieved his own symptoms. It was during COVID-19 quarantine, and the office told him the prescription couldn't be filled unless he made a telehealth appointment to discuss his symptoms. I never knew Fatman to have a steady cell phone, let alone a personal computer, or to live somewhere with reliable internet. Saddled with the precarities working-class and black New Orleanians face accessing healthcare, he couldn't get the time-sensitive medication, and he was denied timely treatment due to rigid healthcare protocols. After speaking to Fat's mother, Paris relayed the story. "He finally had his own place," she said. "He called his mom early in the morning, panicked, saying he couldn't breathe. His brother jumped in the car, and by the time he made it to the apartment, he was gone."

Preparing for Fatman's funeral, I put on some old songs, listening closely for his nasal screams and cheers. The music returned me to the dance floors and stages we'd shared. He'd taken such pride in dancing and shaking. All Fat needed was "dat beat" to carry his mind and his body away. "Sometimes I can get so loose!" he'd say. All these things moved through my mind as I drove to the viewing. I'd known Fat's family for years at this point; I knew how close they were and how much they embraced him. Yet I still had the fears so many queer people have. I worried they wouldn't honor him or represent him, instead shrouding him in their expectations to create an appropriate image.

When I arrived, Fatman's mother greeted me outside with tears in her eyes. She needed my help, she said, holding up a white carnation flower with a pin through it. "I just can't go up to him—I can't touch him," she told me. "Please, would you?" I took the corsage inside. When I approached Fatman's casket, I had to pull back a black veil before I could clearly see him. Some of the grief I'd held on to for days—and the fears I'd arrived with—dissipated, replaced by relief.

Fatman was dressed like he was on his way to the club. He was decked out in a black mesh jacket and matching pants, silver chains around his neck, his face beat with makeup. His nails were painted; they'd left his blond extensions in. As I pinned the flower to his lapel, I said, "Hey, friend. Now I know they better have you in some black mesh."

As part of Fat's homegoing, a balloon release was happening near his aunt's house; the balloons floated off as I pulled up. A wake of sorts was going on at the family home. Crowds gathered in the yard, on the porch, and inside with a huge spread of food. I recognized family members, old boyfriends, and people from the club scene. An indoor stereo played bounce; eventually someone arrived and set up a system with large speakers on the porch. As the sun went down, the music got louder. A few of Fat's cousins joked about his dance moves and began to emulate him. Before long, people were shaking, twerking, and popping, holding the banisters on the porch and leading up the steps. One of Fat's ex-boyfriends was giving it his all. The scene—dat beat pouring from the speakers and people taking to the rhythm, memorializing Fatman—filled me with a mix of joy, sadness, nostalgia, and profound beauty. It reminded me of the jazz funerals I'd seen, processions leaving the cemetery while dancing to a second-line band. Neither kind of memorial was an odd sight in New Orleans.

The religious studies scholar Elizabeth Pérez (2016) has identified twerking as part of a family of African diasporic sacred dances associated with life-giving and death-witnessing; she points out that twerking's popular reductive sexualization reflects an ahistorical perspective that disassociates booty-shaking from sacred kindred dances across the Caribbean and West and Central Africa.[4] Moments like Fatman's repast certainly aren't solely secular; they exemplify how rhythm and dance, even the oft-sexualized performance of twerking, play a role in spiritual and communal connection. As Pérez and others explain, collective release can be particularly vital for politically embattled communities of the African diaspora. Getting "loose" through twerking and shaking may relate to our need for healing and catharsis in ways we haven't accounted for—because that looseness represents a threat to the body-soul divide within the church, while also suggesting very old colonial fears of the primitive savage.

Like the mind-body divide, communal forms of ecstasy have been tightly regulated within Western culture. But these collective moments of embodied pleasure articulate a mix of spirituality and erotic power that offers catharsis, joy, and transcendence to those who've been alienated because of their flesh. Loving the flesh has a deep historical significance to the descendants of people who endured enslavement—and to queer and trans people, whose "unnatural" relationship to their bodies should be determined not by other people, but through their own deeply felt sense of connection to the sacred and the divine.

Like the black gospel mothers who inspired much of twentieth-century rock and roll through the creation of visceral and immediate forms of sanctified joy, black queer and trans bounce artists are the unsung generators of popular culture at the turn of the century. Just as gospel greats like Thomas Dorsey wrote songs expressing an urgency of need, artists like Big Freedia raise the bottom by prayerfully asking for spiritual healing in the here and now of our flesh, however alienated or traumatized through dark histories and endless disasters. Through a bottom-epistemological lens, bounce acts as a network wherein the music, clubs, and labor of artists counter conservative interpretations of theology. Post-Katrina bounce in New Orleans reveals that black urban cultural aspects that some treat as ephemeral and meaningless, and even as pathological examples of oppression's impact, must be situated within both historical/global understandings of systemic power and African diasporic practices of healing and resistance. Radical fellowship, sanctuary, and spiritual joy can be found in the bottom.

Not long before Oscar's death, over ten years earlier, he'd dreamily shared an observation with me: "Bounce can be very hypnotizing, and it can be very overwhelming at times. When you hear that music, it will do something to you—to where it sends something into you, to where you have no choice but to move. It's about what you do with it. . . . It's almost like if I was to see my long-lost cousin or a long-lost family member, and immediately I see them, and of course it's going to send something through me that's indescribable."

Though I didn't quite understand what Oscar meant at the time, it's clearer now that bounce holds a sacred—and yes, *indescribable*—power over me and other listeners. Each time I drive into New Orleans, I feel a sense of joy, but also regret for the friends I've lost. To hear the sound of bounce is indeed like feeling the passing of a familiar, fleeting spirit.

ACKNOWLEDGMENTS

The road to completing this text was anything but linear and had its ups and downs. Finishing it would not have been possible without the support, guidance, and love, and care of many people. I am grateful for every relationship this work has brought into my life.

To New Orleans, you have given me more than I could ask for, and this book is my humble act of gratitude and solidarity. Thank you to Vockah Redu (Javocca Davis), Clarence Mosley, Jody Shepard, Rosie Hickerson, Randi Sylve, Legacy Nicole, Big Freedia, Sissy Nobby, Katey Red, Rusty Lazer, Alison Fensterstock, Jayna Jenson, Aubrey Edwards, and Lefty Parker. Thank you to the many friends and community members who supported and inspired me, especially Mayaba Liebenthal, Elizabeth Steeby, Victor Pizzaro, Pai Palomo, Jennifer Whitney, Janick Lewis, Aesha Rasheed, Kate Paxton, Jordan Flaherty, Ellery Neon, Reimoku Smith, and Fari Nzinga.

Thank you to Mark Johnson at Brotherhood Inc. and Deon Haywood at Women with a Vision. My love to everyone at the Community Book Center, especially Jennifer Turner, Vera Warren-Williams, and Denise Graves. Thank you to those who have left us too soon, including Glendell Weir, Oscar Phillips IV, Donte Jarrell Brown, and Ethan Clark. My appreciation goes to the owners and staff at the various bars and clubs that contributed to my fieldwork: Club Fusions, Club Vibe, and The Page.

This book came to fruition through the support and guidance of Duke University Press. I want to thank my editor, Kenneth Wissoker, for believing in the project and encouraging me through the challenges of the pandemic. Thank you for the thoughtful and thorough feedback of the anonymous reviewers, and to all the editors who contributed their time and energy to this project and its earlier versions, including Scott Weble, Katherine Pace, and Anne Mathews. Anne, after twenty years of collaboration between us, I can't wait to see what's next.

This research began among a dynamic community of scholar-activists at the University of Texas at Austin. I am grateful to all the teachers and advisors who gave me their time and support throughout the years. I would like to extend my sincere appreciation to Christen Smith, João H. Costa Vargas, Omi Joni L. Jones, Lyndon Gill, and Edmund T. (Ted) Gordon. Thanks to my mentor, Jafari Sinclaire Allen, for taking a chance on me. You not only showed me the extent to which I could further my education, but you also shared your friendships, home, and other resources in support and care for me. Hameed S. (Herukhuti) Williams was not based in Austin, but you always picked up the phone and counseled me through so much of this work; I cannot thank you enough.

In addition, other teachers and University of Texas faculty and staff contributed greatly to my well-being and studies, including Maria Franklin, Pauline Strong, Jemima Pierre, Kathleen Stewart, Matt Richardson, Adriana Dingman, and Stephanie Lang. Since my first day at the University of Texas, the Center for African and African Diaspora Studies provided inspiration, early funding for preliminary research and professional development, and, most of all, a home away from home. Thank you to the Department of Anthropology and the Department of African and African Diaspora Studies staff and faculty. My thanks to everyone involved in the creation and legacy of the Austin School.

I would never have seen my way through this process without the camaraderie of so many friends, colleagues, and confidants. I will never forget the years of debate, dreaming, tears, and laughter I have shared with my peers. My special thanks go to Juli Grigsby, Kenyon Farrow, Savannah Shange, Mitsy Chanel Blot, Raquel de Souza, Eunice Garza, Jaime Alves, Gwendolyn Ferreti, Amy Brown, Naomi Reed, Nidra Lee, Melisa Forbis, Tane Ward, Mubbashir Rizvi, Lynn Selby, Maryam Kashani, Beth Ferguson, Leslie McGuiness, Junaid Rana, Jodi Skipper, Pablo Gonzalez, Sarah Imhoud, Martin Perna, Christopher Loperena, Mariana Mora, Sachi Decou, Wura-Natasha Ogunji, Saikat Maitra, Alysia Childs, Elvia Mendoza, Erica Lies, Raja Swamy, Nick Copeland, Ana-Maurine Lara, Damien Sojoyner, Shaka McGlotten, Angeliska Polacheck, Rockie Lynn, and Philip Alexander. William Mosley, thank you for our years-long biweekly check-ins. My gratitude to Celeste Henery and Courtney D. Morris for years of feedback, encouragement, and laughs.

Thank you to the University of California Santa Barbara's Predoctoral Dissertation Fellowship in Black Studies. In particular, thank you to Jeffrey Stewart, Stephanie Batiste, George Lipsitz, Ingrid Banks, Claudine Michel, Douglas Daniels, Christopher McAuley, and Roberto Strongman. Also, my appreciation to Mireille Miller-Young, Eileen Boris, Mahader

Tesfai, Tuyen Nguyen, Karen Buenavista Hanna, Sanibel Borges, and Jonathan Gomez. I wish I could say thank you to Clyde Woods and Cedric Robinson, who left too soon.

Gratitude goes out to my colleagues in the New Orleans area who supported me through my fieldwork and during my first appointment to Tulane University's Gender and Sexuality Studies Program and the Department of Communication. Many thanks to Matt Sakakeeny for your years of guidance. Thank you, Helen Regis, for your open ear and support. I'll never forget Mohan Ambikaipaker and Briana Mohan's generosity.

My thanks to Spelman College. During my time teaching there, I was able to draft and refine many of the arguments and narratives included in this book. Thank you to faculty and staff in the Women's Resource Center at Spelman and to the Department of Anthropology there. I will always cherish the students and young activists I met at Spelman and Morehouse College and throughout the Atlanta University Center.

I would not have been able to finish this book without the time and support provided by Emory University and the Department of African American Studies. Thank you to all the staff and my colleagues, especially Dianne Stewart, Carol Anderson, Walter Rucker, Bayo Holsey, Calvin Warren, Jessica Stewart, Meina Yates-Richard, Pearl Dowe, Michelle Gordon, Kimberly Wallace-Sanders, Crystal Sanders, and Kali Gross. From Tulane to Emory, Beretta Smith-Shomade has been a constant light—thank you. Through the manuscript workshop the department hosted, I was able to transform the book. I cannot thank Jennifer Nash and Martin Manalansan enough for your participation and feedback in the workshop.

I've been fortunate to know some of the most daring artists and thinkers through my time in Washington State. My passion for the arts and social justice was nurtured through the early mentorship of Ester Huey, **Alice Coil,** and Horace Alexander Young. Thank you to my friends, comrades, and accomplices formerly of Luscious Studios, the King Street Collective, and the Infernal Noise Brigade. I will never forget the encouragement and generosity of longtime Washington friends like Paul Rosenthal, D. K. Pan, Davida Ingram, **Alice Coil,** Kathy Kim, and the late Juliana Bradley. And finally, thanks to my Rio de Janeiro friends, including Maga Bo, Monica Avila, Semaj Moore, Lucia Xavier, and Regina Xavier, for taking me in when I needed a change of scenery.

First, thank you to my family and ancestors, who constantly inspire me to honor my past, fight for what I believe, and never take love and kindness for granted. I am grateful to and will always love my mother, Debra Chapman. Thank you for supporting my curiosity and wanderlust, even when I wasn't sure where the path would lead. My love and thanks to my dad, Wayman Chapman. I am grateful for your support and for your instilling in me an appreciation of music. Big hugs to my sister, Shondea Chapman, whose faith and deep memory kept my feet on the ground when I couldn't. My thanks to my extended family, blood and chosen, who inspire me and have supported me in countless ways.

NOTES

INTRODUCTION

Acknowledgment: Parts of "The Black Queer Past" in the introduction appeared in a different form in Alix Chapman, "The Punk Show: Queering Heritage in the Black Diaspora," *Cultural Dynamics* 26 (3): 327–45.

1   Faulty city and state infrastructure, including poorly engineered levees, resulted in the devastating flood that displaced a disproportionate number of working poor black New Orleans residents following Hurricane Katrina in 2005. The black population dropped from 66.7 percent in 2000 to 57.8 percent in 2006. As with the welfare "reform" movements of the 1960s, 1970s, and 1990s, the flood provided powerful governmental and corporate interests with the opportunity to reduce the dense population of poor black residents in potentially profitable areas of New Orleans (Ambrosino 2007; Schram et al. 2003; Hansan and Morris 1999; Smith 2007). According to economist Ben Casselman, "More than 175,000 black residents left New Orleans in the year after the storm; more than 75,000 never came back" (2015).

2   This project joins the work of a number of scholars who, as sociologist Roderick Ferguson writes in *Aberrations in Black*, understand that engaging with Morrison's *Sula* "represented a process of negation in which an apparently non-political literary text about two black women became a resource for epistemological and political practices that could express alternatives to existing social movements." Ferguson continues: "Devising such practices meant resuscitating nonnormative difference as the horizon of epistemological critique, aesthetic innovation, and political practice" (2004, 126). Here, Ferguson speaks to *Sula*'s impact on a generation of black lesbian feminists—including Audre Lorde and Barbara Smith—who saw in its characters a challenge to heteropatriarchal politics and culture, within and without blackness. Referring to Smith, Ferguson adds that despite the book's absence of LGBTQIA+ identities, "black lesbian feminist critique negates the presumption that *Sula* is the private property of Morrison's intentions." Smith's critique, he explains, "is populated with interests

that Morrison could not imagine" in "a world characterized by gender and sexual heterogeneity" (2004, 128).

3   Following Nash, I'm inspired by the groundbreaking work of anal theorists who engage the bottom and anality as an act of queer subversion (Bersani 1987; Dean 2009; Nguyen 2014). I also lean toward thinkers who, like Morrison and Nash, conceptualize the bottom as a site generally constructed as black.

4   Evelynn Hammonds's "Black (W)holes: The Geometry of Black Female Sexuality" (1994) uses astrophysics to discuss black female sexuality as something often perceived as empty, though it's actually full. In "Black Anality," Nash considers how black women's genitalia and sexuality are analogized as black holes in pornography and expands on Hammond's work by "attend[ing] to the 'other' black hole," the anus. Nash explores "how black sexualities more generally, and black female sexualities particularly, become tethered imaginatively, discursively, and representationally to the anus" and describes "how black pleasures are imagined to be peculiarly and particularly attached to *anal ideologies* including *spatiality, waste, toxicity,* and *filth*" (2014, 439). Black sissy figures, as I relate in chapter 4, share this tethering. Like Nash, I approach blackness and sexuality as mutually constitutive.

5   I both draw on and depart from scholarship on the sissy as a black trope and archetype. In *Sissy Insurgencies* (2021), Marlon Ross discusses notions of conduct as a barometer of black masculinities through history; he shows how sissiness informs fit and unfit masculinity in relation to larger social political conditions. Sissy figures in New Orleans are particularly well represented in Ferguson's description (in *Aberrations in Black*) of a black trans sex worker in Oakland. She represents the "general estrangements of African American culture," Ferguson writes, and has been "erased by those who wish to present or make African American culture the embodiment of all that she is not—respectability, domesticity, heterosexuality, normativity, nationality, universality and progress" (2004, 1–2).

6   I see the sissy as both an adjunct to the bottom and—following Darieck Scott's work in *Extravagant Abjection*—an alternative figure of black liberation: "The measure of autonomous or free selfhood is really masculinity, and the Other of the masculine is feminine.... But this does not mean that it is necessarily feminine, or only feminine, merely that it cannot be narrated except as the negation of what it exceeds or overruns" (2010, 19).

7   I use *queer* as an umbrella for nonnormative sexual practices, identities, and worldviews. I do so while understanding the ever-changing power struggles concerning sexual and gendered identity in black communities.

8   Interest in this history was often framed by irony, as if the emergence of a black queer past were a surprising anomaly—despite its ongoing, widespread presence. Figures like Marchan were treated as exceptional "discoveries," in contrast to queer white historical figures, who are more readily absorbed into narratives of white liberal modernity and continuity around sex/gender fluidity.

9   This work owes much to black queer scholar and performance theorist E. Patrick Johnson's explorations of black queer culture throughout the US South in *Sweet Tea* (2008). I build on Johnson's concepts of "quare" studies—sexual and racialized excess that he defines as "incapable of being contained within normative categories of *being*" (2001, 2).

10 Truly valuing and integrating Marchan's life history is difficult because the subject of race, let alone sexuality, is often treated as "conjectural" and "particular," if not totally beside the point. In *Black Gay Man* (2001), Robert Reid-Pharr points out how what's considered "universal" and "particular" needs to be complicated. Discussions of sexuality are frequently seen as tangential: Class is seen as universal, crosscutting all of society, while queerness (for instance) is treated as a "particular" problem for the "naturally" queer subject. The conditions of queerness, however, are still represented and produced within literature and institutions through the machinery of American culture and imperialism.

11 Cash Money Records paid for Marchan's funeral expenses (Wirt 2023).

12 See my article "The Punk Show" (2014) for more on the life and times of Bobby Marchan.

13 Deconstruction and "scholarly" engagement cannot alone account for "embodied meanings that are accessible through ethnographic methods of 'radical empiricism'" (Conquergood 1991, 188). My approach, which juxtaposes performance ethnography and textual analysis, is itself an argument against the binaries that have divided radical black consciousness from everyday lived practices.

14 Coperformance is a method of performance ethnography—a frame "in which performance is accorded status as ethnographic practice" (Kondo 1997, 20). D. Soyini Madison has described coperformance as the act in which "you not only do what subjects do, but you are intellectually and relationally invested in their symbol-making practices as you experience with them a range of yearnings and desires" (2005, 168). This approach accounts for the limits of academic discourse in translating theatrical performance while privileging the researcher's body as a site of experience and meaning (Minh-ha 1989; Madison 2005). Given my access to coperformers' theatrical performances alongside my quotidian experiences working and living in New Orleans, I needed a methodological frame that would incorporate my

multiple experiences and observations. These techniques allowed for a self-reflexive critique of my own experiences as a black queer scholar working within a community while moving between positions of insider and outsider (Abu-Lughod 1991; Hill Collins 1990).

15 Simply "observing" music and dance would not suffice. I had to develop other senses and embodied forms of dialogue. As Conquergood states, "Listening is an interiorizing experience, a gathering together, a drawing in, whereas observation sizes up exteriors" (1991, 183). Also see Veit Erlmann's "But What of the Ethnographic Ear?" ([2004] 2020).

16 Again, Morrison's work in *Sula* informs my approach: The novel deals with issues of residential segregation, gentrification, and black people's precarious assimilation into the nation.

17 The film *Faubourg Tremé: The Untold Story of Black New Orleans* (Logsdon 2008) speculates that the setbacks to black activism in the wake of *Plessy v. Ferguson* constituted a crisis for political action and a turn from formal activism to a reinvestment in cultural performance. It was during this same period that brass bands, jazz funerals, and the first Mardi Gras Indians began challenging the dominance of white supremacy in public space. These incursions of black performance into white public space were not altogether welcome, even as they came to define the cultural identity of the city. In "Textures of Black Sound and Affect" (2024), anthropologist Matt Sakakeeny considers the impact of musician renegades, like Charles "Buddy" Bolden, whose insurrectionist impulse contributed to a radical vision of black working-class life. Sakakeeny argues that the structures of feeling that run through jazz funerals and related performances might not always make explicit contestations of antiblack violence—but they do generate a significant "atmosphere" of liberation and mutual aid.

18 Although the term "sissy" has vernacular roots that preceded black queer performance in bounce, some artists felt that Nobby's popularity in the years following Katrina led new listeners to use the term "sissy bounce" more often because of the sound's association with Sissy Nobby. I use "sissy bounce" and simply "bounce" interchangeably, but more often I use the former when referring to the cross-cultural context that occurred after Katrina.

19 In "Black Noise, White Fears: Resilience, Rap, and the Killing of Jordan Davis" (2018), musicologist William Cheng writes, "Perceptions of loud blackness metamorphosed into fictions of criminal threat. Physical and sonic excess made flesh. Flesh unmade by bullets." Such a moment speaks to the fact that the disciplining of black bodies—and also resistance to antiblackness—occurs not only through a field of vision, but as contestation over sound and the sensory landscape as a whole.

20 Bounce represents a particular sound, characterized by a mixture of two principal beats: the Brown beat and the Triggerman. These rhythms

originated in the South Bronx and migrated to New Orleans in the early 1980s. Music scholar and filmmaker Matt Miller, in his book *Bounce*, describes the music as having "a particular mid-tempo rhythmic feel created by a propulsive, syncopated bass drum pattern in combination with layered, continuous percussive elements such as handclaps or simple melodic lines and often featuring particular sounds sampled from other recordings" (2012, 1). Miller's book and 2007 documentary (with Stephen Thomas) situate bounce in local black musical traditions; Miller's work also addresses the economic and racialized tensions affecting the local music scene while covering attempts by national record labels to commercialize and assimilate bounce.

21 Prior to Miller's 2012 book, there'd been very little written documentation of bounce, and even less on black queer bounce performers. Roni Sarig's book *Third Coast* (2007) had described the emergence of Southern rap and its assimilation into national hip-hop culture, offering some of the first scholarly documentation of bounce music. Sarig noted Katey Red in particular: "Take Fo', which has remained a pre-eminent bounce label, broke new ground by signing Katey Red, a transvestite rapper who called himself (herself) 'the Millennium Sissy'" (261).

22 My analysis is informed by Steven Gregory's *Black Corona* (1998), a book that significantly defines and rethinks "community" and collective political action. Exploring the political formation of black identities in New York, Gregory explains that "the social construction of identity or the 'fixing' of racialized, gendered, and other subject positions within a given social order is not only political, it is also the precondition of politics" (13). Gregory's counterhistory challenges the trope of the "black ghetto" and inner-city black communities as morally bankrupt and homogeneous.

23 *Sula* uses the counterintuitive to drive forward alternative notions of personal and communal vitality (Morrison 1973). This is most effectively represented in the various ways black women are narrated as physical and symbolic penetrators of black men. A bottom epistemology is a process of relearning and redressing what's generally considered *illegible* and *unproductive*. To touch, feel, and care for what's in and of the bottom goes against nationalist, racist, homophobic, classist, and misogynistic rhetoric—all of which share concerns about proximity to the dirty Other, imagined as an encounter that cannot be recovered from.

24 Musical performance is an honored form of cultural expression in New Orleans with a well-documented relationship to black radical resistance (Roach 1996; Sakakeeny 2024; Sublette 2008, 2009). This is exemplified in performances of the Black Masking Indians, second-line bands, and

25   others (Blank 1978; Hair 1976; Mugge 2007; Regis 2006). Performance brings the body, the discourse of place, and community together.

25   In *The Shock Doctrine* (2007), Naomi Klein situates the response to Katrina within a critique of neoliberalism and disaster capitalism. In *Development Drowned and Reborn* (2017), Woods counters Klein's framework, arguing that the history of New Orleans and the region reveals practices of economic violence that precede the development of neoliberal ideology and are better explained through a critique of plantocracy. We must consider how both colonial structures and more contemporary economic trends have led to housing segregation and gentrification over time.

26   Chapter 3 will discuss how property values and residential segregation have followed patterns of subsidence.

27   This bottom sensibility is not unique, but part of a network of minoritarian cultural expressions spread across racial, ethnic, and queer diasporas. In Chicano and Latino vernacular, for instance, the bottom relates to concepts of *rasquachismo* and *sucio*. Chicano scholar Tomás Ybarra-Frausto defines the former as "a visceral response to lived reality," "a working-class sensibility," and "an underdog perspective"—a view from *los de abajo*. An attitude rooted in resourcefulness and adaptability yet mindful of stance and style." He further elaborates: "*Rasquachismo* presupposes the world view of the have-not, but is also a quality exemplified in objects and places (a *rasquache* car or restaurant) and in social comportment (a person can be or act *rasquache*)" (1989). Capitalism creates surplus populations of have-nots who carry with them the trace of *los de abajo*—the ones from below, the uninhabitable, sites that merge bodies with the dirty (*sucio*). Deborah R. Vargas writes, "Queer surplus tastes and smells *sucio* and cultivates a presence and lingering perseverance of queer sex and joy within neoliberal hetero- and homonormative violences. By extension, the queer surplus of *sucias*—dirty and filthy nonnormative genders—demonstrate capital's contradictions" (2014, 1).

28   In "Why Katrina's Victims Aren't Refugees," Adeline Masquelier discusses debates over the use of the word. "Many U.S.-born citizens have never experienced invasion by an alien power," she writes, "and to them 'refugeeness' essentially connotes 'otherness'" (2006, 738).

CHAPTER 1. *CATCH DAT BEAT*

Acknowledgments: Parts of the section "*Catch Dat Beat*" appeared in a different form as "The Punk Show: Queering Heritage in the Black Diaspora," *Cultural Dynamics* 26 (3): 327–45; parts of "Kinship, Care, and Renewal" appeared in "Katrina Babies: Reproducing Deviance in the

Future Unknown," in *Navigating Souths: Transdisciplinary Explorations of a US Region*, edited by Michele Grigsby Coffey and Jodi Skipper (University of Georgia Press, 2017); parts of chapter 1 on performance and the stage appeared in "Passing the Mic: Black/Queer/Femme Poetics in New Orleans Bounce Music," *Women & Performance: A Journal of Feminist Theory* (Oct. 12, 2025): 1–16.

1. These unofficial, vernacular performances are a useful means of critiquing engagement by black queer people with prescribed notions of belonging. As E. Patrick Johnson (1998) discusses, performance is used to contest scripts about belonging within the home, the church, the "club," and the "street."

2. This dilemma is taken up by Toni Morrison in her book *Playing in the Dark: Whiteness and the Literary Imagination* (1992). She argues that a "dramatic polarity" is created by skin color, wherein white narratives reify blackness as the Other, or "not-me" (38).

3. In *Beautiful Bottom, Beautiful Shame* (2006), Kathryn Bond Stockton points out that the black men of *Sula*'s Bottom are unable to experience the polarization of sexual divisions of labor—the economic basement—because of difficulties gaining employment at all. This is partly true—Jude, for example, works as a server but hopes to gain a masculinized position as a laborer, escaping the feminized servility of waiting tables. This resonates with the political economy of New Orleans: the service economy overdetermines most forms of labor while depending on black culture and performance.

4. Martin F. Manalansan uses the concept of "cultural citizenship" to discuss how gay men of the Filipino diaspora navigate questions of belonging and place as they move through the world. He writes that cultural citizenship "is constituted by unofficial or vernacular scripts that promote seemingly disparate views of membership within a political and cultural body or community. Citizenship requires more than the assumptions of rights and duties; more importantly, it also requires the performance and contestation of the behavior, ideas, and images of the proper citizen" (2003, 14).

5. In *Times Square Red, Times Square Blue*, black gay scholar Samuel Delany discusses two modes of social relations: contact and networking. Contact happens when diverse cross sections of people are "thrown together in public spaces through chance and propinquity" (1999, 128). Unstructured and unplanned, contact can happen across class, race, and other forms of difference. Networking, on the other hand, is usually more formal or planned; it tends to happen within institutional contexts, between homogeneous groups. Networking and contact aren't binary oppositions, but differences of scale, high and low; all networking begins in moments of contact, but not all

	moments of contact become networks. Legacy's circumstances of rescue—involving the help of strangers within the public sphere—are excellent examples of points of contact as forms of social reproduction and regeneration. As Delany points out, "More ordinary sorts of contact yield their payoff in moments of crisis" (125).
6	Legacy's story parallels experiences documented in *What Lies Beneath: Katrina, Race, and the State of the Nation* (South End Press Collective 2007). In one report, Sharlie Arpollo Vicks, a transgender woman, survived Hurricane Katrina; upon finding shelter in Houston, she was separated from her family and arrested and jailed for using the women's shower at a detention center (Carter 2007, 58).
7	Documenting illicit sexual economies in New York's Times Square on the cusp of corporate gentrification, Delany notes that encounters in those contexts "were encounters whose most important aspect was that mutual pleasure was exchanged—an aspect that, yes, colored all their other aspects, but that did not involve any sort of life commitment . . . what greater field and force than pleasure can human beings share?" (1999, 56).

CHAPTER 2. GET IT HOW YOU LIVE

1	Even Morrison draws from this history. In *Sula*, the origin story of Nel and her mother, Helene Wright, links New Orleans to a sexual economy with unusual customs. Helene is born of a Creole sex worker in the Sundown house, a red-lit brothel she spends her life getting far away from. Nel is defined by the double binds of her mother's heteronormative respectability and her grandmother Rochelle's nonnormativity. Rochelle—sensual, exotic, ethnically different, and perhaps a gold digger (as inferred from her interest in her estranged dead mother's home)—is narrated as a painted canary, smelling of gardenias, with an earthy animalism that suggests her bottom proximity in contrast to Helene's high morals and habits.
2	Redbone's hypocrisy can be found in the contradiction of being a nonnormative subject who leverages desire—in this case, the exclusionary "masc for masc," "no fats, no femmes" standard—while also maintaining enough normative masculinity to still "belong." This was no surprise to me; narratives of black freedom and uplift are often tied to the performance of a successful masculinity (Scott 2010), and appropriate and fit masculinity is still often defined against the shadow of the sissy (Ross 2021).
3	This escape is a matter of effacing the bottom—not only geographic bottom locations, but also what Stockton calls "another locale, a place one can visit, even with others . . . the body's own bottom" (2006, 71).

4   "Even the whores were better then"—thus Morrison qualifies the erotic autonomy of sex workers in the neighborhood of the Bottom who are replaced and erased by black people's efforts at assimilating into dominant culture (1973, 164). Prostitution and queerness share a similar sexual history in their resistance to black heteronormativity and nationalism. In "This Immoral Practice," Martin Summers writes, "Homophobia in black nationalist thought has performed a similar function as homophobia within ultranationalist and fascist movements throughout the twentieth century. . . . Homophobic ideologies within nationalism are intimately connected to its patriarchal underpinnings" (2003, 22). Summers's analysis of homophobia, patriarchy, and heteronormativity in black liberationist thought dovetails with M. Jacqui Alexander's arguments in "Not Just (Any) Body Can Be a Citizen" (1994). Alexander, like Summers, points to the homosexual and the prostitute as the embodiment of erotic autonomy. They are sexual outlaws who cross structural and symbolic boundaries.

5   Black feminist scholar Joy James states that not everyone can normalize themselves toward these notions of success and winning, nor should they have to: "The normalization process is itself constricted and disciplined by the imaginary of the norm—the white, male, propertied heterosexual. . . . One must recognize that some bodies cannot be normalized no matter how they are disciplined, unless the prevailing social and state structures that figuratively and literally rank bodies disintegrate" (1996, 28).

6   I'm borrowing feminist scholar Marilyn Frye's framing from her essay "Oppression." "The root of the word 'oppression' is the element 'press,'" Frye writes. "Something pressed is something caught between or among forces and barriers which are so related to each other that jointly they restrain, restrict, or prevent the thing's motion or mobility. Mold. Immobilize. Reduce" (2000, 1).

7   In *The Dozens: A History of Rap's Mama* (2012), music journalist Elijah Wald discusses this game of banter as a poetic form of African American wordplay that is a primary source of modern rap.

8   This narrative is couched in the Reagan era's response to HIV/AIDS, which framed the issue as a matter of moral deficit and lack of conformity to the nuclear family model. In *The Boundaries of Blackness: AIDS and the Breakdown of Black Politics* (1999), political scientist Cathy J. Cohen discusses how a black middle class, emerging in the 1970s, was defined against nonheteronormative subjects like queers and HIV-positive people while also filling a regulatory position as an unofficial arm of the state. This script is also an extension of preexisting black matriarchy discourses, which *Sula* (1973) engages through Morrison's focus on the Peace family, a household led by three generations of black women who are all suspect for their lack of conformity.

9   Marlon Bailey's (2009) research on house and ballroom culture's relationship to community-based HIV/AIDS awareness and prevention highlights tensions between outside "interventions" and effective alternative strategies created by community members themselves—what he calls "intraventions."

10   In his essay "Is the Rectum a Grave?" (1987, 212), Leo Bersani speaks to this way of thinking, explaining that gay men and women are assumed to "abdicate power" through the feminized sexual passivity that's associated with anal penetration.

11   As Jennifer Nash explains, "Two representational modes through which blackness and anality become tethered [are] the production of anal space as analogous to ghetto space, and the representation of black sex as wasteful" (2014, 443).

12   In *Sounding Like a No-No*, Francesca T. Royster discusses the influence of black musicians like Stevie Wonder on children of color in the 1970s and '80s, via programs like *Sesame Street*. These musical performances, she states, "served as a way of unlearning the bodily lessons of assimilation into a white culture" (2012, 61–62).

13   This issue is taken up in Dwight McBride's 1998 piece "Can the Queen Speak?" He discusses the ways black intellectuals essentialize notions of racial authenticity in the name of moral and representational authority that deprives the subaltern, or "the queens," of their right to speak. The events I observed have led me to ask, Does the queen *want* to speak?

14   The desire or need to essentialize subjects' racial and sexual consciousness to fulfill positivist and empirical notions of scholarly evidence and political argument is also taken up by Cathy J. Cohen (2004) in her critique of Robin D. J. Kelley and Jim Scott. Does black studies essentialize, qualify, and represent black consciousness and political possibilities because of a concern and focus on blackness as a wellspring of knowledge and information or an implicit preoccupation with critical investigation of Western society and its institutions?

15   In the fourth chapter of *Aberrations in Black* (2004, 110–37), Roderick Ferguson highlights the ways Toni Morrison challenged these pathologizing black matriarchy discourses; he also details how black lesbian feminists of the 1970s were inspired by her alternative vision of black life and family.

CHAPTER 3. BACK OF TOWN

Acknowledgment: Parts of chapter 3 appeared in "Passing the Mic: Black/Queer/Femme Poetics in New Orleans Bounce Music," *Women & Performance: A Journal of Feminist Theory* (Oct. 12, 2025): 1–16.

1. These and other black women in bounce—some of whom still perform—all deserve further study and listening.
2. The low-lying geography of this bottom is reversed in Morrison's fictional Bottom, which is ironically located up in the hills. While the two places are different in topography, they're similar demographically: Both are less habitable sites of racial and classed segregation, in contrast to predominantly white neighborhoods.
3. European travel writers depicted even the famous Congo Square, despite its status as a major site of African diasporic autonomy in the New World, as essentially a "ghetto" at the time (Sublette 2008). It's essential to consider these past inequalities alongside modern-day political and economic reconstruction in relation to cultural production. There is an intimate relationship between gentrification and black cultural performances such as bounce.
4. Here, I elaborate on black feminist scholar Katherine McKittrick's work in *Demonic Grounds: Black Women and the Cartographies of Struggle* (2006). Outlining the poetics of landscape in Édouard Glissant's work, McKittrick points out how "geographic expression, specifically, saying, theorizing, feeling, knowing, writing, and imagining space and place," can be used to map black struggles throughout the diaspora and through time (xxi).
5. Morrison informs McKittrick's and my own interest in questioning "how places and spaces of blackness can be recovered when they were formerly identified as irrelevant and/or non-existent" (McKittrick 2006, 32).
6. As McKittrick writes, "Naming place is also an act of naming the self and self-histories" (2006, xxii). Black women's poetics, she explains, counter dominant geographies; they "expose the racial-sexual functions of the production of space and establish new ways to read (and perhaps live) geography" (143). Written and unwritten, a poetics of landscape privileges the ways language can help us narrate place and space in ways that improve our lives and give us agency and power. Traditional geographies, on the other hand, assume that places and spaces are tangible and self-evident, which creates access (such as in the original development of public housing projects, and more recent attempts to decentralize poverty) while obscuring how these spaces rely on white, patriarchal, heterosexual, and classed vantage points.
7. Raymond Williams's 1977 work *Marxism and Literature* speaks to the continuous function of cultural expressions like these; while they are fixed forms, they're also reanimated through the viewer's interpretations. They do not simply exist; they also act on readers of text, who then go on to express what's been perceived.
8. The US Department of Housing and Urban Development decided to reduce the number of public housing units in 2006, and in 2007, New

Orleans's city council approved the demolition of four housing developments totaling approximately 4,500 units. State officials and private contractors razed or remodeled most of the city's major public housing complexes, replacing them with "mixed-income" developments (Luft 2006). In the mass displacement that occurred in the wake of Hurricane Katrina (throughout Louisiana and in adjacent states), many were able to rely on their own wealth, family, and churches to secure support. People without access to such resources had to fall back on social services to mitigate the loss of kin and regular social networks eroded by the erasure of the safety net. When public housing recipients face neoliberal privatization of public services, their life chances are greatly affected by the whims of capital rather than human need.

9   Even in multiethnic and queer neighborhoods, these beliefs and practices persist, informed by neoliberal notions of community where identity follows practices of consumption while privileging "difference" within private domesticity (rather than public life).

10 The expansion of the gig economy and Airbnb led to legal battles throughout the mid-2010s. Tourists and recent transplants, often from more rural and suburban cities, demanded that noise ordinances be changed so they could enjoy staying in urban neighborhoods with mixed commercial and residential spaces. Cultural norms like public parading and procession impeded touristic commodification of space.

11 In "*État de Siège*: A Dying Domesticating Colonialism?" Ghassan Hage expands Frantz Fanon's critique of settler colonialism to consider a "dying domestication," which he describes as "the final stages of an equally colonial mode of instrumentalizing, dominating, and exploiting the natural world, as well as differentiating oneself from it" (2016, 38). I consider the ways racial-sexual difference has been constructed as "dirty" and seen as a threat to domesticity.

12 In *Cities of the Dead* (1996), Joseph Roach provides a thorough account of Latrobe's time in New Orleans while discussing black performance as a memory-making practice.

13 Certain predominantly white low-lying adjacent communities in Saint Bernard Parish (such as Arabi and Chalmette) have similar ecological conditions that have also led to repeated evacuations—but those regions' brick homes, alongside other socioeconomic factors, have allowed their white residents to return and remain.

14 Fred Moten references the work of Saidiya Hartman (1997) to discuss this crossroads in terms of a cut, or a break. He describes Hartman's exploration of the "massive discourse of the cut, of rememberment and redress, that we always hear in narratives where blackness marks simultaneously both the performance of the object and the performance of humanity" (Moten 2003, 1–2).

15   Here I'm speaking to characters like Jude Greene and BoyBoy Peace (Nel Wright and Eva Peace's husbands). Jude abandons Nel while BoyBoy and Eva are estranged. Neither man wants to commit to family or life in the Bottom. World War I soldiers and veterans Plum Peace and Shadrack, similarly, live in pain and despair. By contrast, there's a pleasurable *oneness* in Nel and Sula's girlhood bond, and in the experiences of the Deweys, Eva's three adopted children. This oneness—characterized by Sula's deathbed observation that "we were two throats and one eye and we had no price" (147)—might be understood as the power of collectivism over the individual ego.

CHAPTER 4. TOUCHING THE RIM

1   In *Sula*, the Bottom is not a homogenously black neighborhood. Not unlike the geographic bottom in chapter 3, it's also a diverse space where various forms of white difference that conflict with white domesticity are segregated. Morrison conveys this through the character of Tar Baby—a "mountain boy" and alcoholic looking for someplace to die, "not quite alone"—and in a brief reference to Irish immigrants who are also alienated by the white Protestant community of Medallion (but still see themselves as better than their black neighbors). These figures are presented as nonnormative; their inability to assimilate leads them to the Bottom.

2   Carla Kaplan's *Miss Anne in Harlem: The White Women of the Black Renaissance* (2013) describes the pattern of white women crossing racial lines, defying social conventions, and breaking taboos to participate in the Harlem Renaissance. Similarly, Ann Powers's *Good Booty: Love and Sex, Black and White, Body and Soul in American Music* (2017) discusses how gospel quartets destabilized the color line in post–World War II Memphis when white teens began attending black churches, sometimes on dates, because it was the "groovy" and "in" thing to do. The text also describes Elvis sneaking away from his home church to perform in historically black congregations, noting that he and other early white rock icons were musically influenced by their illicit proximity to blackness.

3   In "Katrina Babies: Reproducing Deviance in the Future Unknown" (2017), I discuss Hurricane Katrina's mass displacement of black communities, and the fact that the return and growth of white heteronormative nuclear families in New Orleans was taken as a sign of hope and rebirth. I counter that such framings marginalize forms of social, rather than biological, reproduction that are key to black and queer kinship and futurity.

4   In her book *Queer Phenomenology* (2006), Sarah Ahmed describes the sense of disorientation as closely related to the process of racialization. Racism reduces the black body to an object among objects in the environment. The black body is not erased as much as the white body extends itself through space—the space of the environment and its objects (including objectified black bodies). This white self-extension is in part determined by a history in which whiteness is scripted as the inheritor of the sociopolitical landscape. In proximity to whiteness, we're made to remember this relationship and are "put in our place": no longer subjects oriented by surrounding objects, but other objects whose conscious selves are reduced.

5   Matt Miller's *Bounce: Rap Music and Local Identity in New Orleans* (2012) explains that record labels from outside New Orleans had attempted to work with and sign artists but found the cultural threshold (and the threat of violence in a city known for high murder rates) too formidable a barrier.

6   See, for example, "Sissy Bounce Rap from New Orleans" (Fensterstock 2012).

7   In "Setting the Historical Stage: Colonial Legacies," the authors share legal scholar Dorothy Roberts's observation that "even before the African slave trade began, Europeans explained the need to control Africans by mythologizing the voracious 'sexual appetites' of Blacks" (Mogul et al. 2011, 6). These myths of aggressive and "deviant" (i.e., queer) black sexualities formed a common sense that served as an excuse for the slave trade and settler colonialism.

8   In "Punks, Bulldaggers, and Welfare Queens" (2005), Cathy J. Cohen shows how queer identity movements (and, I would argue, other forms of so-called progressive movements) have the potential to limit transformative action addressing the political needs of groups marginalized by class and race. Without a radical critique, queer political claims (such as the fight for gay marriage or inclusion in the military) cannot account for the racial consciousness of nonwhite people (within and outside a movement) who are "always and already" queer in that they are racially nonnormative. This leads us to Cohen's call for a politics of transformation: "In using the term 'transformational,'" she writes, "I mean a politics that does not search for opportunities to integrate into dominant institutions and normative social relationships but instead pursues a political agenda that seeks to change values, definition, and laws that make these institutions and relationships oppressive" (29).

9   Black women and queer people weren't the only people bending over and dancing to bounce music, and this is particularly interesting given the overlapping visibility and cultural resonance of bounce and HIV/AIDS. Nationally, the 1990s saw an erasure of androgynous expres-

sions of black masculinity—as had been popular in the funk and disco work of musicians like Rick James, Parliament-Funkadelic, Prince, and the Time—in favor of a more militant hip-hop masculinity. Although no one would deny the violence and gangster culture of 1990s New Orleans, I believe a persistent investment in locality, the carnivalesque, and the effacement of certain national trends facilitated an attachment to residual interpretations of black masculinity.

10   *Where They At: A Multi-Media Archive of New Orleans Bounce*, curated by Aubrey Edwards and Alison Fensterstock, included photos, oral histories, and video documenting the history of the genre. It toured in the winter and spring of 2010.

11   Big Freedia, more than any other artist, was associated with sissy bounce, and rightly so. Many listeners have taken issue with Beyoncé's decision to use Big Freedia's samples but not visually feature the artist. Despite Big Freedia's absence, however, I believe the "Formation" video uses her vocal presence to make a statement about what is actually visible onscreen.

12   In "Compliance Is Gendered" (2006), Dean Spade reveals how systems of surveillance and discipline attempt to regulate the sexual and gendered practices of low-income women who rely on public welfare programs for their autonomy and survival. Spade writes that public relief systems operate "through moralistic understandings of sexuality and family structure to force recipients into compliance with sexist and heterosexist notions of womanhood and motherhood" (218). The media's treatment of Freedia employed stereotypes that have followed black women; her troubles with the system also prove that social welfare reform is very much a queer issue. As Spade states, "The purpose and result of vilifying welfare recipients and focusing on sexual morality and gender role transgression is the creation of coercive policies designed to force poor people to obey rigid gender and family norms" (223).

CHAPTER 5. RAISING THE BOTTOM

1   This chapter owes much to E. Patrick Johnson's 1998 essay "Feeling the Spirit in the Dark," and Jafari Sinclaire Allen's 2009 piece "For 'the Children' Dancing the Beloved Community." Both scholars explore the black queer club and house music as sites of alternative sacred fellowship, where the body and soul find union.

2   As sexologist and black funk studies scholar Herukhuti has shared, analysis and deconstruction are only part of the work of decolonization, since those practices are often dissatisfying on their own (2016). He

calls for an epistemological blueprint that synthesizes various Afrocentric aesthetics while disrupting respectability politics, even within the field of black queer studies.

3   In *Dancing in the Streets*, historian and activist Barbara Ehrenreich writes, "Durkheim's notion of collective effervescence and [anthropologist Victor] Turner's idea of communitas each reach, in their own ways, toward some conception of love that serves to knit people together in groups larger than two. But if homosexual attraction is the love 'that dares not speak its name,' the love that binds people to the collective has no name at all to speak" (2007, 14).

4   Exploring the sacred capacities of these dances, Pérez references Judene Antoinette Small's 2012 take on Jamaican dancehall, a cultural form Small describes as "the contemporary reenactment or resurgence of traditional West African trance practice." She explains that the music and dance of dancehall merge the sacred and secular "through trance and catharsis . . . which create an individual and collective release that empowers the people of the garrisons [politically controlled urban neighborhoods in Jamaica]" (4–5).

REFERENCES

Abu-Lughod, Lila. 1988. "Fieldwork of a Dutiful Daughter." In *Arab Women in the Field: Studying Your Own Society*, edited by Soraya Altorki and Camilla Fawzi El-Solh. Syracuse University Press.

Abu-Lughod, Lila. 1991. "Writing Against Culture." In *Recapturing Anthropology: Working in the Present*, edited by Richard G. Fox. School of American Research Press.

Adams, Thomas Jessen, and Matt Sakakeeny, eds. 2019. *Remaking New Orleans: Beyond Exceptionalism and Authenticity*. Duke University Press.

Adams, Vincanne. 2019. "Neoliberal Futures: Post-Katrina New Orleans, Volunteers, and the Ongoing Allure of Exceptionalism." In Adams and Sakakeeny, *Remaking New Orleans*.

Agid, Shana. 2007. "Locked and Loaded: The Prison Industrial Complex and the Response to Hurricane Katrina." In *Through the Eye of Katrina: Social Justice in the United States*, edited by Kristin A. Bates and Richelle S. Swan. Carolina Academic Press.

Ahmed, Sara. 2006. *Queer Phenomenology: Orientations, Objects, Others*. Duke University Press.

Alexander, M. Jacqui. 1994. "Not Just (Any) Body Can Be a Citizen: The Politics of Law, Sexuality and Postcoloniality in Trinidad and Tobago and the Bahamas." *Feminist Review* 48:5–23.

Allen, Jafari Sinclaire. 2003. "Counterpoints: Black Masculinities, Sexuality, and Self-Making in Contemporary Cuba." PhD diss., Columbia University.

Allen, Jafari Sinclaire. 2009. "For 'the Children' Dancing the Beloved Community." *Souls* 11 (3): 311–26.

Allen, Jafari Sinclaire. 2011. *¡Venceremos? Sexuality, Gender and Black Self-Making in Cuba*. Duke University Press.

Ambrosino, Rosalie, Joseph Heffernan, Guy Shuttlesworth, and Robert Ambrosino. 2007. *Social Work and Social Welfare: An Introduction*. Brooks/Cole.

Anderson, Rhome. 2011. "Big Freedia's Bounce Explosion at DC9." *Washington Post*, May 25. https://www.washingtonpost.com/lifestyle/style/big-freedias-bounce-explosion-at-dc9/2011/05/25/AGovxTBH_story.html.

Ankeny, Jason. n.d. "Bobby Marchan Biography." *AllMusic*. Accessed July 11, 2025. https://www.allmusic.com/artist/bobby-marchan-mn0000085445#biography.

Anthony, Arthé Agnes. 1978. "The Negro Creole Community in New Orleans, 1880–1920: An Oral History." PhD diss., University of California, Irvine.

Austin, J. L. 1975. *How to Do Things with Words*. 2nd ed. Harvard University Press.

Bailey, Marlon. 2005. *The Labor of Diaspora: Ballroom Culture and the Making of a Black Queer Community*. University of California Press.

Bailey, Marlon. 2009. "Performance as Intravention: Ballroom Culture and the Politics of HIV/AIDS in Detroit." *Souls* 11 (3): 253–74.

Bailey, Marlon. 2013. *Butch Queens Up in Pumps: Gender, Performance, and Ballroom Culture in Detroit*. University of Michigan Press.

Berk, Brett. 2010. "New Orleans Sissy Bounce: Rap Goes Drag." *Vanity Fair*, March 11. https://www.vanityfair.com/culture/2010/03/katey-red-starts-a-band.

Berlant, Lauren. 1997. *The Queen of America Goes to Washington City*. Duke University Press.

Berlant, Lauren. 2011. *Cruel Optimism*. Duke University Press.

Bernard, H. R. 2002. *Research Methods in Anthropology: Qualitative and Quantitative Approaches*. Sage.

Bersani, Leo. 1987. "Is the Rectum a Grave?" *October* 43:197–222.

Bertaux, Daniel, ed. 1981. *Biography and Society: The Life History Approach in the Social Sciences*. Sage.

Bhabha, Homi. 2005. *The Location of Culture*. Routledge.

Blank, Les, dir. 1978. *Always for Pleasure*. DVD. Flowers Films.

Blassingame, John W. 1973. *Black New Orleans, 1860–1880*. University of Chicago Press.

Bolton, Ralph. 2005. "Tricks, Friends and Lovers: Erotic Encounters in the Field." In *Taboo: Sex, Identity and Erotic Subjectivity in Anthropological Fieldwork*, edited by Don Kulick and Margaret Willson. Routledge.

Brand, Anna Livia, and Vern Baxter. 2020. "Post-Disaster Development Dilemmas: Advancing Landscapes of Social Justice in a Neoliberal Post-Disaster." In *Louisiana's Response to Extreme Weather: A Coastal State's Adaptation Challenges and Successes*, edited by Shirley Laska. Springer.

Bullington, Jonathan. 2016. "Woman Dies after Being Struck by Car on Loyola Avenue." *Times-Picayune*, October 14. https://www.nola.com/news/crime_police/woman-dies-after-being-struck-by-car-on-loyola-avenue/article_c693b759-c584-58fe-be4b-80e25bc331d2.html.

Butler, Judith. 2004. *Undoing Gender*. Routledge.

Campanella, Richard. 2018. "How Humans Sank New Orleans." *Atlantic*, February 6. https://www.theatlantic.com/technology/archive/2018/02/how-humans-sank-new-orleans/552323/.

Carter, Mandy. 2007. "Southerners on New Ground." In *What Lies Beneath: Katrina, Race, and the State of the Nation*, edited by the South End Press Collective. South End Press.

Casselman, Ben. 2015. "Katrina Washed Away New Orleans's Black Middle Class." *FiveThirtyEight*, August 24. https://fivethirtyeight.com/features/katrina-washed-away-new-orleanss-black-middle-class/.

Certeau, Michel de. 1994. *The Practice of Everyday Life*. Translated by Steven Rendall. University of California Press.

Chapman, Alix. 2014. "The Punk Show: Queering Heritage in the Black Diaspora." *Cultural Dynamics* 26 (3): 327–45.

Chapman, Alix. 2017. "Katrina Babies: Reproducing Deviance in the Future Unknown." In *Navigating Souths: Transdisciplinary Explorations of a U.S. Region*, edited by Michele Grigsby Coffey and Jodi Skipper. University of Georgia Press.

Chapman, Alix. 2025. "Passing the Mic: Black/Queer/Femme Poetics in New Orleans Bounce Music." *Women & Performance: A Journal of Feminist Theory* (Oct. 12, 2025): 1–16.https://doi.org/10.1080/0740770X.2025.2563131.

Che, Deborah. 2009. "Techno: Music and Entrepreneurship in Post-Fordist Detroit." In *Sound, Society and the Geography of Popular Music*, edited by Ola Johannson and Thomas L. Bell. Routledge.

Cheng, William. 2018. "Black Noise, White Ears: Resilience, Rap, and the Killing of Jordan Davis." *Current Musicology*, no. 102. https://doi.org/10.7916/cm.v0i102.5367.

Christian, Barbara. 1987. "The Race for Theory." In *Within the Circle: An Anthology of African American Literary Criticism from the Harlem Renaissance to the Present*, edited by Angelyn Mitchell. Duke University Press.

Coffey, Michele Grigsby, and Jodi Skipper, eds. 2017. *Navigating Souths: Transdisciplinary Explorations of a U.S. Region*. University of Georgia Press.

Cohen, Cathy J. 1999. *The Boundaries of Blackness: AIDS and the Breakdown of Black Politics*. University of Chicago Press.

Cohen, Cathy J. 2004. "Deviance as Resistance: A New Research Agenda for the Study of Black Politics." *Du Bois Review* 1 (1): 27–45.

Cohen, Cathy J. 2005. "Punks, Bulldaggers, and Welfare Queens: The Real Radical Potential of 'Queer' Politics." In Johnson and Henderson, *Black Queer Studies*.

Cole, Johnnetta Betsch, and Beverly Guy-Sheftall. 2003. *Gender Talk: The Struggle for Women's Equality in African American Communities*. One World.

Colten, Craig E. 2005. *An Unnatural Metropolis: Wrestling New Orleans from Nature*. Louisiana State University Press.

Combahee River Collective. 1983. "A Black Feminist Statement." In *Home Girls: A Black Feminist Anthology*, edited by Barbara Smith. Women of Color Press.

Conquergood, Dwight. 1991. "Rethinking Ethnography: Towards a Critical Cultural Politics." *Communication Monographs* 58 (2): 179–94.

Cvetkovich, Ann. 2003. *An Archive of Feelings: Trauma, Sexuality, and Lesbian Public Cultures*. Duke University Press.

Davis, Angela Y. 1998. *Blues Legacies and Black Feminism*. Random House.

Davis, Ujijji. 2018. "The Bottom: The Emergence and Erasure of Black American Urban Landscapes." *Avery Review* 34: 1–7.

Dean, Tim. 2009. *Unlimited Intimacy: Reflections on the Subculture of Barebacking*. University of Chicago Press.

Dee, Jonathan. 2010. "New Orleans's Gender-Bending Rap." *New York Times Magazine*, July 22. https://www.nytimes.com/2010/07/25/magazine/25bounce-t.html.

Delany, Samuel. 1999. *Times Square Red, Times Square Blue*. NYU Press.

Demby, Gene. 2013. "About This Miley Cyrus Business . . ." *Code Switch* (NPR), August 29. https://www.npr.org/sections/codeswitch/2013/08/29/216899758/about-this-miley-cyrus-business.

Dessens, Nathalie. 2007. *From Saint-Domingue to New Orleans: Migration and Influences*. University Press of Florida.

Dupont, Robert L. 2004. "New Orleans: The Case for Urban Exceptionalism." *Journal of Urban History* 30 (6): 881–93.

Durkheim, Emile. (1912) 2016. "The Elementary Forms of Religious Life." In *Social Theory Re-Wired: New Connections to Classical and Contemporary Perspectives*, edited by Wesley Longhofer and Daniel Winchester. Routledge.

Dyson, Michael Eric. 2001. "When You Divide Body and Soul, Problems Multiply: The Black Church and Sex." In *Traps: African American Men on Gender and Sexuality*, edited by Rudolph P. Byrd and Beverly Guy-Sheftall. Indiana University Press.

Ehrenreich, Barbara. 2007. *Dancing in the Streets: A History of Collective Joy*. Palgrave Macmillan.

Erlmann, Veit. (2004) 2020. "But What of the Ethnographic Ear? Anthropology, Sound, and the Senses." In *Hearing Cultures: Essays on Sound, Listening and Modernity*, edited by Veit Erlmann. Routledge.

Ermac, Raffy. 2015. "Fire Destroys Famed LGBT Hotspot in New Orleans." *Out Traveler*, September 21. https://www.outtraveler.com/destination-guide/new-orleans/2015/09/01/watch-fire-destroys-club-fusions-famed-lgbt-hotspot-new-orl.

Evans, Scott. 2022. "Big Freedia Shares Details on Working with Beyoncé on 'Break My Soul.'" Interview with Big Freedia for *Access Hollywood*. YouTube, June 21. https://youtu.be/8e6Ro7ly584&t=197s.

Fensterstock, Alison. 2012. "Sissy Bounce Rap from New Orleans." *Norient*, December 1. Last updated April 10, 2024. https://norient.com/stories/sissybounce.

Fensterstock, Alison. 2013. "Did Miley Cyrus Learn to Twerk in New Orleans? Cheeky Blakk, Other Locals, Weigh In." *Times-Picayune*, August 28. https://www.nola.com/entertainment_life/music/did-miley-cyrus-learn-to-twerk-in-new-orleans-cheeky-blakk-other-locals-weigh-in/article_ecf851aa-7109-5ddd-92c8-128b73ca5b4e.html.

Ferguson, Roderick A. 2004. *Aberrations in Black: Toward a Queer of Color Critique*. University of Minnesota Press.

Ferguson, Roderick A. 2005. "Race-ing Homonormativity, Citizenship, Sociology, and Gay Identity." In Johnson and Henderson, *Black Queer Studies*.

Ferguson, Roderick A. 2007. "Sissies at the Picnic: The Subjugated Knowledges of a Black Rural Queer." In *Feminist Waves, Feminist Generations: Life Stories from the Academy*, edited by Hokulani K. Aikau, Karla A. Erickson, and Jennifer L. Pierce. University of Minnesota Press.

Flaherty, Jordan. 2008. "New Orleans' Culture of Resistance." In *What Is a City? Rethinking the Urban After Hurricane Katrina*, edited by Phil Steinberg and Rob Shields. University of Georgia Press.

Flaherty, Jordan. 2009. "Culture Beat: A New Play Celebrates Bounce Music and New Orleans' Culture." *Facing South*, May 29.

Foucault, Michel. 1980. *An Introduction*. Vol 1 of *The History of Sexuality*. Translated by Robert Hurley. Vintage.

Freeman, Elizabeth. 2010. *Queer Temporalities, Queer Histories*. Duke University Press.

French-Marcelin, Megan. 2019. "Boosting the Private Sector: Federal Aid and Downtown Development in the 1970s." In Adams and Sakakeeny, *Remaking New Orleans*.

Frye, Marilyn. 2000. "Oppression." In *Gender Basics: Feminist Perspectives on Women and Men*, edited by Anne Minas. Wadsworth.

Gautier, Ana María Ochoa. 2016. "Acoustic Multinaturalism, the Value of Nature, and the Nature of Music in Ecomusicology." *Boundary 2* 43 (1): 107–41.

Gladstone, David, and Jolie Préau. 2008. "Gentrification in Tourist Cities: Evidence from New Orleans Before and After Hurricane Katrina." *Housing Policy Debate* 19 (1): 137–75.

Glissant, Édouard. 1989. *Caribbean Discourse: Selected Essays*. Translated by J. Michael Dash. University of Virginia Press.

Gottschild, Brenda Dixon. 2003. *The Black Dancing Body: A Geography from Coon to Cool*. Palgrave Macmillan.

Gregory, Steven. 1998. *Black Corona: Race and the Politics of Place in an Urban Community*. Princeton University Press.

Grey, Stephanie Houston. 2008. "(Re) Imagining Ethnicity in the City of New Orleans: Katrina's Geographical Allegory." In *Seeking Higher Ground: The Hurricane Katrina Crisis, Race, and Public Policy Reader*, edited by Manning Marable and Kristen Clarke. Palgrave Macmillan.

Hage, Ghassan. 2016. "*État de Siège*: A Dying Domesticating Colonialism?" *American Ethnologist* 43 (1): 38–49.

Hair, William Ivy. 1976. *Carnival of Fury: Robert Charles and the New Orleans Race Riot of 1900*. Louisiana State University Press.

Halberstam, J. Jack. 2005. *In a Queer Time and Place: Transgender Bodies, Subcultural Lives*. NYU Press.

Hall, Gwendolyn Midlo. 1992. *Africans in Colonial Louisiana: The Development of Afro-Creole Culture in the Eighteenth Century*. Louisiana State University Press.

Hall, Stuart. 2005. "Whose Heritage? Un-Settling 'The Heritage,' Re-Imagining the Post-Nation." In *The Politics of Heritage: The Legacies of "Race,"* edited by Jo Littler and Roshi Naidoo. Routledge.

Hamburger, Jeff. 2016. "Update: Pedestrian Dies After Being Hit by Car in CBD." *WGNO*, October 13. https://wgno.com/news/local/pedestrian-struck-at-poydras-and-loyola-in-the-cbd/.

Hammonds, Evelynn. 1994. "Black (W)holes: The Geometry of Black Female Sexuality." *differences* 6, nos. 2–3 (Summer–Fall): 126–45.

Hanhardt, Christina B. 2013. *Safe Space: Gay Neighborhood History and the Politics of Violence*. Duke University Press.

Hansan, John E., and Robert Morris. 1999. *Welfare Reform, 1996–2000: Is There a Safety Net?* Auburn House.

Hartman, Saidiya. 1997. *Scenes of Subjection: Terror, Slavery, and Self-Making in Nineteenth-Century America*. Oxford University Press.

Herukhuti [Williams, H. Sharif]. 2007. *Conjuring Black Funk: Notes on Culture, Sexuality, and Spirituality, Volume 1*. Vintage Entity Press.

Herukhuti [Williams, H. Sharif]. 2016. "Introduction to Afrocentric Decolonizing Kweer Theory and Epistemology of the Erotic." *Journal of Black Sexuality and Relationships* 2 (4): 1–31.

Hill Collins, Patricia. 1990. *Black Feminist Thought: Knowledge, Consciousness, and the Politics of Empowerment*. HarperCollins Academic.

Hinson, Glenn. 2000. *Fire in My Bones: Transcendence and the Holy Spirit in African American Gospel*. University of Pennsylvania Press.

Holland, Sharon Patricia. 2000. *Raising the Dead: Readings of Death and (Black) Subjectivity*. Duke University Press.

James, Joy. 1996. *Resisting State Violence: Radicalism, Gender, and Race in U.S. Culture*. University of Minnesota Press.

Johnson, E. Patrick. 1998. "Feeling the Spirit in the Dark: Expanding Notions of the Sacred in the African American Gay Community," *Callaloo* 21 (2): 399–416.

Johnson, E. Patrick. 2001. "'Quare' Studies, or (Almost) Everything I Know About Queer Studies I Learned from my Grandmother." *Text and Performance Quarterly* 21 (1): 1–25.

Johnson, E. Patrick. 2008. *Sweet Tea: Black Gay Men of the South*. University of North Carolina Press.

Johnson, Lucky, dir. 2009. *Catch Dat Beat*. Performed at Walter L. Cohen High School Auditorium, New Orleans, June 5.

Kaplan, Carla. 2013. *Miss Anne in Harlem: The White Women of the Black Renaissance*. Harper.

Keeble, Arin. 2016. "Won't Bow: Don't Know How: *Treme*, New Orleans and American Exceptionalism." *European Journal of American Culture* 35 (1): 51–67.

Klein, Naomi. 2007. *The Shock Doctrine: The Rise of Disaster Capitalism*. Henry Holt.

Kondo, Dorinne. 1997. *About Face: Performing Race in Fashion and Theater*. Routledge.

Kpopstarz. 2013. "Big Freedia Slams Miley Cyrus for VMA Twerking Attempt." Last accessed June 15, 2020. https://www.kpopstarz.com/articles/39734/20130830/miley-cyrus-twerk-big-freedia.htm.

Lewis, Nathaniel. 2017. "Queer Social Reproduction: Co-opted, Hollowed Out, and Resilient." *Environment and Planning D: Society and Space* (October).

Lewis, Peirce F. 1976. *New Orleans: The Making of an Urban Landscape*. Ballinger.

Logsdon, Dawn, dir. 2008. *Faubourg Tremé: The Untold Story of Black New Orleans*. DVD. Serendipity Films.

Lorber, Judith. 2018. "The Social Construction of Gender." *Inequality in the 21st Century: A Reader*, edited by David B. Grusky and Jasmine Hill. Routledge.

Lorde, Audre. 1984. *Sister Outsider: Essays and Speeches*. Crossing Press.

Luft, Rachel E. 2006. "Catastrophe Charity and the Politics of Race: Racism and Antiracism in the Volunteer Flood of New Orleans." Paper presented at *Great Divides: Transgressing Boundaries*, the annual meeting of the American Sociological Association. Montreal, August 13.

Luft, Rachel E. 2009. "Beyond Disaster Exceptionalism: Social Movement Developments in New Orleans After Hurricane Katrina." *American Quarterly* 61 (3): 499–527.

Luft, Rachel E. 2016. "Racialized Disaster Patriarchy: An Intersectional Model for Understanding Disaster Ten Years After Hurricane Katrina." *Feminist Formations* 28 (2): 1–26.

Madison, D. Soyini. 2005. *Critical Ethnography: Method, Ethics, and Performance*. Sage.

Mailer, Norman. (1957) 1998. "The White Negro: Superficial Reflections on the Hipster." In *The Time of Our Time*. Random House.

Manalansan, Martin F., IV. 2003. *Global Divas: Filipino Gay Men in the Diaspora*. Duke University Press.

Manalansan, Martin F., IV. 2005. "Race, Violence, and Neoliberal Spatial Politics in the Global City." *Social Text* 23 (3–4): 84–85.

Masquelier, Adeline. 2006. "Why Katrina's Victims Aren't Refugees: Musings on a 'Dirty' Word." *American Anthropologist* 108 (4): 735–43.

McBride, Dwight A. 1998. "Can the Queen Speak? Racial Essentialism, Sexuality and the Problem of Authority." *Callaloo* 21 (2): 363–79.

McClaurin, Irma. 2001. *Black Feminist Anthropology: Theory, Politics, Praxis, and Poetics*. Rutgers University Press.

McDonnell, John. 2008. "Scene and Heard: Bounce and 'Sissy Rap.'" *Guardian*, September 29. https://www.theguardian.com/music/musicblog/2008/sep/29/sissy.rap.neworleans.bounce.

McGovern, Kyle. 2013. "Watch Big Freedia Set the World Record for Mass Twerking." *Spin*, September 25. https://www.spin.com/2013/09/big-freedia-world-twerk-record-most-people-twerking-simultaneously-video/.

McKittrick, Katherine. 2006. *Demonic Grounds: Black Women and the Cartographies of Struggle*. University of Minnesota Press.

Miller, Matt. 2012. *Bounce: Rap Music and Local Identity in New Orleans*. University of Massachusetts Press.

Miller, Matt, and Stephen Thomas, dirs. 2007. *Ya Heard Me?* DVD. AGH Media Group.

Minh-ha, Trinh T. 1989. *Woman, Native, Other: Writing Postcoloniality and Feminism*. Indiana University Press.

Mock, Brentin. 2016. "Why Big Freedia Shouldn't Do Jail Time over Housing Vouchers." *Bloomberg*, March 17. https://www.bloomberg.com/news/articles/2016-03-17/why-new-orleans-bounce-queen-big-freedia-shouldn-t-do-jail-time-over-housing-vouchers.

Mogul, Joey L., Andrea J. Ritchie, and Kay Whitlock. 2011. "Setting the Historical Stage: Colonial Legacies." In *Queer (In)Justice: The Criminalization of LGBT People in the United States*. Beacon Press.

Morrison, Toni. 1973. *Sula*. Plume.

Morrison, Toni. (1987) 2004. *Beloved*. Vintage.

Morrison, Toni. 1990. "The Site of Memory." In *Inventing the Truth: The Art and Craft of Memoir*, edited by William Zinsser. Houghton Mifflin.

Morrison, Toni. 1992. *Playing in the Dark: Whiteness and the Literary Imagination*. Harvard University Press.

Moten, Fred. 2003. *In the Break: The Aesthetics of the Black Radical Tradition*. University of Minnesota Press.

Moten, Fred. 2007. "Black Optimism / Black Operation." Unpublished paper on file with the author.

Moynihan, Daniel Patrick. 1965. *The Negro Family: The Case for National Action*. US Government Printing Office.

Mugge, Robert, dir. 2007. *New Orleans: Music in Exile*. DVD. Starz Home Entertainment.

Muñoz, José Esteban. 2009. *Cruising Utopia: The Then and There of Queer Futurity*. NYU Press.

Nash, Jennifer C. 2014. "Black Anality." *GLQ* 20 (4): 439–60.

New Orleans Jazz and Heritage Foundation. 2014. "4 Sync Up Keynote Interview: Slim Williams of Cash Money Records." YouTube, April 25. https://youtu.be/I57isbEis-U.

New York Daily News. 2013. "Big Freedia Twerks Her Way into the Guinness World Records." YouTube, September 25. https://www.youtube.com/watch?v=j6Q-MZTaV_o.

Nguyen, Tân Hoàng. 2014. *A View from the Bottom: Asian American Masculinity and Sexual Representation*. Duke University Press.

Nkiru, Jenn, dir. 2019. *Black to Techno*. Frieze/Iconoclast. YouTube, August 7. https://youtu.be/WqVq_QMH46E&.

Nyong'o, Tavia. 2005. "Punk'd Theory." *Social Text* 23 (3–4): 19–34.

Nyong'o, Tavia. 2009. *The Amalgamation Waltz: Race, Performance, and the Ruses of Memory*. University of Minnesota Press.

Omi, Michael, and Howard Winant. 1986. *Racial Formation in the United States: From the 1960s to the 1980s*. Routledge.

Patterson, Orlando. 1998. *Rituals of Blood: Consequences of Slavery in Two American Centuries*. Counterpoint.

Pérez, Elizabeth. 2016. "The Ontology of Twerk: From 'Sexy' Black Movement Style to Afro-Diasporic Sacred Dance." *African and Black Diaspora* 9 (1): 16–31.

Ponderosa Stomp Foundation. 2011. "Booty Green: Reflections on Bobby Marchan." Presentation by Alison Fensterstock, Henry "Palomino" Alexander, "Wild Wayne" Benjamin, and Gerri Hall. Ponderosa Stomp Music History Conference. YouTube, October 24. https://youtu.be/2-6neTB2oqk.

Powers, Ann. 2017. *Good Booty: Love and Sex, Black and White, Body and Soul in American Music*. HarperCollins.

Purnell, Brontez. 2019. Interview. *Monograph* (PBS), June 28. https://www.pbs.org/video/brontez-purnell-muc9hn/.

Ramirez, Remy. 2019. "Big Freedia on Performing with Love and the Power of Prayer." *Nylon*, January 23. https://www.nylon.com/entertainment/big-freedia-interview-holy-ship.

Reed, Adolph L., Jr. 2019. "The Myth of Authenticity and Its Impact on Politics in New Orleans and Beyond." In Adams and Sakakeeny, *Remaking New Orleans*.

Regis, Helen A. 1999. "Second Lines, Minstrelsy, and the Contested Landscapes of New Orleans Afro-Creole Festivals." *Cultural Anthropology* 14 (4): 472–504.

Regis, Helen A., ed. 2006. *Caribbean and Southern: Transnational Perspectives on the U.S. South*. University of Georgia Press.

Reid-Pharr, Robert. 2001. *Black Gay Man: Essays*. NYU Press.

Roach, Joseph. 1996. *Cities of the Dead: Circum-Atlantic Performance*. Columbia University Press.

Ross, Marlon. 2021. *Sissy Insurgencies: A Racial Anatomy of Unfit Manliness*. Duke University Press.

Royster, Francesca T. 2012. *Sounding Like a No-No: Queer Sounds and Eccentric Acts in the Post-Soul Era*. University of Michigan Press.

Sakakeeny, Matt. 2015. "Living in a Laboratory: New Orleans Today." *Books and Ideas* 10. https://booksandideas.net/IMG/pdf/20150910_new_orleans.pdf.

Sakakeeny, Matt. 2024. "Textures of Black Sound and Affect: Life and Death in New Orleans." *American Anthropologist* 126:295–310.

Sarig, Roni. 2007. *Third Coast: OutKast, Timbaland, and How Hip-Hop Became a Southern Thing*. Da Capo Press.

Schram, Sanford F., Joe Brian Soss, and Richard Carl, eds. 2003. *Race and the Politics of Welfare Reform*. University of Michigan Press.

Scott, Darieck. 2010. *Extravagant Abjection: Blackness, Power, and Sexuality in the African American Literary Imagination*. NYU Press.

Sedgwick, Eve Kosofsky. 2003. *Touching Feeling: Affect, Pedagogy, Performativity*. Duke University Press.

Sexton, Jared. 2011. "The Social Life of Social Death: On Afro-Pessimism and Black Optimism." *InTensions*, no. 5 (Fall–Winter). https://doi.org/10.25071/1913-5874/37359.

Small, Judene Antoinette. 2012. "Giv Dem di Dance: An Investigation of the Jamaican Culture Through the Music and Dance of the Dancehalls." Master's thesis, Mills College.

Smith, Lillian. (1949) 1994. *Killers of the Dream*. W. W. Norton.

Smith, Neil. 2007. "Disastrous Accumulation." *South Atlantic Quarterly* 106 (4): 769–87.

South End Press Collective, ed. 2007. *What Lies Beneath: Katrina, Race, and the State of the Nation*. South End Press.

Spade, Dean. 2006. "Compliance Is Gendered: Struggling for Gender Self-Determination in a Hostile Economy." In *Transgender Rights*, edited by Paisley Currah, Richard M. Juang, and Shannon Price Minter. University of Minnesota Press.

Spera, Keith. 2018. "Late Rapper Hits No. 1 with Drake's 'In My Feelings.'" *Associated Press*, August 31. https://apnews.com/general-news-b536191ec937421185c4c9a2b0716bd6.

Stallings, L. H. 2007. *Mutha' Is Half a Word: Intersections of Folklore, Vernacular, Myth, and Queerness in Black Female Culture*. Ohio State University Press.

Stallings, L. H. 2015. *Funk the Erotic: Transaesthetics and Black Sexual Cultures*. University of Illinois Press.
Stockton, Kathryn Bond. 2006. *Beautiful Bottom, Beautiful Shame: Where "Black" Meets "Queer."* Duke University Press.
Sublette, Ned. 2008. *The World That Made New Orleans: From Spanish Silver to Congo Square*. Lawrence Hill.
Sublette, Ned. 2009. *The Year Before the Flood: A Story of New Orleans*. Lawrence Hill.
Summers, Martin. 2003. "This Immoral Practice: The Prehistory of Homophobia in Black Nationalist Thought." In *Gender Nonconformity, Race, and Sexuality: Charting the Connections*, edited by Toni Lester. University of Wisconsin Press.
Summerville, James. 1981. "The City and the Slum: 'Black Bottom' in the Development of South Nashville." *Tennessee Historical Quarterly* 40, no. 2 (Summer): 182–92.
Taylor, Diana. 2005. *The Archive and the Repertoire: Performing Cultural Memory in the Americas*. Duke University Press.
Upton, Dell. 2007. "Sound as Landscape." *Landscape Journal* 26 (1): 24–35.
Vargas, Deborah R. 2014. "Ruminations on *Lo Sucio* as a Latino Queer Analytic." *American Quarterly* 66 (3): 715–26.
Vargas, João H. Costa. 2006. *Catching Hell in the City of Angels: Life and Meanings of Blackness in South Central Los Angeles*. University of Minnesota Press.
Wacquant, Loïc. 2004. *Body and Soul: Notebooks of an Apprentice Boxer*. Oxford University Press.
Wald, Elijah. 2012. *The Dozens: A History of Rap's Mama*. Oxford University Press, 2012.
Walker, Alice. 2011. *The Color Purple*. Open Road Media.
Welch, Michael Patrick. 2011. YouTube interview with Altercation. Last accessed June 15, 2020. https://www.youtube.com/@michaelpatrickwhiteb/ (no longer available).
Wilderson, Frank B., III. 2020. *Afropessimism*. Liveright.
Williams, Jeremy. 2011. *The Rise and Fall of Black Bottom*. Master's thesis, Prescott College.
Williams, Raymond. 1977. *Marxism and Literature*. Oxford University Press.
Wirt, John. 2023. "The Irrepressible Bobby Marchan: From Drag to Rap Promotion and Everywhere in Between." 64 Parishes, February 28. Last updated June 1. https://64parishes.org/the-irrepressible-bobby-marchan.
Woods, Clyde A. 1998. *Development Arrested: The Blues and Plantation Power in the Mississippi Delta*. Verso.
Woods, Clyde A. 1998. "Regional Blocs, Regional Planning, and the Blues Epistemology in the Lower Mississippi Delta." In *Making the Invisible*

Visible: A Multicultural Planning History, edited by Leonie Sandercock. University of California Press.

Woods, Clyde A. 2005. "Do You Know What It Means to Miss New Orleans? Katrina, Trap Economics, and the Rebirth of the Blues." *American Quarterly* 57 (4): 1005–18.

Woods, Clyde A. 2009. "Katrina's World: Blues, Bourbon, and the Return to the Source." *American Quarterly* 61 (3): 427–53.

Woods, Clyde A. 2010. "The Challenges of Blues and Hip Hop Historiography." *Kalfou* 1 (1): 33–54.

Woods, Clyde A. 2017. *Development Drowned and Reborn: The Blues and Bourbon Restorations in Post-Katrina New Orleans*. Edited by Jordan T. Camp and Laura Pulido. University of Georgia Press.

Ybarra-Frausto, Tomás. 1989. "*Rasquachismo*: A Chicano Sensibility." In *Chicano Aesthetics: Rasquachismo*. Exhibition catalog. Movimiento Artístico del Rio Salado. Accessed through the International Center for the Arts of the Americas Digital Archive, Record ID 845510.

INDEX

Page numbers in *italics* refer to figures.

Aberrations in Black (Ferguson), 147n2, 148n5, 156n15
Adams, Vincanne, 100
African diaspora. *See* diaspora
agency. *See* black agency
"Ain't No Mountain High Enough" (Ross), 25
Alexander, M. Jacqui, 154n4
Allen, Jafari S., 134, 161n1
Altercation (dancer), 106–8, 110
anal theory, 6, 19, 48, 147n3, 155n10, 156n11. *See also* twerking
anthropology (discussion of), 4, 12, 47, 149nn14–15
Armstrong, Louis, 13, 91–94
Ave Girls, 76–78
"Avenue Girlz 2Gs" (Vockah Redu and the Cru), 2
"Azz Everywhere" (Big Freedia), 19–20, 114

"Baby Got Back" (Sir Mix-a-Lot), 105
back of town, 72–74, 77, 79, 82, 85, 89–94. *See also* black geographies; structural neglect
"Back o' Town Blues" (Armstrong), 91–92
"Back That Azz Up" (DJ Jubilee), 106
"Back That Thang Up" (Juvenile), 105
Bailey, Marlon, 155n9
Bamboula, The (Kemble), 86
Beautiful Bottom, Beautiful Shame (Stockton), 6, 153n3
Beloved (Morrison), 136–37
Bersani, Leo, 155n10

Beyoncé, 12, 15, 32, 115–17, 121, 134–36
Big Freedia (Freddie Ross), 9–12, *10*, 17, 19–20, 24, 36–40, 56, 66–67, 93, 103–11, 114–19, 121–23, 131–36
Big Freedia (TV show), 118–19
Big Sean, 114
black agency, 44–47, 64–65, 69–70
"Black Anality" (Nash), 6, 148n4
black capitalists, 116–17, 121
black church, 122–26, 130–33, 135, 137–38
Black Corona (Gregory), 151n22
black funk. *See* funk studies
Black Gay Man (Reid-Pharr), 149n10
black geographies, 13–15, 19–22, 74–76, 79–93, 100, 157n6, 159n1. *See also* back of town; structural neglect
Black Masking Indians, 151n24
blackness (discussion of), 6, 8, 17–21, 27–28, 32, 69, 82, 84–90, 105, 116, 119–20, 156n11, 158n14. *See also* pathology; queerness (discussion of)
"Black Noise, White Fears" (Cheng), 150n19
black queer club scene. *See* dance clubs
Black queer studies, 17, 125, 161n2
black queer vernacular, 5, 69
black studies (discussion of), 20, 156n14
"Black (W)holes" (Hammond), 148n4
black women, 19, 32–34, 77–78, 116, 123, 125, 148n4, 157n6. *See also* femininity; masculinity; misogyny
BlaqNmilD, 93
"Blood on the Leaves" (West), 14
blues, the, 93

blues epistemology, 18–19
"Blurred Lines" (Thicke), 113
"Boadicea" (Enya), 15
Bolden, Charles "Buddy," 150n17
bootstrap ideology, 117
bottoming (sex), 55
Bounce (Miller), 150n20
bounce music (background on), 1, 4, 8, 11, 13–15, 20, 73–78, 82, 94–95, 150n20, 151n21. *See also* black women; *Catch Dat Beat* (Johnson); sissy bounce (background on); specific artists
Boundaries of Blackness, The (Cohen), 155n8
BP oil, 35–36
"Break It Down" (Sissy Nobby), 13
"Break My Soul" (Beyoncé), 134
Brown, James, 26, 133
Brownlee, Caresha "Yung Miami," 93
Buck, 10th Ward, 38–39

Campanella, Richard, 87
"Can the Queen Speak?" (McBride), 156n13
caregiving, 25–31, 111, 120–21. *See also* informal labor; kinship
Cash Money Records, 1, 7, 83. *See also* Williams, Bryan "Birdman"; Williams, Ronald "Slim"
Casselman, Ben, 101
catastrophes. *See* Hurricane Katrina; oil spills
Catch Dat Beat (Johnson), 36–40, *37*
"Center of Thy Will" (Clark Sisters), 135
Chapman, Alix, *10*
Cheng, William, 150n19
Chev off da Ave, 56
Chris, Gotty Boi, 38
Christian, Barbara, 5
"Church Girl" (Beyoncé), 135–36
Cities of the Dead (Roach), 158n12
City Girls, 93
Clark Sisters, 135
Club Fusions, 126–31
Club Vibe, 126
Cohen, Cathy J., 17, 81, 155n8, 156n14, 160n8

collective asshole, the, 96–97
collective effervescence, 131
collective release, 140
colonialism. *See* settler-colonialism
Color Purple, The (Walker), 65
community. *See* kinship
community-based organizations (CBOs), 52–54
Conquergood, Dwight, 150n15
contact, 153n5
coperformance, 12, 22, 149n14
cultural appropriation, 98, 104–7, 114, 118–19, 121
cultural citizenship, 153n4
cultural pathology. *See* pathology
cultural reciprocity, 107
culture of poverty. *See* poverty
Cyrus, Miley, 12, 113–14, 118

dance (discussion of), 61–62, 68, *86*, 90, 139–41. *See also* twerking
"Dance (A$$) Remix" (Big Sean), 114
dance clubs, 15, 24, 34, 49–53, 124, 126–31, 134. *See also specific dance clubs*
dat beat, 15–16, 135, 150n20
Davis, Angela Y., 18–19
Davis, Jordan, 14
decolonization, 20
Delany, Samuel, 18, 153n5
Dem Hoes, 52
Demonic Grounds (McKittrick), 157n4
Development Drowned and Reborn (Woods), 92, 152n25
diaspora, 21–22, 24, 125, 139–40, 153n4, 156n3, 157n4
disaster capitalism, 97, 100–101, 104. *See also* Klein, Naomi
displacement, 29–31, 35, 40–42, 45–48, 64, 80–83, 89, 98, 102
DJ Jubilee, 106
DJs (discussion of), 15–16
Dorsey, Thomas, 136, 140
Dozens, The (Wald), 155n7
drag shows, 7–8, 36–37, 130
Drake, 1, 12, 93–94, 121

Durkheim, Émile, 131
Dyson, Michael Eric, 124–25

Eddie, 66–69
emasculation, 68. *See also* masculinity
Enya, 15
epistemology of the bottom, 6–7, 17–22, 26–28, 36, 48, 60, 69–70, 125–26, 136, 151n23, 152n27. *See also* raising the bottom (discussion of); sissy bounce (background on)
État de Siège (Hage), 158n11
"Excuse" (Big Freedia), 106
"Explode" (Big Freedia), 134–36
Extravagant Abjection (Scott), 148n6

Fanon, Frantz, 158n11
Fatman, 11, 29–36, 57–61, 64, 97–100, 107–12, 138–39
Faubourg Tremé, 150n17
fellowship, 126–29, 140
FEMA, 42, 45
femininity, 6, 28, 55, 106, 148n6. *See also* black women; masculinity
Fensterstock, Alison, 104
Ferguson, Roderick A., 6, 42–43, 125, 147n2, 148n5, 156n15
Fire in My Bones (Hinson), 122
Flaherty, Jordan, 42
"Formation" (Beyoncé), 115–16
Franklin, Aretha, 133
Freedia. *See* Big Freedia
freedom (discussion of), 51, 54, 57
French-Marcelin, Megan, 79–80
Freud, Sigmund, 6
Frye, Marilyn, 155n6
Fugees, 15
funk studies, 20

Gallo, Terrelle. *See* Sissy Nobby.
gatekeeping, 109, 112
Gautier, Ana María Ochoa, 89–90
gender identity, 55–57, 65, 111–12, 116
gentrification, 24, 29, 97–98, 101, 104–6, 109, 119–20, 154n7. *See also* housing

geographies. *See* black geographies
Glissant, Édouard, 157n4
Good Booty (Powers), 159n2
gospel music, 122–23, 133, 135, 140, 159n2
Gotty Boi Chris, 38
Gregory, Steven, 151n22

Hage, Ghassan, 90–91, 158n11
Hammond, Evelynn, 148n4
Hartman, Saidiya, 158n14
Hathaway, Donny, 133
healthcare, 52–53, 62–65, 92, 138
Herukhuti, 20, 161n1
Hinson, Glenn, 122–23
hip-hop, 1, 4, 8–9, 13–15, 58, 83, 93, 104–5, 114–15, 151n21, 160n9
HIV/AIDS, 52–55, 81, 125, 130, 155nn8–9
Holly, Buddy, 118
homophobia, 2–4, 32, 51–52, 69, 103, 105–6, 154n4
Hot Boys, 58
housing, 78–82, 87–93, *88*, 100, 119–20, 157n8. *See also* gentrification; the projects
Howlin' Wolf, 13
Hudson, Kate, 62
Hurricane Betsy, 89
Hurricane Katrina, 4, 7, 12, 15–17, 22–24, 41–45, 47–48, 81, 88–89, 95–102, 147n1. *See also* displacement; FEMA; reconstruction; survival tactics

informal labor, 30–36. *See also* caregiving
infrastructural (urban transformations), 18–19, 23, 85, 101. *See also* structural neglect
"In My Feelings" (Drake), 93–94
institutional racism, 30
"Is the Rectum a Grave?" (Bersani), 155n10

Jackson, Mahalia, 133
Jackson, Michael, 56
Jay Electronica, 14
Johnson, E. Patrick, 149n9, 152n1
Johnson, Lucky, 36–40

"Josephine Beat" (Sissy Nobby), 14–15
Juvenile, 14, 56, 83, 105

Kanye. *See* West, Kanye
Kaplan, Carla, 159n2
Katey Red. *See* Red, Katey
Kelley, Robin D. J., 156n14
Kemble, Edward Winsor, 86
Killers of the Dream (Smith), 96
Kilo, 13
kinship, 4, 17, 24, 28, 31–32, 39–44, 60. *See also* caregiving
Klein, Naomi, 152n25
Knowles, Beyoncé. *See* Beyoncé

Latrobe, Benjamin Henry, 86–87, 89–92, 94, 158n12
Legacy, 41–45, 153nn5–6
Lil' Kim, 72
Lil Wayne, 1, 8, 83
Lorde, Audre, 20, 48, 133, 147n2
Lowe-Bridgewater, Renetta Yemika. *See* Magnolia Shorty
Luft, Rachel, 102

Madison, D. Soyini, 149n14
Madonna, 118
Magnolia Shorty, 71–74, 72, 76–78, 82, 93–94
Mailer, Norman, 103
Manalansan, Martin F., 153n4
Manicure Records, 8
Marchan, Bobby, 7–9, *8*, 148n8, 149n10
Marxism and Literature (Williams), 157n7
masculinity, 6, 28, 33, 50, 55–56, 94, 148nn5–6, 154n2. *See also* emasculation; femininity; patriarchy
Masquelier, Adeline, 152n28
McBride, Dwight, 156n13
McKittrick, Katherine, 92, 157nn4–6
Miller, Matt, 13, 17, 150n20, 160n5
Minaj, Nicki, 1, 114–15
minstrel performances, 24, 28, 118, 120
misogyny, 55, 69, 104–6. *See also* black women

Miss Anne in Harlem (Kaplan), 159n2
Moe, 57–61
Morrison, Toni, 5–7, 25, 48–51, 73–74, 94, 136–37, 147n2, 150n16, 151n23, 153nn2–3, 154n1, 154n4, 156n2, 156n15
mortality rates, 92
Moten, Fred, 158n14
Motown, 20
Ms. Tee, 38
mutual aid. *See* kinship
Mystikal, 8

Nash, Jennifer C., 6, 97, 147n3, 148n4, 156n11
"Neoliberal Futures" (Adams), 100
neoliberalism, 4, 42–43, 80, 97, 100–101, 120, 152n27, 157n8
networking, 153n5
New Orleans (discussion of), 22, *88*, 89, 100
"New Orleans's Gender-Bending Rap" (Fensterstock), 104
Nicky da B, 52
Nixon, Richard, 79
Nobby. *See* Sissy Nobby
"Not Just (Any) Body Can Be a Citizen" (Alexander), 154n4
Nyong'o, Tavia, 69, 103

oil spills, 35–36
106 and Park (BET TV show), 58–61
"Oppression" (Frye), 155n6
Orlando's Society Page, 126
Oscar, 62–66, 138, 140–41

parading culture, 16, 56, 76
Paris, 97–103, 108–13
"Partition" (Beyoncé), 15
pathology, 6–7, 17, 21, 23–24, 26, 28, 36, 42–46, 52–54, 68–70, 80–81. *See also* blackness (discussion of); queerness (discussion of)
patriarchy, 33. *See also* black women; femininity; masculinity
Pérez, Elizabeth, 139–40

Perry, Tyler, 36
Pigott, Adam "BlaqNmilD," 93
Playing in the Dark (Morrison), 153n2
Plessy v. Ferguson, 92–93, 150n17
popular culture, 8, 12, 18, 73, 91, 96, 102, 113–15, 140
poverty, 53, 64, 68–69, 74
power, 4–5, 12, 19, 36, 40, 45, 54, 65, 70, 110, 155n10
Powers, Ann, 123, 159n2
Presley, Elvis, 118
privilege, 84–85
projects, the, 1–8, 13–15, 71–76, 88. *See also* housing
public health, 52–55
public housing. *See* the projects
"Punk'd Theory" (Nyong'o), 103
"Punks, Bulldaggers, and Welfare Queens" (Cohen), 17
punk shows, 7, 16. *See also* sissy bounce (background on)
"Punk Under Pressure" (Red), 49, 51
Purnell, Brontez, 16

quare studies, 149n9
queerness (discussion of), 17, 19, 32–33, 36–37, 69, 111, 116, 125, 148nn7–8, 149n10, 154n4. *See also* blackness (discussion of); pathology

racial topography, 20–22
Rainey, Ma, 19
raising the bottom (discussion of), 2, 5. *See also* epistemology of the bottom
Rashad, Phylicia, 93
rasquachismo, 152n27
"Ready or Not" (Fugees), 15
Reagan, Ronald, 42, 80, 155n8
reconstruction, 12, 79, 92, 98, 100–102, 120
Red, Katey, 12, 17–19, *18*, 38, 49, 51–52, 56, 103, 111, 114, 117–18, 131, 151n21
Redbone, 49–51, 55, 154n2
Reed, Adolph L. Jr., 117
Reid-Pharr, Robert, 149n10
representational passageways, 97

residential segregation. *See* housing
respectability (discussion of), 19–20, 22, 39, 51, 65, 100
Roach, Joseph, 87
"Roll Call" (Vockah Redu and the Cru), 75–77
Rose, 123
Rosen, Jody, 118
Ross, Diana, 25–26
Ross, Freddie. *See* Big Freedia
Ross, Marlon, 148n5
Royster, Francesca T., 156n12

safe spaces, 105, 118, 120, 134
Sakakeeny, Matt, 120, 150n17
Sarig, Roni, 151n21
Scott, Darieck, 6, 45, 148n6
Scott, Jim, 156n14
settler-colonialism, 85, 87, 91, 125, 158n11, 160n7
sex work, 12, 49–51, 59, 80, 92–93, 148n5, 154n1, 154n4
Shock Doctrine, The (Klein), 152n25
Shorty, Magnolia. *See* Magnolia Shorty
sickle cell anemia, 62–65
Simone, Nina, 133
Sir Mix-a-Lot, 105
sissies (discussion of), 6, 24, 36, 68–70, 148nn5–6, 150n18. *See also* caregiving; femininity
sissies at the picnic, 125
"Sissies at the Picnic" (Ferguson), 6
sissy bounce (background on), 1–8, 16, 21–22, 69–70, 96–97, 101–7, 111–18, 120–21, 150n18. *See also* bounce music (background on); epistemology of the bottom; minstrel performances; popular culture; punk shows; twerking; *Where They At* (music exhibition); specific artists
Sissy Insurgencies (Ross), 148n5
Sissy Nobby (Terrelle Gallo), 12–15, 38, 40, 69, 104, 150n18
"Site of Memory, The" (Morrison), 73–74
Smith, Barbara, 147n2

INDEX | 179

Smith, Bessie, 19
"Smoking Gun" (Magnolia Shorty), 75, 93
social justice, 4, 47
social mobility, 50–51
social reproduction, 48
social wealth, 23, 27, 32, 69
social welfare, 42–43, 60, 69, 72, 78–81, 119
Sounding Like a No-No (Royster), 156n12
sound studies, 14, 84, 86–87, 89–90, 150n19, 158n14. *See also* Moten, Fred
spiritual erotic, 122–23, 133–38
Stallings, L. H., 20
Stockton, Kathryn Bond, 6, 153n3, 154n3
"Stop Pause (Jubilee All)" (DJ Jubilee), 106
stripping, 49–50
"Strokin' Part 2" (Marchan), 7–8
structural neglect, 30, 46–48, 79–82, 85, 89. *See also* back of town; infrastructural (urban transformations)
structural oppression, 53
Sula (Morrison), 5–6, 25, 48, 50–51, 94, 147n2, 150n16, 151n23, 153n3, 154n1, 158n15, 159n1
Summers, Martin, 154n4
superstructural (urban transformations), 18
survival tactics, 42–43
Sweet Tea (Johnson), 149n9

Tader, 57–58, 60–62, 138
"Take My Hand, Precious Lord" (Dorsey), 136
Tee, Ms. *See* Ms. Tee
10th Ward Buck, 38–39
"Textures of Black Sound and Affect" (Sakakeeny), 150n17
Tharpe, Sister Rosetta, 133
Thicke, Robin, 113
Third Coast (Sarig), 151n21
"This Immoral Practice" (Summers), 154n4
Thomas, Stephen, 17, 150n20
Times Square Red, Times Square Blue (Delany), 18, 153n5, 154n7

trans people, 4, 6, 17, 28, 33, 40–41, 51, 55–56, 69, 81, 111, 123, 128–30, 140
transphobia, 2–4, 17, 51–52
twerking, 2–4, 9, 12, 15, 24, 55, 61–62, 66–68, 97, 104–15, 118, 120, 139–40. *See also* anal theory; dance (discussion of); sissy bounce (background on)
2 Live Crew, 105

Uncle Luke, 105
"U Need a Perm" (Vockah Redu and the Cru), 25–29
Upton, Dell, 90

Vargas, Deborah R., 152n27
violence, 14, 17, 74, 78, 82, 84, 106–7, 112, 130–31, 152n27
Vockah Redu, 27, 81–83, 111–12, 122–23, 138
Vockah Redu and the Cru, 1–4, 9, 11–12, 14, 19, 22–23, 25–29, 51–67, 70, 72, 75–78, 97–103, 108–14, 138–39. *See also* Ave Girls; black women; Eddie; Fatman; Legacy; Moe; Oscar; Paris; Rose; sissy bounce (background on); Tader; specific songs

Wald, Elijah, 155n7
Walker, Alice, 65
Wayne, Lil. *See* Lil Wayne
"We Can't Stop" (Cyrus), 113
welfare. *See* social welfare
West, Kanye, 14, 133
What Lies Beneath, 153n6
"When You Divide Body and Soul, Problems Multiply" (Dyson), 124–25
Where They At (music exhibition), 10, 27, 71–72
white audiences, 27–28
"White Negro, The" (Nyong'o), 103
white vice, 21, 92
"Why Katrina's Victims Aren't Refugees" (Masquelier), 152n28
Williams, Bryan "Birdman," 8–9. *See also* Cash Money Records

Williams, H. Sharif. *See* Herukhuti
Williams, Raymond, 157n7
Williams, Ronald "Slim," 8–9. *See also* Cash Money Records
Williams, Trishell. *See* Ms. Tee
Williams, Tyronne, 130
women. *See* black women

Wonder, Stevie, 156n12
Woods, Clyde, 18, 92, 152n25

Y2 Katey Millenium Sissy (Red), *18*
Ya Heard Me? (Miller and Thomas), 17
Ybarra-Frausto, Tomás, 152n27
Yung Miami, 93

www.ingramcontent.com/pod-product-compliance
Lightning Source LLC
Chambersburg PA
CBHW020241170426
43202CB00008B/175